Project Clarity

Fleur Elizabeth

First published 2025 by FE-ED Pty Ltd

Produced by Independent Ink

Copyright © FE-ED Pty Ltd 2025

The moral right of the author to be identified as the author of this work has been asserted.

All rights reserved. No part of this publication may be reproduced, stored in a retrieval system or transmitted in any form or by any means available now or in the future without the prior written permission of the author, nor be otherwise circulated in any form of binding or cover other than that in which it is published and without a similar condition being imposed on the purchaser.

Cover design by Catucci Design
Edited by Christine Egner and Daina Lindeman
Internal design by Independent Ink
Typeset in Greycliff CF by Post Pre-press Group, Brisbane

ISBN 978-1-7642293-0-2 (paperback)
ISBN 978-1-7642293-1-9 (epub)
ISBN 978-1-7642293-2-6 (kindle)

To Judith and Genevieve

From the very bottom of my heart, thank you. You guided me to truly understand myself, to set healthy boundaries, and to heal. Through different stages of my life, you helped me connect with my inner child and accept every piece of myself, even the parts I thought weren't all that pretty. This book is my way of giving back what you gave me – the wisdom that everything I need is within me, found in acceptance.

Disclaimer

The content you're about to dive into is a reflection of a coaching approach I've carefully developed. It draws upon my experiences in performance and nutritional health coaching, and blends in techniques from Acceptance and Commitment Therapy (ACT), Motivational Interviewing, and Dialectical Behaviour Therapy (DBT). It's important to understand that this is a coaching program, not clinical therapy.

Think of this book as a supportive companion, whether you're looking to enhance your current medical plan or simply wanting to explore new paths for personal growth. I believe strongly in the connection between mind and body, and this book takes a holistic approach to that connection, particularly as it relates to our relationship with food and drink. My aim is to provide you with a solid foundation for making choices that lead to a balanced and healthy life.

Please remember, the information shared here is not a replacement for the guidance of your doctor or therapist, including psychologists, counsellors, or psychiatrists. This book isn't intended to be a substitute for any ongoing or future therapy you might be undertaking, especially trauma therapy.

This book is not a clinical treatment for mental health conditions such as mood disorders, eating disorders, body dysmorphia, or alcohol addictions, particularly those related to sexual violence, abuse, or mental abuse.

 **AN IMPORTANT NOTE:** Change Talk Coaching, the Change Experience Series of books, and I as the author, publisher, and creator of this book cannot be held responsible or liable for any effects that actions taken or drugs used may have on your body or mental wellbeing as a result of engaging with this material.

The information provided is for educational purposes only and should not be interpreted as recommendations for self-administering drugs or any form of medication. Always discuss your medication with your doctor or therapist, and only take medication prescribed specifically for you. If, at any point, the content brings up difficult emotions or triggers past experiences, please reach out to your doctor or therapist immediately. Your wellbeing is my priority.

Contents

Preface
The Book Series Structure   3
When Comfort Becomes a Crutch   14

Let's Begin
1 Drawn to a Cause   21
2 Is This You?   25
3 Bravely Sharing   41
4 Start with Intention   43

Your Past Challenges
5 Be Trauma-Informed   49
6 What the?   62
7 When Your Body Reacts   71
8 Not My Secret Anymore   75

Change
9 The Change Experience   83
10 Helpful Strategies   91
11 Motivational Change   96
12 The Art of Change   104
13 Your Future Self   111
14 Your Progress, Your Reward   124
15 My Trauma Experience   127

Your Values
16 Life Is Automatic   141
17 The Roots of Your Truth   145
18 Living Your Truth   153

19	Choosing Your <u>New</u> Values	162
20	My Values Experience	181
21	Living By Your Values	184
22	Reflection Time	205

Your Relationship with Food and Drink

23	The Hidden Language of Desire	213
24	My Trauma Experience	232
25	Reflection Time	238
26	Your Food and Drink Reality	244
27	The Social Maze of Change	252

Stress, Sleep, and Your Food and Drink

28	When Stress Takes Over	265
29	Reflection Time	269
30	The Sleep-Food Dance	274
31	Your Sleep Toolkit	279
32	Your Plate, Your Rules	287
33	Your Food Story	301
34	Drink: The Silent Destroyer	318
35	Staying On Course	329
36	My Trauma Experience	333
37	Drinkies Discovery	337
38	Reflection Time	343
39	From Here to Clarity	349
40	Until We Meet Again, Friend	355

| Appendix: Methodology | 361 |
| References and Research | 363 |

Preface

THE CHANGE EXPERIENCE
Heal your past, transform your today

Project Clarity
The trauma-informed woman: *Unmask hidden wounds, end automatic coping habits and embrace your authentic self.*

- Why I'm here
- Is this you?
- Trauma defined
- Strategies for change
- Change is hard
- Your Future Self
- Life is automatic
- Family influences
- Values – your past and future
- Living by your values
- Your relationship with food and drink
- Stress and sleep

A New Perspective
The emotionally resilient woman: *Recognise your triggers, cultivate self-acceptance and embrace emotional health.*

- Becoming friends with your emotions
- Repetitive cycles
- Grounding techniques
- Searching for happiness
- Your emotions invalidated
- Adverse Childhood Experiences
- Emotional regulation
- Triggers defined
- Trigger, behaviour, consequence
- Triggers – gaslighting
- Your liberation toolkit
- How to trust yourself, self-empathy, embrace mistakes, self-acceptance

Liberated Connection
The energetic woman: *Set healthy boundaries, honour your needs and embrace your feminine power.*

- Change can be tough
- Embracing your energy
- Healing hypervigilance
- Removing chaos
- Energy Vampires
- Boundary setting
- Barriers to change
- Energetic conflict resolution
- Getting what you want in life
- S.M.A.R.T Energy focused
- Become your Future Self

I.
The Book Series Structure

A Brief Guide of What to Expect
This is Your Personal Change Experience Journey

Welcome to The Change Experience: a unique, three-part series created to help women heal from their past, transform their present, and build the skills they need to create lasting, authentic change in their adult lives.

I've created this series as a personal guide for women who have navigated life's challenges and still feel the impact of traumatic experiences. Healing starts with unpacking what trauma means and understanding how it became a part of who you are. This delicate process helps us see how it plays out in our adult lives.

This work has many layers, just like we humans do. To avoid feeling overwhelmed, we'll tackle the puzzle over three books, breaking it down into manageable steps so you're not trying to take it all in at once.

First, I'll help you become trauma-informed, appreciating how adult struggles are most commonly rooted in childhood experiences. We'll then move toward a deeper emotional awareness, understanding how those past events play out in your adult life. Finally, you'll build the essential life skills needed to dissolve the barriers keeping you stuck in old narratives.

Throughout the series, I weave in real-life stories and relatable examples of the challenges women face after trauma and how these experiences manifest in their adult lives. With courage and vulnerability, I share my own journey, offering a deep sense of understanding and inspiring hope for those who, like me, may have suffered in silence for far too long.

The backbone of this series is a practical roadmap with the building blocks for developing self-awareness, self-acceptance, and healing, empowering you to step into a life where you can trust your choices and find genuine peace. I know that lasting change requires more than just understanding – it needs new skills and a viable way to put them into practice. My insightful guidance offers thought-provoking questions and strategies to help you break free from self-destructive patterns and cultivate a new normal where you feel good in your own skin again.

My very conversational writing style makes this an intimate journey between us. This book is a safe space where you don't have to walk alone. Whether the echoes of past trauma manifest as a reliance on unhealthy coping mechanisms, overwhelming anxiety, persistent negative self-talk, or suffering the insidious manipulation of gaslighting – I will hold your hand throughout. My goal is to offer you a clear, compassionate, and ultimately liberating path toward healing and reclaiming your life.

My friend, I invite you to stay the course with me through this powerful three-part series directly addressing the multifaceted experiences of women navigating the aftermath of life's difficult challenges. Life will not be the same for you when you have honed the skills needed to break free from unhealthy cycles and build a life defined by genuine happiness, profound peace, and enduring joy. As the great philosopher Joseph Campbell once said, "Doors will open where before there were only walls."

Book One: *Project Clarity*
The Trauma-Informed Woman: Unmask Hidden Wounds,
End Automatic Coping Habits & Embrace Your Authentic Self

Ah, I'm so glad you've found your way to this book. It's truly a passion project of mine, straight from the heart. I created it with women in mind who, like me, have experienced some of life's challenges. You might wonder about the title? Well, when I work with my coaching clients, helping them to see how their past influences their present and guiding them towards emotional awareness and authenticity, I often give our work a name, like "Project Ruby" – that was the name of a beautiful client. And as I was working with a new client while writing this book, the idea for the title, *Project Clarity*, was sparked. So, you could think of this as your own personal project, a chance to really understand what's happening in your life and find clarity along the journey.

Perhaps a little voice inside you whispered that it was time to explore how your past might be influencing, or rather uncomfortably shaping, your present. My intention is to gently shine a light on those challenging life experiences, bringing awareness to the often unseen and misunderstood impact of trauma – not only the big, painful events, but also those early life moments when, perhaps, your needs weren't always fully met. Together, we'll tenderly explore how the patterns and values we absorbed from our families can sometimes lead to automatic reactions, triggers, and cycles that no longer feel quite right.

Imagine, for a moment, having real clarity on what truly lights you up today, what's really important to just you, beyond what you might have taken on from others – and knowing you can follow that truth or take care of that need without fear, guilt, or shame. This book is a warm invitation to lovingly uncover your authentic values and begin that beautiful journey towards the woman you envision becoming, the life your heart truly desires – your Future Self. By taking a kind, compassionate look at how past challenges might be gently woven into current struggles with things like food, drink, sleep, or stress, you'll start to see the real impact of those ingrained habits, with understanding and grace.

With some thoughtful reflections and gentle, practical exercises, you'll begin to build new, "must-have" life skills and nurture a kinder relationship with yourself, and around food and drink too. You'll learn to honour your own unique process of change and see with clarity the costs of staying where you are, versus the beautiful possibilities of moving forward.

Clarity is what we all need in life to be authentic and to consciously choose actions that resonate with our values and what is right for our Future Selves. I'm here with you every step of the way, holding your hand and offering you my tried-and-tested ways and psychologically proven strategies to gently step back into the driver's seat of your life. I'm giving you a clear path to understanding how your story has been shaped by the events of your past, and within your own deeply intimate Change Experience, you can transform all of that. You can show up fully, fostering a deep, loving awareness of yourself and take those brave, gentle steps toward a future filled with intention, self-compassion, and the embrace of the magnificent you that is there, just waiting to emerge!

Book Two: *A New Perspective*
The Emotionally Resilient Woman: Recognise Your Triggers, Cultivate Self-Acceptance & Embrace Emotional Health

My second book, *A New Perspective*, is your guide to becoming a more emotionally resilient woman. It offers an empowering journey towards a more gentle and self-accepting view of yourself, helping you understand your emotional landscape and the intricate patterns that shape your life. This is the next step to unpacking how your unmet childhood needs and past experiences have shaped the behaviours you see in your adult life today.

Emotions can be scary for some, so we begin with grounding techniques to navigate potential triggers with greater ease. *A New Perspective* illuminates the biological underpinnings of repetitive behavioural cycles, encouraging self-compassion over shame. You'll discover why quick fixes for happiness don't last and how to find real joy and peace. The book explores how early emotional experiences affect you today and offers practical tools for self-regulation, leading to balance and taking control of your choices. Understanding the significant role of adverse childhood experiences in shaping adult behaviours and overall wellbeing becomes a key aspect of this exploration.

In *A New Perspective*, you will come to appreciate the transformative power of befriending your emotions and embracing your shadows, recognising this as a vital starting point for healing and liberation. You'll gain more clarity on your automatic behaviour patterns – including triggers, consequences, and the impact of emotional manipulation such as gaslighting. Equipped with practical life skills from the "Liberation Toolbox", you'll learn to build trust, cultivate self-empathy, learn from mistakes, utilise grounding techniques, and embrace self-acceptance. Ultimately, this book is a compassionate guide to achieving *A New Perspective* on your life and emotions, empowering you to become a more balanced, liberated woman, living with greater peace and joy.

Book Three: *Liberated Connection*
The Energetic Woman: Set Healthy Boundaries, Honour Your Needs & Embrace Your Feminine Power

The final instalment in the series, *Liberated Connection*, offers a bold alignment with your authentic self. It empowers you to forge your own path, attract what resonates deeply, and explore the profound aspects of your personal feminine journey. Within these pages, you will understand the true essence of feeling liberated and deeply connected. This book acts as a guide, facilitating the full embrace of your innate feminine power, allowing you the confidence to live the life you want within healthy boundaries. Offering a realistic yet compassionate perspective on the process of change, it delivers practical strategies to navigate unavoidable challenges, manage anxieties, and circumvent the recurrence of old patterns.

Make no mistake – none of this is woo-woo stuff. This book is about connecting to your potential by understanding and nurturing your own positive energy to enable change, while keeping your vibration high. Why? Because maintaining a high vibration is crucial for shifting out of the low-frequency states often associated with trauma, such as fear, shame, guilt, and anger. We will gently explore how hypervigilant energy, often a result of past experiences, can sometimes keep you feeling stuck, almost like a victim of circumstance. Together, we will connect to the chaotic energies in your life that might be holding you back, including those draining "energy vampires" – the people whose needs you might habitually put before yours, often at your own expense.

This book offers practical skills to connect with your energy to protect yourself and establish clear, loving boundaries. It is about getting in touch with your own needs, learning to ask for them without guilt or shame, and understanding that building new skills is essential, especially if you have spent a lifetime prioritising others. You will find gentle guidance and reflective questions to navigate the sometimes-tricky path of change, understanding that while it can be tough initially, the long-term rewards of becoming your gloriously worthy Future Self are truly worth it. This book serves as your guide to forging deep connections, your trusted companion on the final leg of your Change Experience journey. It prepares you to move forward in your world. By embracing this path wholeheartedly, you create lasting change and cultivate genuine joy, connecting deeply with your authentic self, liberated from the past, and radiating powerful feminine energy.

How the Books Are Structured

Each book is structured to give you a clear path forward, so you always know what's coming next. Each topic has three main parts:

🔍 **Education:** This part gives you the lowdown on the topic and shows you why and how it's relevant to your life right now.

🔗 **Strategy:** Here, you'll learn practical skills and tools that you can use to adjust, prepare, control, ease, or soothe yourself when faced with challenges, struggles, or emotional storms.

❓ **Questions/Reflection:** At the end of each section, you'll find thought-provoking questions to help you personalise your journey of change. There's also a reflection exercise to help you process what's come up for you.

❗ **AN IMPORTANT NOTE:** How to Approach Questions/Reflections Unlocking Your Unconscious

The purpose of these questions is to help you connect with parts of yourself that are unconscious. They aim to shed light on where your habits and behaviours originate, and why things are unfolding as they are. This might sound straightforward, and the questions themselves may seem simple, but I assure you, sometimes it's not. So, please, give yourself permission to take your time with these exercises.

Be prepared: you might read these questions, and nothing really surfaces for you. You might need to step away from them for a while or simply let the questions sit with you.

You might even read them for the first time and wonder, "Why does she want me to answer this?" It might feel futile or irrelevant. However, I promise you there's a reason behind every question. They are formulated to help you connect with aspects of yourself that aren't at the forefront of your mind. This might be a missing piece of your puzzle that needs to take shape so you can see the whole picture clearly, from a 360-degree perspective.

I often tell people that you might need a crowbar to prise some of this information out from within. This is because you've done such a good job at surviving thus far – that when your system is in hyper-vigilant overdrive (or perhaps in a constant state of fight or flight) – accessing information about yourself can be really tough. And it can take some time.

Effectively, what I'm doing is condensing years of psychological investigation into your former self, your past experiences, your behaviours, your drivers, and your triggers, into three books. Some people take years to work through these types of questions, not just a matter of months. What you're getting here are condensed, super-tuned connection questions, designed to help you navigate this journey of healing and change in a more concise and liberating way.

So, the message here is this: Take your time. Allow yourself the time. Read them more than once. Put them down and come back to them later. Don't worry if nothing magically inspiring appears the first time you read them. The answers might not reveal themselves in question order either, rather unlock in layers as you delve. Allow yourself to sit with what these questions stir within you, and what messages emerge ... in your own sweet time.

Your Journal Companion

Throughout our time together in this book series, I'll be gently inviting you to explore with a series of thoughtful questions. These aren't just any questions; they're designed to help you sink deeply into what truly matters to you right now, and the woman you are today. This is so you can connect with the experiences that lie in your past and the beautifully powerful vision you hold for your Future Self. This journey we're embarking on together calls for a safe and beautiful space for you to capture all your precious reflections. Honestly, this is such a deeply crucial part of what we're creating together. You might be wondering why, and it's because with each question, a powerful next step gently unfolds.

Your Task: To record your reflections, thoughts and answers to my questions, your first task will be to find a journal that feels just right for you. Journals are such deeply personal companions, aren't they? Each of us has such a unique sense of what makes a journal feel truly special. It could be the comforting colour of the cover that calls to you, or the way the paper feels beneath your fingertips, or maybe even the spacing between the lines. Perhaps you're drawn to the freedom of blank pages, with no lines at all! It might be something simple and discreet, easy to tuck away like a precious secret. Whatever whispers to your heart and feels truly good to you, that's absolutely perfect. This is all about honouring your unique preference.

This journal is going to be your trusted companion, travelling alongside you on this unfolding journey. It's the safe haven where you'll pour out your most intimate and perhaps even vulnerable thoughts, so you absolutely get to choose the one that feels like a true extension of yourself. Could you do that for me? Could you take a little moment to go and find a journal that truly resonates with you, the one you'll feel drawn to use as you journey through this book? It's such an important and beautiful piece of your Change Experience here with me, my friend.

One of the most profound parts of The Change Experience is simply hearing your own words. So, as you reflect, I will ask you to please gently read your answers aloud. This is where you truly allow yourself to speak the changes that are already stirring within your heart. It's such a transformative (and even miraculous) way to rewire your brain and those neurological pathways—simply by lovingly acknowledging your own true feelings and choices. You'll be strengthening your inner foundations, bit by bit, and crafting the life you always desired (but have not had the confidence to lead). I'll share more about the science behind this magic later, but please trust me on this: When the words of change come directly from you, and your own ears (and brain) hear your voice speak them, it becomes so much more likely that you'll step into inspired action and make those heartfelt changes.

As you journal, I'd also gently suggest following along with the book's structure, perhaps noting the chapter and the date at the top of each page. If you feel called to, you could also add the exercise title and your personal reflections. This simple act will make it so easy to revisit and reconnect with your own wisdom later on. By the time you reach the end, feeling wonderfully inspired and deeply committed to your own beautiful growth, you'll have all your precious insights captured in one safe and comforting place, ready to be revisited and cherished whenever you wish. This will freely support you in achieving your goals with ease and grace.

Resources

On my website at **www.fleurelizabeth.com**, you'll find helpful resources, including your Health History Assessment. Think of it as your little starting point, a way to understand where your health is at right now. And, please, there's really no need to feel any worry or stress about it! This information is truly here to support you, to help you grow into the amazing person you're becoming. Getting a clear picture of your current health, of where you are today, can really provide a strong foundation, your personal roadmap, for your own journey through this beautiful Change Experience.

Imagine it as just checking in with yourself. Where are you, right here and now? What does your health truly feel like in this moment? This tool helps bring clarity to your health and what areas might need a little extra love and attention. If you can, definitely download it from the internet. It will become a really valuable set of personal insights, helping you develop your values and skills in the upcoming parts of our journey together.

In health coaching, we always begin by gently understanding your health history. That way, we get a clear sense of your starting point and where you're hoping to go. It's similar to planning a journey – knowing your starting point is essential for determining the best path forward. This is your personal journey, and I am here to guide and support you through each step.

Let's do a little sense check, right now. Are you feeling ready to take some affirmative steps to help yourself and your health evolve? Maybe a little bit nervous? Whatever you're feeling is absolutely okay and valid.

Some more reflective questions for you to consider:

1. What does your current health profile feel like and look like to you? Consider your whole being – your physical vitality, your beautiful mental landscape, and your precious emotional wellbeing.

2. What gentle changes, if any, do you feel called to make in your health and overall wellbeing?

3. How might setting this health baseline lovingly support you in gently achieving your heartfelt goals?

4. What does a "healthy you" truly look and feel like from the inside out? What nourishing foods does this version of you enjoy? How does she move her body with joy, and how does she lovingly live her life each day?

These questions provide a valuable starting point for your reflection and will greatly assist us as we work through the material in this book series.

Consider your journal a supportive resource in embracing the changes you are making. This process of personal reflection as you engage with these foundational elements is what I refer to as your "Future Self commitment".

> **Three things to think about before you start:**
>
> 1. Accept that sometimes your biggest critic and bully is you.
> 2. Your pain is often caused by the pursuit of only feeling pleasure.
> 3. You don't have to be ready to change; you only need to be willing.

> Remember, my friend, this is your unique and personal journey. I'm honoured to be a part of it. Let's take this step together, with kindness and compassion for ourselves.

II.
When Comfort Becomes a Crutch

Why Our Past Shapes How We Behave
Moving Beyond Trauma and Automatic Coping

Women who have experienced trauma or complex trauma often share common behavioural patterns and challenges. The brain and body have coping mechanisms, and often, one is a disconnect between your body and your mental state. Many use food and drink to self-medicate, attempting to enhance positive emotions and reduce negative ones. But it is short-lived; it's a quick fix and don't we all know it!

The human journey is one of growth, connection, and contribution. Our purpose lies in experiencing life fully, fostering meaningful relationships, and leaving the world a little better than we found it, through our unique talents and acts of kindness. Sounds good, doesn't it? So why is it that you are looking in the mirror, not liking what you see, and feeling like things aren't working out how you thought they would?

I think you are starting to get the picture now. When you've got a background like ours – one where we've all faced our share of challenges – things can get messy. Triggers stir up emotions, emotions lead to actions, and before you know it, you're turning to food, drink, or substances for comfort. To numb the pain, mask the hurt, and distract yourself from all that uncomfortable stuff that's just too hard to face. You suffer in silence, and always have.

So, like me, I am sure you have used food and drink as a distraction, and perhaps sometimes even a little too often. Your way to exit stage left when the pain, noise, and discomfort get too much is to deflect with these substances. Yep, these are all really common coping mechanisms for anyone who has experienced upsetting events and felt helpless, unsafe, and afraid. It's a biological, physiological response we all share, so you're not alone. We all avoid discomfort and shy away from pain. Why? Because we're rarely taught how to truly deal with pain. And we certainly are never taught what validation means to our human experience, or even how we can validate ourselves and be our own empathetic witness to soothe and prevent our past from making problems in our present. (Don't worry – I will be teaching you all that here!)

On top of this, there's the stigma surrounding words like "trauma", "disorder", "dysfunctional", or, god forbid, "abuse". Nobody wants to talk about it. It's not easy for those who've been through it either. We live in a society where talking about pain, in general, is uncomfortable and not very acceptable, fuelling loneliness, depression, and anxiety – all triggers that drive behaviour. When things get loud, the "toolbox of distraction" seems to work in the moment and once again, you find yourself stuck in a cycle of unhealthy habits. You wonder how you got there, and then one day, you're looking in the mirror, hating what you see, and realise you're living a life you never imagined. You know what I'm talking about, right? It can be a lonely, dark, and scary place, and hard to imagine escaping.

A significant problem is that people who haven't experienced trauma or complex trauma (neglect or physical, mental, or sexual trauma) often underestimate its short- and long-term effects. Some may think they understand, but they have it backward, believing the unhealthy food or alcohol relationship comes first.

When I keep saying you are not alone, I mean it. This is a global humanitarian crisis. Women affected aren't just in certain socioeconomic groups; it happens at every pay grade, in every community and postcode, on every street. Many women suffer in silence, suppressing their emotions and developing destructive behaviours. As they say, "Envy someone until you reach their front door."

What is alarming to know is, eighty percent of women with deep core wounds don't seek help for a number of reasons. They might struggle to admit it due to feelings of shame, they may not fully understand what caused it – perhaps adverse childhood experiences were normalised in their environment. They might have suppressed memories as a survival mechanism, or they may face financial barriers or have trouble accessing government-funded programs. However, increasingly, professional consensus and research now support the path of self-healing more than ever. This advocates that women who struggle managing their emotional triggers, have problems regulating their behaviour, or numb the pain with food and alcohol as a way of coping can heal in their own private space with the right tools.

> So, when I talk about how women suffer in silence, you can see why, right?

My friend, the message here is this:

If you've suffered any form of life challenge, or significant events of trauma, your struggles with eating and drinking habits can be complex. Change is hard, especially when trying to do it solo, and many factors are at play: biology, social culture, your self-perception, and more.

Your survival mechanism can unfortunately manifest in destructive behaviours. You may spiral into patterns of overeating, binge eating, strict rules around eating, not eating enough, purging, control issues with over-exercising, and body image issues. The mirror can be a dangerous place. These cycles trigger another spiral, becoming a self-fulfilling prophecy of self-loathing.

But – and there is a "but" – I am here to tell you (and bang the drum about it), that healing is possible. Change is possible, and it is all within your reach. You just have to be willing to try. And try, you will! Allow me to explain how.

> I'm validating and acknowledging this because so many women, like you and me, have experienced it. You're not alone. I'm going to be right here with you.

Your Personal Change Experience

This book invites you into a deeply personal exploration, a chance to gently unravel the layers of who you are and what has shaped your journey. Come with an open heart and a willingness to look within, to question ingrained habits, and to truly connect with what your soul desires. This is not about quick fixes; it is about embarking on a path of profound self-discovery, guided by the warm understanding that I, too, have walked this very road.

Within these pages, we will embark on a journey to build a stronger, more loving connection with your authentic self. We will gently explore how you have arrived at this moment, bringing clarity to your experiences so that things begin to make sense. From this foundation of self-awareness, you will naturally find the desire and motivation to make changes that truly resonate with you. Together, we will build the skills and find the support you need to step into a happier, healthier version of you, your Future Self – living the life you deeply want and deserve.

As we delve deeper, we will explore topics that touch so many of us: understanding the impact of our experiences, the intricate dance between our emotions and our eating and drinking habits, and how these can affect our sleep and overall health – mental and physical. We will also gently shine a light on our relationship with alcohol, opening a new door to change and shifting those deep-seated, automatic behaviours into more conscious choices, aligned with values that are chosen by you and are right for your path in the here and now. This book is your companion; I am your companion, offering clarity into who you are and why you are the way you are.

> **"I want you to know you are not alone in your being alone."**
> – Stephen Fry

With practical insights and a supportive voice as you navigate change, I am in your corner to help you embrace progress and cultivate a more nourishing and joyful relationship with food and drink.

Are you ready? Okay, let's do this!

Let's Begin

1.
Drawn to a Cause

My Heart Unveiled
A Colourful Journey of Resilience and Hope

Hello to you, and my most heartfelt welcome. It's with a heart both full and very real that I share my story with you here. This isn't just a narrative; it's my life, my truth, the very essence of who I am today. It's a story of navigating through the storms of childhood trauma, of making what felt like every mistake under the sun, of losing myself, and then, oh, the joy of finding my way back. And now, here I am, reaching out to you, hand-in-hand, heart-to-heart. I'm opening up my life, all of it, so you can understand what truly drives my passion for this work. Later in this book series, I'll share even more truths, some of them not pretty at all, but all of them mine.

Like so many of you, I've walked a path with its fair share of shadows and light. Growing up, I found myself tangled in a web of mental abuse and manipulation within my own family. Can you imagine the confusion of feeling adored one moment, only to be met with harsh attacks – physical, mental, and emotional – the next? Then, the sexual violence at the hands of men with whom I should have been safe. This push-and-pull, this constant gaslighting, eroded my ability to trust others and, most heartbreakingly, to trust myself. It led me down a path of battling bulimia, struggling with my body image (my weight would swing wildly: super skinny, then chubby, and then very overweight). I always found myself in chaotic relationships and situations, like a magnet for drama. I often turned to alcohol, all while carrying the heavy weight of self-blame and shame. On the outside, I might have seemed bright and bubbly – "Fleur Jazz Hands", I used to call myself, the life of the party – but behind closed doors, I felt so incredibly alone and unlovable.

These experiences fuelled a cycle of destruction – with food, with alcohol, and with my choices. Now, this might sound incredibly self-absorbed, but at the time, I didn't fully feel responsible for my "mess". To a large degree, I lived in denial that there was a mess. I'd wake up the next day and be "fabulous" again, covering up the evidence of my disaster. Everything felt so automatic, and honestly, I felt like a victim of my circumstances. How could anyone blame me for what was happening?

It wasn't until my world completely blew up that things changed. I was thrown onto a cement step by a family member in a dramatic rage, and I later required a hip replacement. In recovery, my therapist asked me, "What was your role in this situation?" Those words, I can honestly say, changed my life. There it was, the concept of self-responsibility, and finally, I had to learn how to embrace it.

> **"Hope is being able to see that there is light despite all of the darkness."**
> – Desmond Tutu

So, here's the beautiful, hope-filled part: Healing is possible. With the help of a wonderful coach and a compassionate therapist, I began my journey toward self-love and inner peace. It wasn't easy, not at all. Change is often messy, and it can be downright painful when you're still seeking validation from others. But something magical happened when I realised my worth didn't depend on anyone else's approval. My choices were my own, and so too were my values. No longer was I living under the influence of what my family felt was best for me. I could choose, I could decide, in my own authentically compassionate way. Solidifying my values was another massive breakthrough. And then, slowly, the uphill climb became a gentler, more joyful stride.

Healing also meant looking back, facing those difficult memories, and accepting what had happened. It meant taking responsibility for my part and seeking guidance to truly master the art of acceptance. I dove deep into understanding the dynamics of abuse and learned to connect with my inner child through meditation, changing the hurtful narrative she once believed. I learned to set those all-important healthy boundaries, reclaimed my power, and finally started putting my needs first. Saying "no" became a powerful act of self-care. It took time, but, oh, how I emerged stronger, more resilient, and deeply, truly in love with the woman I've become.

My professional life has been a vibrant tapestry, from the fast-paced world of telecommunications sales and marketing to fulfilling my dream of becoming a chef and restaurateur and opening an award-winning place in Singapore. But even amidst success, I faced heartache, betrayal, and those dark moments when suicidal thoughts crept in. Alcohol and anxiety felt like constant companions. Thankfully, kind souls reached out and helped me find my way back to the light. I learned invaluable lessons about trust, self-responsibility, and the heavy cost of self-sacrifice.

That chapter led me to explore food chemicals and create concepts for international brands. By 2018, I had two decades of experience leading teams and deep knowledge of the food industry. Wanting to help people truly understand what they were putting into their bodies, I retrained as a nutritional health coach. And then, I realised I needed to go deeper, to address the psychology behind food choices, the patterns that lead to self-loathing and unhealthy eating. That's how my coaching business evolved, and The Change Experience approach was created – a platform and place where women can understand how their past is impacting their world today. To heal, to learn new skills, to embrace change, even with all its challenging moments, to find peace and joy, liberated and living the life they truly desire. To learn more about my coaching practice, please go check out my website: **www.fleurelizabeth.com**.

Creating this new space for healing – the online videos, the book series, the coaching (and my podcast that will be launched next) – it all came from that burning desire to share my story, to let other women know they are not alone. I needed to break the silence, lift the shame, and offer hope. Sharing trauma stories can be intense, and I know it can be confronting for some. But I don't want these to be secrets anymore. That's why my marketing slogan is: "This is not your secret anymore." I want women to feel safe to speak their truths, to release those secrets that keep us trapped and afraid.

Today, at fifty-one, I'm living a quieter life here in Australia with my three fur babies and beautiful life companions. I spend my days writing, gardening, and cooking. I'm a motivational speaker, author, coach, and a fierce advocate for change. I want to help women move from feeling trapped to feeling empowered and confident. And if this book reaches the heart of one woman for whom it makes a difference, well, then, that will make my heart sing.

This is my journey, and I share it with you in the hope that it lights a spark in your heart, reminding you that healing is possible and that you're never truly alone.

> I will say it a few times in this book series, "Nothing in life is ever a straight line!"

2.
Is This You?

Welcome, My Friend
Come On In. The Water Is Warm!

If you're holding this book (the first of our three-volume series), chances are, you've felt that tug-of-war with food and drink, and the effects they have on your mind and body. And, honestly, who hasn't? So many of us have been there, and that's why I poured my heart into writing this – to help you navigate this sometimes-tricky relationship and finally find some joy, peace, and ease.

Life throws curveballs, doesn't it? Sometimes you see them coming, and sometimes they just appear out of nowhere, leaving you a little dazed and confused. You just know that something feels off. Life isn't quite what you pictured, and changing those old patterns of behaviour – well, that can feel like an uphill battle. It can leave you feeling like you're the only one facing it, and completely alone. Sigh, that can be a really tough place to be. I truly get it.

Our relationship with food and drink is woven into so many parts of our lives – our work, our relationships, our social lives, our physical and mental health, even how we move our bodies. Stress, joy, struggle, pain, love, happiness, heartbreak, and excitement – they all play a role. Every experience creates a ripple effect, and most of what we do in this space is automatic, influencing our behaviours and our connection with food and drink. But, if we're being really honest with ourselves, sometimes those automatic behaviours come from us not living in line with what we truly value. That's not always easy to face, I know, but I wonder, does that resonate with you?

Those fad diets promise quick fixes, but they're never really sustainable, are they? And they often miss the heart of the matter – the psychological and emotional parts of what makes us tick. They don't see you as the unique individual you are, with your own story, your own body, your own biology and heritage, and your own emotional makeup.

So, come, let's walk through this together. Let's bravely develop some clarity around how your life experiences and core wounds have shaped you. Let's investigate how they've influenced your relationship with food, drink, or anything else you might use to cope with, or numb and avoid, life's complications. Let's find a deeper understanding, a real connection with your inner self, and build a path forward that truly nourishes you – mind, body, and soul. What do you say?

> I am so honoured to share my life and my lessons with you – including the hard ones. I hope my story gives you the confidence to step out of the shadows and back into the light. This is a safe place for you.

Common Characteristics of Your Core Wound
What Really Happens Behind Closed Doors

I'd love to share a bit about the wonderful women I created this for, and how it might resonate with your story. Let's gently explore some common threads among women who have navigated challenging experiences, sometimes defined as trauma. As you read, please see if any of this feels familiar or touches a chord within you.

It's so common, especially for those of us over mid-thirty, to feel a little uneasy with the word "trauma". Many of us don't realise that some of our challenging life experiences and difficult times do fall under that umbrella, or even fully understand what trauma truly encompasses. I'd like to offer some clarity around this topic for you in the pages of this book. We've often been encouraged to be strong, to power through, to keep a "stiff upper lip", and to just pick ourselves up and carry on. It can feel vulnerable, even a bit shameful, to admit our struggles publicly. And, honestly, sometimes it seems like others shy away from those who have been through difficult times. That stigma can still linger in social settings.

Thankfully, mindsets are shifting and evolving. But for a long time, those older ways of thinking were the norm, and many of us were raised with those values ingrained within us.

Given all of this, many of us may not fully realise the impact of past experiences on our present lives. It's not always easy to say, "I'm struggling." I can truly relate to that. It's hard to acknowledge something when you're not even sure what it is, or how it might be affecting you.

Please take a moment, and with kindness towards yourself, read through this and see how it might offer some clarity on what's going on with you, and how you may find a connection with your own journey.

The False Self

When life throws us truly difficult, heart-wrenching challenges – events that leave us feeling utterly helpless and isolated – our brains have an incredible way of stepping in to protect us and help us keep moving forward. If you've navigated a traumatic experience of any kind, whether in childhood, your teens, or young adulthood, your brain might have created a "protective persona" or a "false self". This is the brain's way of helping us survive, a way for our psyche to cope with overwhelming experiences. This resourceful persona gently shields us, while the trauma gets tucked away deep inside, sometimes even leaving us feeling numb. And so, we carry on, doing our best to navigate life as if everything is alright.

It's important to know that many of us may not even realise this shift in persona has occurred. We might be completely unaware that we're living behind this protective layer our brain so cleverly created. For some, this can show up as feeling somewhat detached, almost robotic, or disconnected from emotions and pain. For others, it might manifest as being exceptionally vibrant, always putting on a cheerful and outgoing face.

Is This You?

- I'm a people pleaser.
- I hide behind a false self, keeping up appearances to the outside world.
- I cry behind closed doors.
- I find it hard to trust people.
- My health is up and down.
- I use food and alcohol to numb feeling overwhelmed.
- I don't like the mirror much.
- I'm hypervigilant.
- I fall into repetitive cycles.
- No one was there to validate or support me when I was vulnerable.
- I get lost in emotional storms.
- I carry shame because of what's happened.
- I get triggered and react.

And for others still, it might drive a persistent need for high achievement, always striving to excel in everything. In whatever ways it expresses itself in you, please know that the person who experienced those challenging events is still there, living behind this persona, where you now navigate your life.

You might find, as so many others do, that when triggered or facing an emotional storm, you fall into automatic behaviours. These might take the form of high-risk activities, erratic choices, attention-seeking actions, or extreme behaviours related to food or alcohol, to avoid the pain and numb the feelings that are bubbling up.

The Absence of the Healing Power of an Empathetic Witness

Perhaps, in the past, that supportive presence of an empathetic witness felt absent. Maybe no one validated your experience, offered reassurance, or comforted you when you were afraid. It's perfectly alright to acknowledge those feelings. First, this was not your fault. It's okay if you feel like you didn't have someone there for you when you were vulnerable. It's half the battle just recognising that critical fact that shapes your life responses to the events you encounter.

Please remember, this lack of support wasn't a reflection of your worthiness either, even though it might have become the basis for some of those inner-critic stories you tell yourself, like "I'm not worthy." I will gently guide you through a healing process that involves recognising your own worthiness and treating yourself with that same compassion you craved in the past.

When we experience severely challenging or frightening events that leave us feeling vulnerable, helpless, and alone, our brains create a story about what happened. This is how trauma can become imprinted in the emotional centre of the brain – like a tattoo (it can be permanent!). Often, these deeply held narratives take root in childhood when our developmental needs weren't met by caregivers. Instead of being that empathetic witness, offering a sense of safety and security, caregivers may have been absent, dismissive, or neglectful.

However, things can unfold differently when someone is there with us during those difficult times, offering comfort and reassurance. If someone soothed your fear, told you that you were going to be okay, addressed your needs, or let you know that it wasn't your fault, then that experience takes on a different form in your brain. Instead of a deeply embedded trauma, it becomes a difficult experience that you went through, rather than an event that resurfaces with the same fear, pain, and anxiety every time you encounter something similar. This is the profound difference that having an "empathetic witness" can make. This person, quite simply, can truly change the course of your life.

Triggers, Behaviours, and Consequences

We all have triggers – those moments that, in some way, echo past experiences and stir up a strong emotional response within us. It can sometimes feel like an emotional whirlwind.

These triggers can lead to automatic behaviours and actions we take without even fully realising why. Unfortunately, often these automatic responses can take us down a path of destructive patterns, ways we might try to avoid, numb, or suppress the pain that surfaces from the trigger. And when these behaviours play out, there are consequences. Some of those consequences might be positive, but often, they present their own set of challenges.

These cycles can feel automatic and repetitive, like we're caught in a loop. And because they're automatic, and because we might not be fully aware of our triggers, it can be hard to understand why these things keep happening. It just feels like we're doing the same things over and over, repeating these behaviours and asking ourselves, "Why does this keep happening to me?"

If any of this resonates with you, you're in the right place. I'm here to help you develop the tools to connect with yourself more deeply, to develop clarity and become more aware of your patterns, and slow down those automatic responses. Together, we can create space for more conscious choices.

The Mirror and the Story Within

Those difficult experiences, the ones that feel tied to the past, can sometimes make our relationship with the mirror – and the woman we see reflected there – feel challenging. Sadly, it is these old narratives, like "I'm not worthy," linked to the traumatic experience, that become etched into the way we see ourselves physically. This can, understandably, create another cycle of unhelpful and unkind inner dialogue, filled with judgement about how we look. It's so easy for our minds to play tricks on us and push us toward extreme measures, all to make our bodies into something we think will make us acceptable to ourselves and others.

It truly breaks my heart that so many wonderful women find it hard to love what they see, find reasons to criticise their appearance, and struggle to fully embrace and appreciate who they are. We live in a world where only a tiny fraction of the population fits the "magazine cover model" ideal. The rest of us? We each have our own wonderfully beautiful characteristics that make us whole and uniquely ourselves. However, that persistent desire to be thinner or a different shape, fuelled by the belief that it will make us worthy of love or acceptance, can be a heavy burden to carry day in and day out.

And through this sometimes-painful relationship with the mirror, we often become experts at hiding the struggle we're going through from the outside world. It's hard to admit, isn't it, that we don't truly love our bodies or ourselves entirely? This internal struggle can then start to impact our intimate relationships and our ability to have healthy, fulfilling sexual connections. It can become a very lonely place to be; I know this for sure.

If this is you, again, I will stress, you are not alone. In these pages (and throughout the book series), you will develop a toolbox to construct a gentle approach to the acceptance of self. Accepting who you are, and what you are, is such a powerful gift you can give yourself. And this, my friend, is the skill and the "muscle" that I'm here to help you build, with clarity, kindness, and compassion.

The Heart of a People-Pleaser

It's so understandable. When life has presented challenges, especially those that have left us feeling unseen, unheard, or not valued, it's only natural to seek validation and love in other ways. This can sometimes lead us into people-pleasing patterns. We might find ourselves going out of our way to do things for others, to make them feel good, hoping that in return, we'll feel seen, recognised, and loved ourselves. It can feel like that's the way to earn affection.

However, this beautiful intention can sometimes create a tricky situation with boundaries. We might find it difficult to say "no", and before we know it, we're giving much more than we truly intended or have the energy for. This often stems from experiences in childhood or past relationships where healthy boundaries weren't modelled for us, and where self-sacrifice was highly valued. As a result, we might not have had the chance to learn vital skills, making it hard to implement them now in our daily lives.

A people-pleaser often, with the kindest of intentions, puts everyone else's needs before their own. We might develop a deep-seated guilt, or a feeling that tells us if we don't please someone, we've failed, or that we're still not worthy. It can be hard to find balance and inner peace when everyone around us seems to be getting their needs met but we are left feeling a bit neglected. And, let's be honest, it can sometimes feel like no one is asking about what we need.

Over time, this can lead to feelings of quiet resentment or a low-level anger building inside of us because, ultimately, we're the ones feeling depleted and stretched thin. We might have been conditioned by past experiences to give love in order to receive love, but that love can feel a little hollow when we're running on empty, exhausted, and battling negative self-talk.

If any of this resonates with you, please know that you're not alone. Many of us have been there. You're in such good company, surrounded by a community of understanding women. I'm here to gently guide you as you learn to set healthy boundaries that honour you, develop clarity on what truly matters to your heart, and lovingly prioritise your own needs.

Boundary-setting is an essential life skill – it's your way of showing the world who you are and nurturing your own wellbeing.

Trust

I am the first one to put my hand up to say that navigating relationships after experiencing trauma can be an incredibly difficult and uncomfortable space. What I also know, and would equally like to assure you with, is that trust issues are not a personal failing (I struggled with this for years; I know it's not easy to shift that perception). They arise because trauma can cause our brains to associate anything remotely similar to the traumatic event – be it a time, place, or detail, our relationships with parents or siblings – as a potential threat. And our fear keeps us from ever wanting to experience that deep pain of betrayal again.

Relationships of all kinds can be tricky, especially when traumatic experiences occurred within our family of origin or community. Our trust in those who were meant to keep us safe can be deeply shaken. Naturally, trusting the people who fall under this label becomes a real challenge. Another factor is communication; without trust, it's extremely hard to communicate our needs for fear of repercussion or further invalidation. It can create chaos and confusion in our lives, making even simple problems feel overwhelming. This, in turn, can affect how others perceive us and their willingness to support us.

Alternatively, if we've been unfairly blamed for negative events in the past, we might develop negative beliefs about our ability to make sound decisions or accurate judgements (in essence, we are gaslighting ourselves). This can lead to questioning ourselves constantly, as those past traumatic events seem to confirm our fears and keep us stuck in old patterns. Consequently, we might find it hard to trust our environment and the people around us, anticipating that everyone will treat us with bias.

Sometimes, we may find ourselves giving our trust too quickly, hoping for acceptance and love. We might engage in people-pleasing behaviours, attempting to rewrite that story of mistrust. We could find ourselves placing our trust in the same types of people who have hurt us before, leading to those same patterns being repeated. The flipside of this is we might even subconsciously sabotage trust, as a way of validating our deep inner belief that we can't truly trust anyone at all.

A less discussed, yet very real result of trauma, is the profound damage it does to our ability to trust ourselves. When we lack self-trust, we don't live by our values and we ignore what we know to be important to our health and safety, and our happiness. We might ignore our gut feelings that warn us of danger or when something "isn't right" (but our gut feeling is nearly always right, yes!). We might also struggle to identify what we truly want – often deferring to others – which can lead to negative outcomes. Sadly, this can also leave us feeling unsafe within our own bodies, as we ignore the signals our bodies send, leading to emotional chaos and a lack of impulse control. To avoid this discomfort, we might distract ourselves with rumination and negative self-talk, or by using food, alcohol, or other substances to quiet the noise.

I want to offer more clarity here: My primary goal is not only to simply enable you to trust other people (although I will help you build awareness and skill in how to spot gaslighting and learn how to avoid it) but also to help you open up to trusting yourself. Developing the ability to trust yourself – your choices, your values, and what's important to you – will truly be the foundation for finding joy and peace in your life again.

Navigating the World as a Sensitive Soul

Do you ever feel like you're constantly "on"? Like your senses are heightened, and you experience the world more deeply than others? It's okay, you're not alone. The sensitive souls among us navigate life bound by an armour of hypervigilance. Perhaps you can relate to feeling deeply moved by things that others might easily overlook. Or maybe you startle easily and find yourself constantly scanning your environment, never feeling a sense of safety. This can manifest as a general sense of unease, a jumpy feeling, or even a heightened immune response. Unfortunately, these experiences can sometimes lead to being labelled as "too sensitive" or even a "drama queen", which can feel invalidating when our feelings are genuine and deeply felt.

This hypervigilance can also bring about feelings of shame. When we're told we're too sensitive, it can make us question ourselves and induce feelings of embarrassment and fear. Understandably, many of us struggle in silence, battling an inner critic and racing thoughts, afraid to express what we are feeling. This can sometimes lead to unhelpful patterns with food and drink as we seek ways to cope with the emotional discomfort of feeling triggered.

Often, our hypervigilance is a direct response to past challenging or traumatic experiences. Our brains remember these events and react as if they're happening again in the present. Our nervous system may go into a state of hyperarousal as a protective mechanism. And, if there isn't an empathetic witness during those difficult times, it might leave us feeling unsafe, with our subconscious remaining on high alert. (See how all of this is so intrinsically linked?)

Okay, as someone who was once an extremely hypervigilant lady, I completely understand how difficult this can be. I am a testament that healing is possible, and it can be for you too. When you gain clarity and understand the roots of your hypervigilance and how to tame it, this is where you will begin to create a sense of safety and peace within. I want to help you find a new normal.

Your Physical and Mental Health

It's absolutely true: Those of us who've journeyed through traumatic events in our past often find ourselves navigating some tricky terrain when it comes to our mental and physical health as adults. This is a well trodden path for me. I'd be cruising along just fine, and then, suddenly, I'd feel completely out of sorts. I remember times when people said to me, "There's always something going on with you!" or "You've really been through it with your health lately, haven't you?" Have you ever had moments like that? It can feel so isolating, like no one truly understands.

This is another piece of the puzzle when it comes to navigating life after challenging experiences. In general, being hypervigilant means your adrenal glands are always acting as if you are in fight-or-flight mode. Then, when triggered, our bodies produce a whole lot of cortisol – that's our stress hormone – and our immune system gets a bit overzealous. Essentially, our bodies get tired and worn out. Our sleep goes on strike, our moods become a bit of a rollercoaster, and we find it harder to fend off those pesky bugs and infections. Yet again, we're confronted by those behaviours that pop up when we're triggered. Maybe we turn to food or alcohol, or perhaps other substances that we think will help but ultimately end up taking a toll on our wellbeing.

These ups and downs can have quite a big impact on both our physical and mental health. Physically, those periods of uneven behaviour can sometimes lead to higher acidity in our blood, which can then open the door to other health concerns. We might experience inflammation in our joints, legs, feet, or even our brains. It's been shown that things like arthritis and dementia can be linked to lifestyle choices, especially irregular eating and alcohol consumption.

On the the mental side of things, where anxiety and depression can creep in. Have you ever felt like you're managing alright, just getting through each day, when all of a sudden, something throws you completely off course? You get stuck in a mental fog, start spiralling, and it feels nearly impossible to find your way back. Sometimes, your memory isn't what it used to be, or you might have moments when your mind just goes blank. Or perhaps your short-term memory feels a bit fuzzy, and you can't quite recall what you had for lunch by dinnertime. It's a really tough spot to be in; I truly understand, because I've been there too.

My friends, it's a slippery slope, and if we're not careful, it can slowly and quietly start to affect our health. There can be years of unseen damage happening beneath the surface, until one day, we find ourselves facing a list of health challenges. I have seen this, when one thing starts to go awry, it can create a ripple effect throughout the whole body. This is sometimes called "metabolic syndrome", where one health issue can make us more vulnerable to others.

In this book, which is designed to give you a deeper understanding of your behaviour patterns, I'll share insights into the importance of sleep and practical ways to improve it. Allow me to walk alongside you to guide and bring balance to your mental and physical wellbeing. You'll learn some very effective breathing techniques to help calm you during moments of anxiety, as well as grounding exercises to help you make clear-headed choices during challenging or emotionally charged times. In Book Two, *A New Perspective – The Emotionally Resilient Woman: Recognise Your Triggers, Cultivate Self-Acceptance & Embrace Emotional Health*, we'll delve even deeper into skill-building with grounding techniques. I'll also be sharing guided meditations to help soothe your nervous system and reconnect you with your inner child, so keep an eye out for those. And in Book Three, *Liberated Connection – The Energetic Woman: Set Healthy Boundaries, Honour Your Needs & Embrace Your Feminine Power*, the focus shifts to movement and taking care of your physical self, something I'm incredibly passionate about. So, rest assured, as you journey with me through this entire book series, you'll be developing some powerful "must-have" life skills to support you on your path of evolution and change. We'll explore that together.

Those Private Tears

The impact that past experiences can have on us can hit us out of the blue. One moment, you're doing just fine, and the next, it feels like you've been hit by a speeding freight train that's run head-on into a massive brick wall. Bang! Explosion, uncontrollable tears, hyperventilating, and fog – just so much confusion mixed with so much pain. Oh gosh, I remember those times so vividly.

It's really vulnerable to admit, isn't it? The sheer intensity of tears when we get caught in an emotional storm can feel utterly debilitating. Tears streaming down your face like marbles bouncing down your cheeks, and that visceral, whole-body feeling, where everything seems knotted, torn up, and so, so painful. It's a lonely place, these moments often happening behind closed doors when no one is looking. And sometimes, there's just no one there to offer a comforting hug or nurturing words.

Sometimes, you might find yourself needing to cry where someone can hear you, almost like a cry for help. But ultimately, you feel a sense of shame about it, don't you?

Remember earlier when we talked about the false self – that persona we create because our brains have decided that the impact of what we experienced was too much for us to handle, so it gets locked away and buried deep within? It maybe a great survival mechanism, but what's actually happening is our brain re-registering something that reminds it of that past experience, and suddenly, all those feelings, memories, and emotions get unlocked, as if it's happening all over again, right in that very moment. Hence, the flood of tears. Does that offer some clarity?

Some might call this a "product defect" and want to ask for a refund, but sadly, my friends, this is just the way our brains work. Your brain is trying to protect you, even if it doesn't feel like it is.

> Exhale. Take a breath for me, okay?

The Weight of Shame

It's completely understandable to feel a lot of shame about what happened in the past and the path life has taken. Sometimes, it can feel like you're held captive by those experiences, like a victim trapped there, held back by what was challenging. This isn't the life you envisioned, the life you truly wanted, not at all. And the things you feel you've missed out on because of those past events can make those feelings of shame and unworthiness seem even heavier.

It's likely you've felt, and will continue to feel, moments of shame at various times. This feeling might linger with you over your morning coffee or stay for days. Sometimes, you might just want to curl up and disappear when those waves of shame wash over you. Shame can make us feel like we're not good enough, and the instinct to hide away is perfectly natural.

And because shame often brings emotional pain, it's also understandable to feel angry, sometimes even directing that pain away from yourself.

That deep-seated feeling of being worthless, that "toxic shame" – there's that old narrative creeping in again, right? See how it touches so many areas of your life? It happens when we internalise the poor treatment towards us by others and turn it into a belief about ourselves.

It's tough. It's a really, truly tough place to be. But you're here now, taking a brave step on this journey with me. We'll work together on this mission to enhance your clarity, to understand and gently examine those feelings of shame so that you can begin to release them. We'll gently shift thought patterns, allowing you to move forward.

> **"As traumatised children, we always dreamed that someone would come and save us. We never dreamed that it would, in fact, be ourselves as adults."**
> – Alice Little

By developing self-acceptance skills and normalising mistakes as part of being human, you can discover a new sense of normal – one that embraces imperfections and recognises the value of learning and growth from every experience.

Your Core Wound

To begin, let's gently connect with the essence of your core wound. Think about the experiences you had growing up, and how they have shaped you until now. This is a short but powerful exercise to help you gain some clarity on the emotions tied to your past. Grab your journal, and let's dive in together.

Place your hand on your heart

I'd like you to read each question below aloud, and then say the very first word that comes to your mind, also aloud. Then, jot that word down.

1. What's one thing you received from Dad that you didn't truly want?

2. What's one thing you received from Mum that you didn't truly want?

3. What's one thing you longed for from Dad, but never received?

4. What's one thing you longed for from Mum, but never received?

5. Now, take a moment. What's the overarching theme or feeling that connects those words? (Say this in one word.)

6. Next, give me ten different single words that reflect what you needed back then. What did your heart truly yearn for? (You can write the word, and why it is relevant to your story.)

Hold onto these words; we'll revisit them later in Book Three: *Liberated Connection* – it will make sense when you get there, trust me! For now, just know that this is your first step towards uncovering the roots of deeper connection, empowering you to step out of the shadows and into the light again.

...

3. Bravely Sharing

What Happens Behind Closed Doors
My Intimate Connection Through Storytelling

My friend, I want you to know, from the bottom of my heart, that this has been my journey too. My struggle, my fight, my path to where I stand today. It hasn't always been easy, and I'm opening up to you in a way that feels both vulnerable and incredibly freeing.

Throughout this book series, I'm sharing pieces of my soul, stories that have shaped me, that are the very foundation of who I am. I'm inviting you into the deepest parts of my life, the spaces where trauma, both seen and unseen – sexual, physical, and mental – took root. It's through these stories that you'll truly understand why I'm here, why this work – this connection with you – means everything to me.

My hope in sharing these raw, unfiltered moments is that you'll see yourself reflected in my experiences. That you'll understand, with a knowing deep in your bones, that you are not alone. I want to shed light on some of the triggers that sent me spiralling, that fuelled unhealthy patterns, especially with food and drink. For me, one of those major trauma responses was bulimia, a battle I fought for so many years, starting when I was just fifteen. But this isn't just about the struggle; it's about the healing, about finding my way to peace, and I'll share that with you too.

> "Time and health are two precious assets that we don't recognise and appreciate until they have been depleted."
>
> – Denis Waitley

When I first started using social media to share snippets of these stories about difficult moments in my life, something incredible happened. A wave of women reached out, each with their own echoes of pain and resilience. They said, "This happened to me too." Hearing that, seeing that connection, it was … humbling. These women, with their kind and compassionate words, shared that my storytelling allowed them to finally acknowledge their own experiences. That it made them realise they weren't alone, and that they too could and needed to talk about it.

It's astounding, and honestly heart-wrenching, how many of us have carried our burdens in silence for so long. We didn't have a safe space, a place to be heard without judgement. While it pains me to know so many of you have faced such heartache, there's a profound truth in this shared experience. It's prevalent, it's real, and the fact that my vulnerability can be a bridge to connection for you … well, that's everything I could have hoped for. I truly wonder, will these stories resonate with you in the same way?

I do need to give you a gentle warning. My stories are raw and intense. They can be triggering. What happened to me wasn't pretty. I want you to be in the driver's seat. I want you to choose when, and if, you're ready to walk this path with me.

Anywhere I share a personal story, a piece of my trauma, it's titled "My Trauma Experience". That way, you'll know what's coming, and you'll have the power to decide if you're ready to delve into that chapter. If you want to save it for a time when you're in a safe, quiet space, know that it's absolutely okay to do so.

The most important message I want to convey is this: I leave this entirely with you. You have a choice. That is your free will.

If you do find yourself feeling activated or triggered by anything you read, please know that I've provided grounding techniques. I want you to have the tools to navigate your emotions with gentleness and care.

This is from me to you, with love.

4.
Start with Intention

Setting Your Intentions
A Must-Have Life Skill

Setting an intention for your day, or how you want to approach working on yourself, is a powerful tool. It's like retraining your brain and telling the universe your desires and what you want in life – a process known as "calling it in".

It's a way to get your thoughts and intentions out there, helping you connect and allowing the clarity to motivate action towards what you need. It is important to be clear and specific in your intentions. This is your form of energetic communication to your authentic self and to the world.

I was first introduced to this concept by a very smart man called Mike Dooley. Google him; he's famous. One of the stand-out things I learned from him was the concept that "thoughts become things, so we must choose the good ones!" He believes that the laws of physics are simply that what you think, you create. Your thoughts create energy that attracts what they say. Dr. Joe Dispenza (a world-renowned neurosurgeon who teaches change through changing our neuropathways) also teaches the same thing. Both gentlemen and I advocate that you must get into the habit of ensuring your mind isn't clogged with negative thoughts. You have the power to crowd these out with thoughts about the good things you are going to do for yourself in life. Be conscious of the fact that the thoughts you create will affect the outcomes you want for yourself.

Setting intentions is key to having a good experience and getting the most out of the investment and energy you are putting into this time we are spending together here. It's about defining how you'll approach this book every time you pick it up and inviting positive energy into the experience.

So, set your intentions for your path forward and ask yourself, "How do I want to feel at the end of this?"

> **"Every journey begins with the first step of articulating the intention and then becoming the intention."**
> – Bryant McGill

I've found that setting a daily intention has changed my life. The self-doubt is gone, and it's transformed every experience because I'm clear with my intention – to myself and out to the universe – on how I'll show up and the experience I'll have each time I do something.

Whether it's walking the dog, driving to an appointment, working on my book, or having dinner with a friend, I decide what's important to me, how I'll show up, and the experience I'm inviting into my life. Then, I simply verbalise my intention (I like to tell the universe), and I use this phrase to go with it, " ... and this will be effortless," and it always is. Effortless.

Think about: What are you going to "call in" that meets your needs? How do you want to show up every day? Wouldn't you love to make this effortless and enjoyable? How will you feel after learning new skills to stop automatic coping mechanisms and find balance and peace in your life? How do you intend to feel when you have clarity on your habits with food and drink and can take back control?

> I always use the words "<my intention> will be effortless"; it is incredible how things that were once hard work seem to be easy and just flow now!

If it works for me, it can work for you, too. That's why I'm sharing this golden nugget with you. Wouldn't you love to feel like a life of chaos has changed into a life that is effortless? So, take a moment to write down your intentions for your Change Experience.

Let me help you take the uncomfortable out of this and bring the world you want to live in into this. Here are some helpful questions to guide you through the process.

Questions to Ask Yourself

Remember: Read your answers aloud so you hear yourself speak the words – so you believe what you say.

1. How would you like to feel after you have completed a chapter and learned some useful empowerment tools? Can you set an intention, articulating how you will feel with each new skill you learn?

2. Knowing your learning style and that you're applying yourself to personal improvement work, could you set an intention for the best way to make sure you get the most out of this process?

3. In your life, you may sometimes face barriers or challenges with balance that may interfere with the flow of this self-work. How might you set an intention to work through those barriers and overcome them?

4. Being aware of your personal stressors, could you set an intention for the best way to manage your anxiety to get the most out of your Change Experience and stay balanced?

To recap, get comfortable with setting and then focusing on your intention for each task you embark on. This will help you create a mindset for what you want for yourself while working on this personal work and beyond. It will become your new normal, and a new, healthier automatic behaviour. So, the message here is this: Practising setting an intention is a must-have life skill to bring into your life and use every day.

> **"Never underestimate the power you have to take your life in a new direction."**
> – Germany Kent

By the end of this book, I would like you to check in with yourself. Ask yourself in what ways you have already noticed the shifts in your perspective and how the world around you is looking. Notice the signs that indicate you are progressing towards embracing what you truly desire for your life.

This is all extremely powerful stuff to visualise, connect to, be clear about, and call in. How nice it would be if your intentions felt effortless! What have you got to lose? Give it a go!

Your Past Challenges

5.
Be Trauma-Informed

Your Core Wounds
So, What Are Trauma and Complex Trauma Really?

To help you gain clarity and come to terms with the word "trauma" and its effects on your life, I wanted to gently take you through a process of defining what it is, common occurrences of how and where it happens, and what the results are in a person's mental and physical condition. In this chapter, we will explore the nuances of trauma, particularly the distinction between single-incident trauma and the more pervasive complex trauma that can develop within a family environment. We'll delve into how these challenging life experiences, often normalised in childhood, can have lasting impacts on adult life, potentially leading to a realisation that past experiences have shaped your present in ways you hadn't fully understood.

 Please approach this information intellectually, as knowledge, rather than emotionally, to avoid potential distress or triggering of past wounds. If you find yourself experiencing emotional discomfort, please pause and return to this chapter when you feel more grounded.

Understanding Trauma vs. Complex Trauma

Trauma, at its core, is more than just a bad experience; it's a deeply distressing or disturbing event that rocks our sense of safety and wellbeing. It's like a storm that sweeps through our lives, leaving us feeling utterly overwhelmed. There are two main types we often talk about: single-incident trauma and complex trauma. Let's explore them together, shall we?

🔎 Single-Incident Trauma

This kind of trauma stems from one specific, isolated event – a sudden jolt that makes us feel intensely unsafe or in danger.

Examples of single-incident trauma:

- A car accident where you truly feared for your life.
- Witnessing something violent and feeling helpless.
- A natural disaster, like a terrible fire, flood, or storm, that turned your world upside down.
- Being robbed or assaulted, leaving you feeling violated.
- Being sexually assaulted or raped.

It's like a lightning strike. Afterward, we might experience things like:

- **Flashbacks:** These aren't just memories; they make us feel like we're right back in that moment, reliving it all over again.
- **Nightmares:** Troubling dreams that replay the trauma (sometimes called night terrors).
- **Hypervigilance:** Feeling constantly on edge, as if danger is always lurking.

- **Avoidance:** Trying to steer clear of anything that reminds us of what happened – places, people, or activities that trigger memories.

These events can shatter our sense of security and leave deep emotional wounds.

🔎 Complex Trauma: The Weight of Many Burdens

Complex trauma is different. It arises from repeated or prolonged exposure to hurtful experiences, often within relationships that should be safe. It's especially tough when it happens in childhood.

Some examples of complex trauma:

- Growing up in a fractured home, leading to divorce. (Observing parents' volatility, verbal abuse, and gaslighting.)
- A family environment whereby it is normalised to have repeated jokes made at your expense, mean and demeaning nicknames, or constant put-downs.
- Growing up in an environment where you were used as the scapegoat and blamed when things went wrong, even when it was not your fault.
- Parents who are too busy, unavailable, or caught up in their own health challenges, addictions, and mental health problems.
- Growing up with a parent who is physically or emotionally unavailable or neglectful.
- Living in a home with domestic violence.
- Witnessing or enduring physical or sexual abuse.

Imagine growing up feeling like you're always walking on eggshells, where your basic needs aren't met. It's like living in constant "survival mode". You can never really relax because you are constantly on guard, in fear of the next hurt to take place.

Common Characteristics:

- **Chronic Unpredictability:** Life feels chaotic, leaving you constantly anxious.

- **Emotional Neglect:** Your feelings are ignored or dismissed, making you feel invisible.

- **Lack of Safety and Security:** Never feeling truly safe or secure.

- **Interpersonal Trauma:** Hurt from those who should care for you.

- **Difficulty Regulating Emotions:** Struggling to understand and manage your feelings.

- **Negative Self-Image:** Feeling like you're not good enough or don't measure up.

Complex trauma can profoundly impact a person's development, affecting their ability to form healthy relationships, regulate their emotions, and maintain a positive sense of self. The next level of issues is that complex trauma can cause people to be highly erratic, become involved in high-risk behaviours, have addictive personalities, and develop issues with food and alcohol disorders. This constant feeling of being on guard, unsafe, and never being able to relax (ultimately always feeling unsafe) can lead to a range of long-term mental and emotional health challenges.

I hope this helps you understand more about where trauma actually comes from and the distinctions between single-incident and complex trauma. From here, we can start the process of appreciating the diverse ways in which trauma can shape a person's life. In this case, yours.

Where Does Complex Trauma Start for a Child?

Remember I mentioned earlier that not everyone realises they have been affected by complex trauma, but they know something isn't right? I'd like to share some examples to help you get a better understanding of how a child can experience complex trauma at home. This is Project Clarity, right?

🔍 **Inconsistent Discipline and "Walking on Eggshells":** A parent alternates between harsh punishment (sometimes physical) and permissive freedom to break the rules (neglect). This creates an environment where the child is constantly anxious, never knowing where they stand or what will trigger a negative reaction. This instils a pervasive feeling of being unsafe and an inability to relax, a true hallmark of complex trauma.

🔍 **Emotional Invalidations and Put-Downs:** A parent regularly dismisses the child's feelings ("You're too sensitive," "Stop being dramatic") or uses belittling language ("You're so stupid," "Why can't you be more like your sister?"). This undermines the child's sense of self-worth and creates a deep feeling of not being good enough. The child never feels like they are accepted for who they really are.

🔍 **Lack of Boundaries and Enmeshment:** A parent overshares adult problems with the child, relies on them for emotional support, or invades their privacy. This blurs the parent-child role, leaving the child feeling overwhelmed and responsible for managing adult emotions, taking care of the parent's needs first (they act like the parent), which prevents the child from being allowed to be a child and go through normal developmental stages. This creates another sense of a lack of safety.

🔍 **Mixed Messages and Gaslighting:** A parent's words and actions don't align, or they deny the child's perception of reality ("That didn't happen," "You're imagining things"). This creates confusion and distrust, making the child doubt their own beliefs (and the constant "there must be something wrong with me" feeling), hindering their ability to trust their own judgement.

🔍 **Unpredictable Moods and Emotional Volatility:** A parent's moods shift rapidly and unpredictably, from loving to enraged, without the child really understanding why. This creates a constant state of hypervigilance in the child, as they try to anticipate and avoid the parent's outbursts, and they are unable to ever truly relax or feel safe.

🔍 **Lack of Empathy and Emotional Neglect:** A parent consistently fails to recognise or respond to the child's emotional needs, dismissing their sadness, fear, or anger. This conveys a message that the child's feelings don't matter, leading to a sense of isolation and unworthiness, and more of the negative self-talk like, "There must be something wrong with me."

🔍 **Conditional Love and Acceptance:** A parent only shows affection or approval when the child meets certain expectations (e.g., academic performance, obedience). This teaches the child that their worth is conditional, leading to anxiety and a constant need for external validation.

🔍 **Public Humiliation and Ridicule:** A parent makes fun of the child in front of others, revealing private information or embarrassing the child. Their trust in their intimate relationship is violated, and they don't feel like they can express themselves anymore. This destroys the child's sense of safety and dignity, leading to shame, social anxiety, and the need to isolate and withdraw from people because of a fear of being hurt.

🔍 **Absence of Consistent Routines and Structure:** A chaotic home environment with no clear routines or expectations creates a sense of instability and insecurity. This makes it difficult for the child to regulate their emotions and develop a sense of predictability. Again, there are no signals of safety here.

🔍 **Parental Rejection of the Child's Identity:** A parent actively rejects the child's desires, interests, or personality traits – their basic need to be seen. They may criticise the child's gender identity or sexual orientation and shame them. This communicates that the child is fundamentally unacceptable, leading to deep feelings of shame, self-hatred, and a lack of acceptance. Creating a false self-persona is a common hiding place for a child.

Childhood Trauma of Any Kind

You may be shocked to read this, but it is true: The Centers for Disease Control and Prevention's 2019 study on "adverse childhood experiences" (ACEs) revealed that childhood wounds and neglect are the single most preventable cause of food disorders and alcohol abuse. What's even more scary, studies have shown that these experiences in childhood also significantly contribute to chronic disease, a reduction in life expectancy, and suicidality.

Psychologists involved in the study believe that if we could remove childhood trauma from our communities, we'd see a dramatic reduction in negative outcomes; alcoholism would be reduced by two-thirds, suicide by half, domestic violence by two-thirds, and sexual violence against women by half.

> Jeez, I have to wonder, when you know all of this, how is there not more focus on teaching people how to become healthy parents!

ACEs can stem from many things that are often overlooked. Perhaps you were neglected, not honoured, or simply not seen as a child. It could be that you were denied basic needs like security, trust, nutrition, love, and community. Maybe a parent was always absent and never had time for you, or perhaps your parents divorced or separated, and their broken home left you feeling like it was your fault. Or perhaps you endured even more horrific experiences: beatings; molestation; verbal, sexual, or mental abuse; manipulation; gaslighting; or the constant cycle of being built up and torn down. Or, like many children, you were made to feel like the stress of your parent or caregiver was caused by you and your behaviour.

Witnessing abusive dialogue between caregivers, experiencing or witnessing violence, or living through a particularly frightening and upsetting event can all cause trauma. It can also be caused by caregivers with food disorders, alcoholism, or mental imbalances and disorders. Suicide, trouble with authorities, court cases, or jail sentences within the family also fall under this banner.

Words can be the cruellest and most damaging form of trauma, leaving scars that the outside world doesn't see. While a broken bone, a black eye, or even rape is physically visible and recognised for its severity, vicious, clever, and manipulative words inflict a pain that's indescribable and immeasurable. That pain may go unnoticed.

> **"Survivors of abuse show us the strength of their personal spirit every time they smile."**
> – Jeanne McElvaney,
> *Healing Insights: Effects of Abuse for Adults Abused as Children*

I will go into more detail about this later, but this is just a light to shine on the place where problems that you are experiencing now can come from. Irregularities in behaviours, emotional rigidity and inflexibility, and an inability to take responsibility for your behavioural outcomes are all rooted in your childhood experiences.

On a deeper and potentially scary level, left untreated, exposure to these experiences in childhood (ACEs) can be linked to negative outcomes later in life, including chronic disease, mental health issues, impulse control problems, and even the ability to maintain employment and relationships.

Ten Basic Needs of Children: A Foundation for Healthy Development

People who imprint on a child often have no idea of the devastating ripple effect their words, actions, and behaviours – which are experienced as horrible things – have on that child's life. There are ten basic needs that every child requires to grow into a healthy and functional adult. Tragically, when these needs aren't met, the effects can last a lifetime.

A child's healthy emotional and psychological development hinges on the consistent fulfilment of a set of fundamental needs. These aren't just "nice-to-haves"; they are absolutely crucial building blocks for a secure, confident, and well-adjusted individual. When these needs are met, children are empowered to thrive. I want to be clear: When these needs aren't met, the impact can be profound and long-lasting.

1. **Safety: A Sanctuary from Harm**
   First and foremost, a child requires a deep-seated sense of safety. This isn't just about physical safety, though that is obviously paramount. It's also about emotional safety – knowing they are protected from harm and that their wellbeing is a top priority. A child who feels safe can relax, explore, and learn without the constant fear of being hurt or abandoned. When safety is absent, a child is often in a state of hypervigilance, always on guard, which can severely hinder development.

2. **Basic Needs: The Physical Building Blocks**
   Basic survival needs, such as a roof over their head, access to nutritious food, and adequate clothing, are absolutely essential. These provide the physical building blocks for healthy growth and development. A child who is hungry, cold, or lacks basic necessities cannot focus on learning, playing, or forming healthy relationships. Neglecting these basic needs creates immense stress and insecurity.

3. **Respect and Value: Recognising Their Worth**
   Beyond the physical, a child's emotional wellbeing is deeply intertwined with their sense of self-worth. They need to feel respected and valued as individuals, and have their thoughts and feelings acknowledged and considered. When a child feels respected, they learn to respect themselves and others. Being dismissed or ignored can lead to feelings of worthlessness and a lack of self-esteem.

4. **Validation: Understanding Their Inner World**
   Validation of a child's emotions, even when they seem irrational to adults, is crucial for them to understand and regulate their feelings. When a child's emotions are validated, they learn that their feelings matter. This helps them build emotional intelligence and develop healthy coping mechanisms. Invalidating their feelings can lead to confusion, self-doubt, and difficulty managing emotions.

5. **Acceptance: Unconditional Love**
   Being accepted for who they are, without conditions or judgement, allows children to develop a strong sense of identity. Children need to know that they are loved and accepted for their unique selves, not for what they do or achieve. Conditional love can create anxiety and a constant need for external validation.

6. **Belonging: Connection and Community**
   A sense of belonging and feeling part of a "tribe", whether it's family, friends, or a community, provides a crucial support network. Children are social beings and need to feel connected to others. When they feel like they belong, they are more likely to develop healthy social skills and a sense of community. Isolation and exclusion can lead to feelings of loneliness, depression, and low self-esteem.

7. **Consistent Rules: Structure and Security**
   A stable and predictable environment is vital. Consistent rules and boundaries provide a framework for understanding expectations and navigating social interactions. This sense of structure fosters a feeling of security and helps a child learn self-discipline. Inconsistent or absent boundaries can create confusion and anxiety.

8. **Honesty and Trust: Building Reliable Relationships**
   The ability to be honest without fear of reprisal and to trust that their caregivers will act in their best interests are cornerstones of healthy relationships. Children need to feel that they can trust the adults in their lives. Dishonesty and broken promises can damage a child's ability to trust and form healthy relationships in the future.

9. **Clear Communication: Avoiding Mixed Messages**
   Clear communication, free from mixed messages, ensures that a child understands and can rely on the information they receive. Mixed messages can be confusing and create distrust. Open and honest communication helps children feel secure and understood.

10. A Sense of Justice: Believing in Fairness

Finally, while the world is not always fair, a child needs to have a general sense that life is just. This allows them to develop a sense of hope and belief in their ability to shape their own future. When children feel that the world is unpredictable and unfair, it can lead to feelings of helplessness and hopelessness.

When these fundamental needs are consistently met, children are empowered to grow into emotionally balanced, resilient, and compassionate adults. The absence of these needs being met, however, can have lasting and damaging effects on children's mental and emotional health.

> One of the saddest realities is that negative childhood experiences often leave an unconscious imprint on a person, leading to dysfunction in adulthood without a realisation of the root cause.

Three-quarters of these children will become the same type of person as the parents (or abusers) that they grew up with – in other words, they repeat the same patterns. Those who don't may spend their lives attracting these tricky (mentally disordered) types, subconsciously trying to change the ending to their childhood trauma, only to continue suffering.

Our lives often run on autopilot. We're conditioned by the people we grew up with, adopting their values and beliefs, which shape our automatic behaviours as adults. We may not even realise that what we're doing is out of alignment with what we truly want for ourselves. (I will explore this topic in greater detail in Book Two of the series.)

By slowing down and examining our behaviours, we can gain clarity to identify the underlying values and belief systems that drive them. Only then can we question whether these values truly belong to us or if they're inherited. This process of choosing and redefining our values as adults is crucial. It allows us to align our actions and behaviours with our true selves.

Thankfully, with the increased focus on mental health and complex trauma, people are becoming more interested in understanding their childhood experiences as a lens to understand their adult selves. It's incredibly healthy to be curious about your upbringing, the people you grew up with, the dynamics of those relationships, and the impact they had on you.

> The next time you find yourself doing something "destructive", ask yourself: "Is this action or behaviour aligned with my values?" At some point, you have to make a choice: move towards the person you want to be or fall back into old, unwanted patterns that keep you stuck.

Neglect

I want to touch on this topic because neglect is one of the major reasons people suffer from the effects of complex trauma, without recognising it. Let me explain.

Childhood neglect, a deeply painful form of maltreatment, happens when a caregiver consistently fails to provide for a child's most basic needs – physically, emotionally, and developmentally. Sometimes this is glaringly obvious, like not providing enough food, a safe place to live, or necessary medical care, or leaving a child all alone in unsafe situations. Other times, it's quieter, but no less damaging. It might look like emotional unavailability, where a child's cries for comfort are consistently ignored, their feelings dismissed, or where they simply don't receive the age-appropriate interaction and stimulation they so desperately need. Imagine, if you will, a parent who, caught up in their own struggles, is physically present but emotionally miles away, rarely engaging in meaningful conversations or showing the affection a child needs to thrive.

This ongoing lack of responsiveness can create a profound sense of abandonment and worthlessness in a child's heart. They begin to believe, deep down, that their needs simply don't matter, leading to deep insecurity and a real struggle to form healthy, trusting relationships later in life. This consistent failure to meet a child's needs, especially their emotional ones, forms the very foundation of complex trauma. The child often exists in a state of constant hypervigilance, always hoping their needs will finally be met, but sadly, that rarely happens. This ongoing stress is incredibly disruptive to healthy brain development and can lead to a range of mental health challenges as the child grows, including anxiety, depression, PTSD, difficulty regulating emotions, and even personality disorders. All of which directly correlate with irregularities and dysfunction in relationships with food and/or use of alcohol.

6.
What the?

Is There a Problem?
Why People Don't Realise They Are Suffering From Complex Trauma

It's astounding how many people I've met – clients and acquaintances alike – who genuinely believe they had a perfectly fine childhood. Yet, they grapple with deep-seated feelings of unworthiness, struggle with setting healthy boundaries, experience recurring health issues, or find themselves reaching for a bottle of wine or a six-pack of beer every night. Some of these individuals, even into their fifties and sixties, turn to drugs (cocaine at every dinner party, or pingers for a boogie), all while insisting they're "happy people". Ironically, they are often the first to judge or shame others for showing mental health vulnerabilities or visible struggles.

Understand me clearly: This isn't about pointing fingers or apportioning blame. Not at all. What I want to say here is that what I described above is actually the norm these days, and people who break free from these cycles are the outliers. My aim is to change that, to make it more normal to bravely step back into the light and motivate more people to join this movement of change.

My intention is to help you gain a clearer understanding of whether you might have normalised certain experiences that are now manifesting as destructive behaviours, leaving you confused about the "why". This is not about blame, shame, or dwelling in victimhood. It's about empowering you to truly understand yourself, to acknowledge and accept what is there, and to give it form so you can reclaim your power. I hope I can make this process less scary and intimidating for you now.

First, we have to address an elephant in the room – why is it that the "why" is so hard for people to connect to? Well, it's incredibly common for people to live with the lasting effects of complex trauma without ever identifying the root cause. Let me explain how the "unknown" or lack of awareness often arises from deeply ingrained psychological processes.

🔎 Normalisation

Children adapt to their environments, even when those environments are harmful. If neglect, emotional abuse, or inconsistent care is "normal" within their family system, it becomes their only point of reference. They learn to accept these conditions as their reality.

Common phrases like "It wasn't that bad," "Every family has its problems," or "My parents did the best they could" are often used to rationalise and minimise the impact of traumatic experiences.

🔎 Survival Mechanisms

Dissociation: As a way to cope with overwhelming stress, the mind can dissociate, creating a separation between thoughts, feelings, and experiences. This can manifest as gaps in memory or a feeling of detachment from one's own life.

Internalising Blame: Children often believe they are responsible for their caregivers' behaviour. This internalised blame can persist into adulthood, making it challenging to recognise oneself as someone who experienced trauma.

Emotional Suppression: In order to navigate a challenging environment, children often suppress their emotions. They can become adults who have difficulty recognising and processing their emotional landscape, or who are unable to connect to past memories.

🔎 Lack of Awareness and Education

Complex trauma is a nuanced concept, and many people simply aren't familiar with its symptoms.

Society tends to focus on visible, acute trauma (such as physical abuse) while overlooking the more subtle yet deeply damaging effects of emotional neglect and chronic stress.

🔍 Shame and Stigma

Survivors of complex trauma often carry deep feelings of shame, making it incredibly difficult to acknowledge their experiences or reach out for help. They may fear being judged or labelled as "weak" or "damaged".

🔍 Impact on Development

Complex trauma significantly impacts brain development and the nervous system. As a result, the very tools needed to recognise trauma are often themselves affected.

Ultimately, the conditions that lead to complex trauma also create significant barriers to recognising it. This is why so many individuals can live with the repercussions of complex trauma for years, even decades, without ever fully understanding the underlying cause of their struggles.

🔍 Family Loyalty

One of the most significant – and often heartbreaking – barriers to recognising and addressing childhood trauma is the incredibly powerful pull of familial loyalty. It's something I've seen so often: Children, and even adults, often unconsciously feel the need to maintain a positive image of their parents, even when those parents were the very source of harm. This need can stem from a deep-seated fear of disrupting the family unit, that feeling of obligation to honour our elders that's ingrained in us, or the deeply held belief that criticising one's parents is just plain wrong.

It creates an inner conflict – the difference between our beliefs and our actions, between our experiences and that loyalty. To try to make it all okay, people often minimise or deny what happened, sometimes even taking on the shame and blame themselves. It's like if we just pretend it didn't happen, we can avoid the emotional storm of facing our parents' actions and the potential fallout of speaking out. But in the end, we often end up sacrificing our own wellbeing just to keep that perceived sense of family peace. It's a tough spot to be in, and one that takes real courage to work through.

> Take a moment and ask yourself:
> Does any of this feel familiar? It's okay if the answer doesn't make sense yet. The purpose of this work is for you to unearth what's happening inside and begin to connect the dots, giving you more clarity. I'm right here with you, every step of the way.

The Unhealthy Automatic
What Needs to Be Let Go

When we talk about change, a crucial piece of the puzzle is to have clarity on how our earliest experiences shape us, particularly our childhood need for connection and safety. As children, we are inherently dependent. We rely on our families or caregivers to meet our needs – we simply can't do it alone. So, what happens when those parents or caregivers aren't able to provide that connection and meet those needs? Perhaps they're overwhelmed, dealing with their own struggles, or simply don't know how to be present. The child then struggles to feel safe and connected, and subconsciously, their brain registers that their needs won't be met. This deep need for connection is so fundamental that if it isn't fulfilled in a healthy way, a child will seek connection with something else. This is often where complex trauma coping mechanisms begin. All the while, they still yearn to connect with their parents or caregivers.

When a child tries to connect authentically and is met with rejection, they internalise that rejection. They start to believe there's something wrong with them. So, they learn to "fawn". They learn to be what they think others want them to be. They become experts at reading others' needs, priorities, and beliefs, all in an attempt to finally feel connected. The inner dialogue becomes, "If I'm going to get my needs met, I need people to connect with, but the only way to do that is not by being authentic; it's by being fake." They begin to believe that their true self prevents connection.

Now, if projecting this "fake self" and attempts at people-pleasing doesn't work, the child will try anything to get their caregivers' attention, even if it means acting out. Because any attention, even negative attention, feels better than none at all. If being a "nightmare kid" or constantly in trouble brings attention, then that's what they'll do. If being sick or in pain is how they get attention, then that becomes the pattern. Anger, violence, rebellion – they'll resort to whatever gets them noticed.

When children grow and realise they don't fit in at home, and don't have a sense of belonging, they'll search for that connection elsewhere. Whether it's seeking out the "cool kids", gangs, or other groups, they'll do what it takes to fit in and have their needs met. The underlying belief remains the same: They must conform, fawn, and be a chameleon – inauthentic – because that's the only way they know how to get their needs met. They might find a form of attachment, but it's not secure because it's based on conformity, not genuine connection. So, they continue to search for other things that give them a feeling of connection.

They might focus on an imaginary friend, a teddy bear, a bike, a blanket – something that becomes special and almost like a companion. This object replicates the feeling they're supposed to get from connecting with another human being. (I had an imaginary friend named Mr. Noisy Norman; he was my best friend, but no one could hear him except me.) They might turn to activities that help them disconnect from their day-to-day existence, escaping into a fantasy world. Video games, stories, and even physical activities like sports can become ways to escape pain. And then there's food – eating sweet foods, salty foods, or a lot of food, as a way to soothe the pain of disconnection.

These activities become habits because of the feelings they create; they become lifelines, essential for feeling happy and having needs met. They are the coping mechanisms that protect a child from further hurt.

As these children observe the world around them, they develop beliefs about what will bring true happiness and success, images that are often surface-level, soulless, status-driven, or materialistic. Images of what they should be and should have in order to have connection. These new attachments, formed with unhealthy beliefs, won't provide a true, secure path to having their needs truly met by people around them. Sure, there can be temporary highs, or a replication of a good feeling, but they leave the soul empty. (For example, acquiring an income that allows them to be lavish, overly generous, and buy people's attention). Yet, they continue these patterns because, in their mind, it's creating something positive. Sadly, these surface-level dependencies lead to heartache. They form the roots of those automatic, risky, erratic, or destructive behaviours with food and drink later in life.

> In simple terms, these childhood images and attachments become the autopilot for life. It's why unhealthy patterns keep happening, why you feel like you have no control. An automatic life ultimately leads to unhappiness.

If any of this resonates, here's the crucial step: If you're committed to change and living the life you truly want, you have to let go of the unhealthy activities, the unhealthy people, the unhealthy groups. You must be willing to release those childhood attachments and those old-school coping mechanisms. Gaining clarity on those childhood attachments and coping mechanisms is what the aim of the game is here.

Let's Look at an Example

A key part of this is discerning between the healthy and unhealthy aspects of an attachment. For instance, you can have a healthy relationship with food, but you need clear boundaries around when, what, how much, and with whom. This prevents sliding back into unhealthy patterns.

> **Trading the unhealthy ...**
> When I'm stressed, I go to the XXX restaurant with my friend Katy (who trauma dumps on me and manipulates me), and we over-order. We drink excessively, and I spend the entire time listening to her problems instead of addressing my own. I leave feeling depleted, drained, and wake up feeling awful.

For healthy ...

When I'm stressed, I go to the XXX restaurant with my new friend Louisa (who shares my values). We order mindfully, enjoy our meal, and have a genuine conversation. We listen to each other, share our feelings, and create space for each other. I leave feeling connected and grateful, and I wake up feeling refreshed.

Do you see the difference?

Then, apply this to other areas of your life. When is people-pleasing healthy, and when is it unhealthy? When is humour healthy, and when is it used to avoid pain or put yourself down? Often, those who lacked secure connection in childhood become very controlling of their environment and those around them in adulthood. So, observe yourself and ask, "What is healthy control (in behaviour where you can feel safe, not fear-based), and what is healthy letting go (like allowing someone else to take the lead)?"

Questions to Ask Yourself

Remember: Read your answers aloud so you hear yourself speak the words – so you believe what you say.

Exploring Your Childhood

Here's a set of questions crafted to encourage introspection into what your experiences were like growing up. Using your favourite journal, write your answers to each question.

1. **Your Earliest Memories:** Thinking back to your early years, how would you describe the overall feeling you had within your family? Did it feel like a safe haven, a place where you truly belonged?

2. **A Sense of Security:** In those formative years, did you feel a deep sense of safety and security? Did you feel like you had a soft place to fall, no matter what?

3. **Full Attention:** Did you often feel like you had your parents' undivided attention? Like they truly saw and heard you, not just physically but emotionally too?

4. **Finding Your Place:** How did you feel you fit into the dynamic of your family? Were you the one who spoke their mind, or did you tend to keep to yourself? Or maybe something in between?

5. **Availability:** How accessible did your parents seem to you? Did they feel like a comforting presence you could turn to, or were they often distant or preoccupied?

6. **Seeking Attention:** As a child, did you ever find yourself "acting out" to get attention, even if it was negative attention? It's okay to be honest; many of us did!

7. **Validation and Support:** Did you feel truly validated by your parents? Did you feel like they understood your needs and supported you in being yourself?

8. **Protection in Vulnerability:** When you felt stressed or vulnerable, did you feel like your parents were there to shield and protect you?

9. **Expressions of Love:** How would you describe the love that each of your parents expressed towards you? Did it feel genuine, warm, and consistent?

10. **Trust and Reliability:** Did you feel you could trust what your parents said and rely on them to be there when you needed them?

11. **Guidance on Right and Wrong:** Did your parents teach you the basics of right and wrong, providing a moral compass as you navigated the world?

12. **Clear Expectations:** Did your parents communicate their values and expectations clearly, so you knew where you stood?

13. **Acceptance for Who You Were:** Did you feel truly accepted by your parents, for exactly who you were as a child, quirks and all?

14. **Freedom of Expression:** Did your parents encourage you to express yourself freely and to be your authentic self?

15. **Nurturing Curiosity:** Did your parents encourage your curiosity, your sense of wonder, and the depths of your imagination?

16. **Guidance for Your Best Life:** Did your parents offer guidance and insight into how to live a fulfilling and happy life?

17. **Wisdom and Balance:** Did your parents teach you how to make wise choices, avoid unnecessary trouble, and find balance and joy in life?

These questions are designed to be thought-provoking and encourage deep reflection. The aim here is to create a safe space for you, my friend, to explore your past and gain some initial valuable insights. This may feel a little challenging, so please take your time with it.

> My intention is that connecting to these elements from your past will help you sail through and get even more value from the exercises to come.

7. When Your Body Reacts

How Your Brain Tries to Protect You
Understanding the Science Behind Your Body's Response

When trauma occurs, it's common for individuals to experience heightened sensitivity and reactions that may seem exaggerated or even aggressive to others. To gain clarity on why this happens, let's explore four key areas of the brain and how they function in the context of trauma.

Understanding the Impact of Trauma

🔍 **The Data Analyst (Thalamus):** This part of the brain gathers data from both the external world (through your five senses) and the internal world (your body's systems and sensations). It packages this information and sends it to other brain regions for further processing.

🔍 **The Emergency Centre (Amygdala):** Responsible for threat detection, this area receives information from the thalamus and triggers the body's fight-or-flight response.

🔍 **The Security Guard (Sympathetic Nervous System):** This system prepares the body for action in response to perceived threats, leading to a fight-or-flight response.

🔍 **Mission Control (Medial Prefrontal Cortex):** This area receives information from the thalamus and assesses whether a threat is real, allowing for a more thoughtful and measured response.

🔍 **The Trauma Response:** In a traumatic situation, the thalamus repeatedly sends messages to the amygdala that there is danger. This, in turn, activates the sympathetic nervous system, putting the body into a constant state of alert. This can lead to hyperarousal, hypervigilance, and a heightened sensitivity to potential threats.

🔍 **The Impact on the Mind and Body:** Trauma can have a profound effect on both the mind and body, leading to feelings of weakness, oversensitivity, and worthlessness. It's important to remember that these feelings are a normal response to an abnormal situation. The brain is simply trying to protect you from further harm.

Fight, Flight, Freeze, or Fawn
Understanding Your Brain's Response to Trauma

You've probably heard of the "fight-or-flight" response – it's your body's physiological reaction to a threat, preparing you to either face it head-on or run away. But there's more to your brain's survival mode than just those two options. Let's explore how your brain reacts in the face of danger and how it might be impacting you today.

🔍 **Your Brain's Alarm System:** Your autonomic nervous system is responsible for regulating your body's internal functions. It has two main parts: the sympathetic nervous system (the go pedal) and the parasympathetic nervous system (the brakes). When you feel threatened, your sympathetic nervous system revs you up, releasing adrenaline and getting your heart pumping.

🔎 **Fight or Flight: The Body's Call to Action:** In fight-or-flight mode, your body tenses up, your heart races, and stress hormones flood your system. You might feel a swirl of emotions like fear, anxiety, and anger. But what happens when there's no one to fight or nowhere to run? These physical changes and pent-up emotions can leave you feeling incredibly uncomfortable and on edge.

This is often when we turn to unhealthy coping mechanisms, like using food or drink to numb the discomfort and avoid those overwhelming feelings.

🔎 **Freeze: Stuck in Shock:** Sometimes, the fight-or-flight response doesn't kick in. Instead, your brain's signals become so intense that your body shuts down. This is the "freeze" response, where you feel stuck, frozen, or paralysed. Your heart rate and blood pressure drop, and you might feel weak or unable to move.

🔎 **Fawn: The People-Pleaser's Response:** Another response to danger, especially common in children or those who have experienced abuse, is the "fawn" response. This involves trying to please the abuser or appease the threat to avoid conflict or further harm. As adults, this can show up as people-pleasing behaviour, difficulty setting boundaries, and neglecting your own needs in order to gain approval.

The Aftermath: Unhealthy Patterns and Cycles

So, my friend, the truth is, these trauma responses can lead to unhealthy patterns and cycles, like overeating, restricting food, or developing a negative body image. These patterns are often driven by our emotional triggers and can create a self-fulfilling prophecy of self-loathing. Can you appreciate what I am saying?

Breaking the Cycle

When you start to gain more clarity and understand all of this, you can start to see why you're trapped in a loop, feeling like you go round and round again in the cycle of irregular food and drink choice patterns. It's a lonely and sometimes dark place, and it can be tough to get out of. Alone and scared – what a horrible place to be. I understand how you feel, and I'm sure many of you have previously experienced this once or twice and possibly it is a regular occurrence.

> **"When the whole world is silent, even one voice becomes powerful."**
> – Malala Yousafzai

I'm also here to tell you that you can recover from this; you can move forward, out of these cycles, and create a new pattern of behaviour. With the right tools and the right focus, you can make a change. I am living proof of lasting change, as are millions of people around the world who have taken responsibility for their health, choices, and healing from past experiences. Have faith; you can do this too.

Getting your head around all of this can be a lot, so take your time. If you're feeling exhausted, take a break. When you read something that you don't completely understand, note it down, and go back to it when you're feeling refreshed.

> So, the message here is that understanding your brain's response to trauma is the first step in breaking free from these unhealthy patterns. Remember, you are not alone, and I'm here with you.

8.
Not My Secret Anymore

My Trauma Experience
Violated, Vulnerable, and Helpless as a Young Girl

This is what happened to me in a family and friends' environment. I was violated as a young girl, in a place that should have been secure, a place of trust. This experience would drive a lifetime of distrust, hypervigilance, and the creation of my "false self-persona" to hide behind.

When I was eight, we lived on a farm in regional Victoria, Australia. As a family, we took a trip to visit some family friends for lunch on a neighbouring property. Our mothers were besties, and as far as couples go, this foursome knew how to have a wonderful time. They all liked to drink; the men looked after the barbecue, and they would sit together, roaring with laughter out in the garden.

There were three of us kids in my family and three boys in our friends' family. Their eldest was my bestie, and he was a year younger than me. Their youngest was only a baby. My two family members were older and significantly larger in size than the rest of us. Game time was controlled and dictated by the eldest and the biggest.

The lunch was long, and our parents wanted to "kick on", to keep drinking and have an adult talk, so I think they ushered all of us kids into the bunkroom to go have a nap while they carried on partying with their shenanigans.

There were five of us in this bunkroom, aged from thirteen or fourteen down to five. The baby was put in a different room. We were too boisterous. When the parents left, it was suggested that playing a game was a good idea. I was on the top bunk and only wanted to sleep, but I was jostled and told to pay attention.

I was the only girl in the group of five. I remember being cradled by one of them from behind, with their hand on my shoulder in the adolescent, childlike way of offering support in what was turning out to be a "Lord of the Flies-type" scenario. A group of people led down a path through the forces of one powerful individual. Completely scared to death but following his lead anyway.

It was suggested it would be fun to play a game of putting their fingers inside me.

I can assure you that every person in that room knew that what was going on was wrong. But they didn't have the ability to do anything about it because the influence of this character was too overwhelming. Too influential. Too frightening. What would be the ramifications if they didn't do as he said? No one wanted to find out what would happen if they didn't do what this character said. So, they were complicit. They had no idea of the consequences this game would have on my life. They were all children.

I remember the burning sensation. I remember the shame. I remember the fear. I remember no one was there who could stop what was happening or help me.

From then on, I started to wet the bed. Every night. For years. I had to have a plastic cover under my sheets because I kept ruining the mattress. I could not sleep in a room by myself without the light on. Next came the imaginary friend. Mr. Noisy Norman. He was my friend that I could trust. We had our own special place that I could retreat to with him.

My brain, doing its best to protect me, completely blocked that memory out. The trauma was just too much for my young self to handle. For years, my behaviour felt automatic, like I was driven by something I couldn't see or understand. I did so many things without really knowing why. That deep-seated violation, buried under layers of subconscious reactions and a heavy weight of shame, led me to create a "false self", a persona I hid behind.

I think I dreamt of being a girl who was always happy and carefree. I became her, that character, a larger-than-life version of myself. I'd sing on any stage – even if it was just a step in the garden, or in my imagination – entertaining my family with my own little shows, complete with imaginary audiences, toys, and dolls. Later on, this turned into me dancing on tables in pubs and nightclubs as an adult.

It really messed with my understanding of intimacy and connection, causing some pretty unhealthy patterns in my life. My actions, especially in the sexual area, were often driven by that buried shame, leading to overly sexualised behaviour based on this deep-down belief that my worth was all about my sexuality. This led to me constantly flirting, having one-night stands, and sex with strangers, a desperate search for something I couldn't even put into words. All made worse by a feeling of being disconnected and numb, because of the psychological impact of the trauma and my inability to process it.

When I drank, I often found myself battling significant anger issues, sometimes bursting out with abusive language directed at a man who, perhaps unknowingly, reminded me of my perpetrators. And in those lonely moments, drinking by myself, the anger would surge, leading me to shout profanities at the walls in my apartment. Then I would crumble and cry. Sobbing, in hysterical tears, grappling with a pain that had finally found its voice.

Through the help of my therapist, I came to realise that my constant need to please people, to the point of exhaustion, most likely began with this experience. I was always searching for validation, desperately trying to regain a sense of worth that felt completely taken away. Because this violation occurred in a place where I should have felt safe, with people I should have been able to trust, it created a deeply painful belief that I wasn't enough to be protected, that I wasn't worthy of support. My understanding of trust was utterly distorted, not only by this event but by the wider pattern of abuse within my family. This insidious breakdown of trust showed up in my adult life as constant hypervigilance, an inability to truly relax, and a persistent feeling that I had to perform, to be "good enough", to keep myself safe. It was like my very foundation of safety and deservingness had been shattered right from the start.

It's true, the brain can lock away trauma, completely erasing it from your conscious mind. Yet, when triggered by something profoundly significant, those locked-away memories can suddenly resurface.

The night after Dad passed away, a series of events unfolded, leading to a verbal argument with the very person who hurt me years before. This escalated into a physical altercation, resulting in a fractured hip and, eventually, a hip replacement. (You can find more about my recovery journey in my book *HIP: Seven Ways to Heal*.) That incident became a turning point, brutally unlocking the floodgates of my memory. I was suddenly watching a movie reel of my life, all the trauma surfacing. That moment felt like a massive explosion of truth. The shame, the pain, the awful reality, all the secrets we'd kept for years, and the way we all carried that darkness and stayed silent – it made me sick to my core. I tried to drink that pain away; I really did. I was just surviving, completely unaware of the triggers or drivers that were in control. I was unable to stop the destructive patterns with food and alcohol because they had become my only way of coping.

As the shame felt so overwhelming, it felt impossible to share. I confided in a friend, who listened in disbelief and asked, "Are you sure?" This reinforced my gut feeling and long-held hesitation to trust my own reality, which was tragically confirmed when I later shared my story publicly.

When I tried to talk to my immediate family about what happened, I was met with gaslighting and denial. They said it was all in my head, that it never happened. When I reached out to my extended family, they dismissed me too. The narrative became that I was mentally unstable. I felt utterly invalidated. Then, one person, a woman who'd known me my whole life, from within my family, said she believed me.

Through all the work I subsequently did to unpack my past, I learned a powerful lesson: I would never get validation from those who refused to acknowledge my truth. That validation had to come from myself. And no matter what they said, or how they denied what happened to preserve their reputation, it couldn't change the fact that it did happen.

In recent years, I've been working on "inner-child meditations" and using my powerful feminine energy to go back and connect with – and nurture – my younger self, aiming to heal those old wounds. It's been about reframing and accepting the shame, the horror, the fear, the anger, the humiliation, and the violation I felt. Not to re-live it exactly, but to connect with the experience, to acknowledge the child who got lost in all of it, and to validate her. I can't change what happened, but I can change the story I tell myself about it.

Self-acceptance has been a game changer, a key to finding peace. I've come a long way, no doubt, but the experience has left its marks, signs, and scars. For example, to this day, I can only sleep in the late afternoon if someone I trust is in the house, or with the TV on if I'm alone. This is just one piece of my story, and sharing it is definitely a part of my healing journey. If you've been through something similar, please know you're not alone.

A friend said to me recently, "I have to say, Fleur Elizabeth, it takes incredible courage to share your story. I'm so proud of you for doing this. It's brave, powerful stuff." I looked at her and simply replied, "This isn't my secret anymore; people need to know."

> Using the word "abused" – it took me a fair amount of work with a psychologist to say that word. To admit and then face the fact that I had been abused was a hard, confronting, and incredibly scary task. So, if you struggle with it too, you are not alone; it takes practice, and then you can make room for it with acceptance.

Change

9. The Change Experience

A Heartfelt Journey Within You
Let's Create a Project Clarity Plan

Change is a beautiful, transformative process, albeit a little uncertain at first. So, I'd like to acknowledge your bravery right off the bat. You are choosing to do this, and well done, you, for stepping onto this path. For choosing to develop clarity about who you are and what you want from life. You're familiar with the saying "the fear of the unknown", right? Well, that's often where uncertainty comes from. And then there's that common struggle: "How do I start to change if I don't know what I'm doing? And if I've been doing the same thing for so long?" Sound familiar? Don't worry; These reactions are a completely normal part of the process of change. They aren't roadblocks – they're simply challenges you will learn to navigate with patience.

This is another one of those human experiences where we can get lost without a map. So, I thought I'd unpack a more structured approach to change. This doesn't have to be complicated, so please don't feel intimidated. I'll be taking you through this one heartbeat at a time in this book series, so it will feel like you're simply following along with a music score.

To truly affect change, we need to look at a process of who you are, where you've come from and why, and where you want to go. I think that's easy to follow.

In a more structured sense, the process unfolds in four deeply meaningful stages: Engaging, Focusing, Evoking, and Planning. Let's journey through each one together, exploring how they can be woven into your life.

1. Engaging with Yourself

First, you begin by connecting deeply and authentically with yourself. We've already started this with our conversations. The purpose of the "Engaging with Yourself" stage is to build a strong foundation of self-love rooted in self-awareness. It involves deeply and authentically connecting with oneself, exploring past life challenges, envisioning the Future Self, delving into core values and family history, and completing a health history (you will find this at **www.fleurelizabeth.com**).

2. Focusing on Your Present

The significance of the "Focusing on Your Present" stage is to gain a richer clarity of your current life. It involves exploring what you want out of life right now, examining your relationship with food and drink, identifying what truly matters to you, and understanding why you deeply desire change. This helps to establish a clear picture of your current state in relation to your desired future state. Through thoughtful questions, reflections after each topic, and your own insights, you'll cultivate a richer understanding of who you are and where you stand on your journey today.

3. Evoking Deeper Awareness

From there, I'll gently guide you through the place where patterns, triggers, and the chain reactions of your behaviours come from. The significance of evoking deeper personal connection and self-awareness is that it allows you to identify unique patterns, triggers, and the consequences of your behaviours. It also involves an honest and compassionate look at potential barriers, preparing you for any resistance or challenges that may arise. Having this level of clarity aims to make you feel secure, supported, and not caught off guard.

4. Planning Your Path Forward

This is where a map of your unique and deeply bio-individual world takes shape. The significance of planning your path forward is that it involves creating a personalised roadmap for taking action, building and practising new skills, bravely holding boundaries, normalising mistakes you may make along the way, and making lasting change as the woman you want to be. This stage makes the journey feel less daunting and creates a sense that change and transformation are within your reach, by providing a clearer vision of the path ahead.

> As you consider these changes, I warmly invite you to pause, take a moment, and get your pen ready to reflect. It's vital that these changes resonate deeply with your heart and soul, feeling truly right for your unique, precious journey.

For Your Gentle Consideration

When you're embarking on any change in this process, I encourage you to hold these next questions close to your heart. They will help you assess what's right for you. With a bit of practice, these questions will become a new and positive habit, steering you in the right direction with love and kindness for yourself.

1. What truly fuels your desire for this change?

2. How might you gently and effectively bring this change into your life? What would it feel like for this change to flourish and become sustainable?

3. Taking a moment of honest reflection, how confident do you feel in making this happen? On a scale of 0 to 10, how sustainable does this change feel for you right now?

These questions are a doorway to becoming more conscious of your choices, ensuring this is a change you deeply desire, not one imposed from anywhere else.

Let's also gently consider:

4. Do you have the resources and time to nurture this change?

5. And, importantly, how will you celebrate and acknowledge your progress, the peace, and the balance you create?

> Rewarding yourself along the way is a powerful tool for motivational change. Or in simple terms, life turning out for the better!

· · ·

Through Challenge Comes Growth
Humans Need to Suffer in Order to Change

We often flinch at the idea, don't we? That humans need to experience hardship to truly change. But let's be real with each other – it's a fundamental part of our shared human experience. It's a truth that sometimes we have to navigate through struggle and pain before we finally grab the reins and steer ourselves toward the changes we deeply desire. I know that might not be what we always want to hear, but if we can all gently shift our perspective a little, then the path to change becomes much clearer. Let's explore this together, with open hearts.

Think about Wonder Woman for a moment. What would her story be without the villains she faces, the battles she must win, and the communities she strives to protect? Our heroes resonate with us precisely because they confront adversity head-on, rise to the challenge, and ultimately triumph, bringing light and joy to others.

Now, I've seen firsthand people getting stuck in their struggles. I've witnessed countless people who've been through a truly tough time, a setback, a real disappointment, yet seem to resist any attempt to help themselves. They might say, "Poor me," and get lost in self-pity, sometimes spreading that negativity to anyone who will listen. Round and round they go, the same pattern repeating, stuck in that struggle, unwilling to see that these challenges might be there to help them shift, learn, and grow. Watching this can be exhausting. Often, for these folks (I'll call them our "victims"), their reactions become a defence mechanism. They are afraid of change or even addicted to the adrenaline and the "high" they get from chaos and conflict. Biologically and psychologically, they get stuck, finding a strange comfort in their discomfort. Sadly, this isn't the forward-thinking, proactive approach we need for lasting change.

On the other hand, it's incredibly common for people to lose a job, experience weight changes, go through a relationship breakdown, or face significant trauma that finally spurs them to take charge and pursue change with passion.

> ## Okay, now it's your turn.
> ## Here's a question for you to sit with:
>
> How many times have you felt like you've hit a brick wall, felt resistance against something you really wanted, or stumbled and experienced heartache because, at the time, you truly believed it was right for you, or what you wanted? Then, with time, and perhaps discomfort or pain, something shifted. Suddenly, there was an answer. A new door opened, and things became brighter.
>
> Read this out loud to yourself, so you hear yourself speak these words. Then grab your journal and write your answer down. If you don't have a journal yet, that's okay – just use your iPad or make notes in your phone. But write it down somewhere you can find it again.
>
> Come on now. I'm sure this has happened to you, because I promise you, it happens to all of us.

The Need for Opposition in Our Lives

If everything in life were easy, if everyone loved everything we did, if we faced no opposition or resistance, what would push us to evolve? Life would become monotonous, wouldn't it? A challenge, a nemesis, is what propels us to the next level. Your past, your pain, your fear story – that's the nemesis of your Future Self. When you step back and look at it this way, you see that in this struggle, you have a chance to prove yourself. The pressure from your past fear story, strangely enough, can be the very catalyst for change.

I once said, "I wish I had found myself sooner," but that wasn't possible, because it took time and skills I needed to build to get here. However, one of the missing links I had to develop was right here, in what I am telling you. You see, until I saw my past stories as my enemies, my opposition, what I was avoiding, I couldn't push myself to evolve. And as I always say, what we avoid is where we learn, grow, and become better. It is now my privilege to share my struggles with you, as a way of showing you that my struggles truly changed my life for the better. I will tell you time and time again, I love who I am today. Even when I feel like I have a target on my back from people in my past, it doesn't scare me anymore. Anytime they throw something at me, I relish the chance to demonstrate my superpowers. Because, trust me, we all have them. And with each piece of pressure I face, I know I will learn something else that will help me continue to move forward, in the wonderful flow of life.

The Change Experience approach is about helping you see your life through a new lens. Thinking long-term, taking care of the needs of your Future Self, and taking positive steps now to prevent those big struggles from keeping you stuck, and instead, using them to propel you forward. I'm going to share tools with you that will help you not stop dead at that "brick wall" moment – that moment when you feel like you've hit a crisis because you haven't been paying attention to your needs. And to help you pick yourself up and carry on, like the Wonder Woman you are, to fight another day. Except, it won't always be a fight. It will become more joyous, things will become more effortless, and time will seem to fly by. Just watch.

The education and strategies in this book will help you do just that. You can stay on course and stop that "brick wall" from coming at you full speed. You can break free from that cycle of suffering and reacting, into learning, growing, and evolving. As you

> **"The latest research in neuroscience says that you can change your brain, just by thinking. So then as you begin to think about a new possibility and your brain begins to fire in new sequences and new patterns, and new combinations, and you begin to plan your behaviour, and you begin to review in your mind and mentally who you are going to be in your life. The mere act of mental rehearsal begins to install the neurological circuits in your brain. Now your brain is no longer a record of the past; it's in fact a map to the future."**
>
> – Dr. Joe Dispenza

learn how to identify and connect with your triggers and those automatic behaviours – that "trigger, followed by a behaviour, followed by a consequence cycle" – you'll be back in the driver's seat, right where you belong. (And please know, I've been there many times myself, and I've learned how to stop that pattern. That's why I'm so passionate about sharing this with you.)

Remember, adversity, opposition, and challenges are all forces of energy that are asking you to look inside yourself and push forward, build your tools, sharpen your mind, and transform, again and again and again.

> You are not a one-season flower; you are an energetic being here to keep growing, flourishing, and showing the world the colours of your beauty from within.

10.
Helpful Strategies

When You're Making Changes
You May Need to Shift Your Lens a Little

Shifting your perspective when faced with challenges can make a huge difference in how you experience and overcome them. Here are a few ways to shift your lens:

🔗 **See Challenges as Opportunities for Growth**: Instead of viewing obstacles as purely negative, try to see them as chances to learn, evolve, and become stronger. Remember that adversity, opposition, and challenges are all forces of energy that are asking you to look inside yourself and push forward.

🔗 **Understand Challenges as a Shared Human Experience:** Recognising that struggle is a part of life can help you feel less isolated and more resilient. After all, it's a fundamental part of our shared human experience.

🔗 **Use the "Wonder Woman" Analogy:** Thinking about how heroes face and overcome adversity can provide inspiration and motivation. I used Wonder Woman as an example, suggesting that challenges are what make heroes who they are. Who is your superhero?

🔗 **Consider the Long-Term:** Focus on your Future Self and how overcoming the current challenge will benefit you. The Change Experience approach encourages this long-term perspective to take care of the needs of your Future Self.

🔗 **Identify Patterns:** Recognise repeating cycles of triggers, behaviours, and consequences to understand and change them. This awareness can prevent getting stuck in negative loops.

🔗 **Recognise the "Nemesis":** View your past pain and fear stories as a "nemesis" of your Future Self. By acknowledging and confronting these obstacles, you can drive change and growth.

🔗 **Reflect and Journal:** Take time to sit with your feelings and experiences. Writing down your thoughts can provide clarity and help you find new perspective. I encourage you to use a journal for this purpose.

🔗 **Embrace the "Flow of Life":** Even with challenges, try to find a sense of forward momentum in the wonderful flow of life.

Unlocking Your Inner Voice
The Transformative Power of Your Own Change Talk

You know, what I've always cherished is the belief that real, lasting change isn't something forced upon us. It blossoms from within. It's about discovering your own reasons, igniting your deepest desires, and tapping into that incredible power you hold to create the life you truly envision. And that's precisely where Motivational Interviewing – or as I like to call it, "Change Talk" – comes into play.

While the formal definition speaks of guiding individuals to articulate their own "Change Talk" as the pathway to transformation, for me, it's something far more intimate and profound.

My "Aha!" Moment: Finding the Key to Lasting Change

My journey with Change Talk began as I explored a psychology modality called Acceptance and Commitment Therapy (ACT), which led me to study Motivational Interviewing. I was searching for ways to help people make changes that truly stuck, and then it hit me. This was it. Here was a way to guide people to that sacred space where they articulate their deepest desires, determine what feels right for them, and find the words that resonate with their very soul. It wasn't about me telling them; it was about them uncovering their own unique truth.

In my early days of health coaching, I kept encountering a recurring challenge. People would begin with such enthusiasm, affirming their desire for change. I'd provide them with all the information, the "do's" and "don'ts" about food and drink, and they'd start strong. Yet, the changes wouldn't last. It dawned on me: I was giving them *my* words, *my* instructions. I wasn't connecting with their internal voice of change, their authentic truth.

That realisation sparked a fundamental shift and inspired me to build this platform, and my business called Change Talk Coaching. I created these tools because I believe we all deserve to make decisions from that deep, authentic place within. We need the skills to own our choices and live in harmony with our truest desires.

The Magic of Hearing Your Own Words

In this book series, I've woven together the transformative powers of ACT and Motivational Interviewing, resulting in my own Change Talk method, to create a supportive path for your healing. Each chapter offers questions designed to spark introspection. And here's the magic: I'll encourage you to read each question, and your responses, aloud to yourself. Why? Because hearing your own words has a powerful effect. It creates a profound awareness, a sense of wonder, about your current situation. Then, we'll explore education and solutions to gently propel you forward.

Research consistently shows that lasting change blossoms when you hear yourself make the case for it. This connects your conscious mind to your physical being in a profound and undeniable way.

> ## In your responses, you might:
>
> Connect more deeply with your desire to change, hearing the words "I want ... "
>
> Recognise your ability to change, when you hear yourself say, "I can ... "
>
> Uncover your reasons for change, when you hear yourself say, "If I don't change, it will cost me ... "
>
> Express your need for change, when you say, "I must change this because I want ... "

Choosing Your Own Path with Self-Compassion

We all know that little rebellious streak that arises when someone tells us what to do, even when we know they're right. It's human nature to resist being dictated to. So, the essence of Change Talk is empowering you to hear your own voice of change, to speak that change into being. This is a process of posing thoughtful questions, sharing relevant insights, and creating space for you to discover your own answers.

Yes, reading your responses aloud might feel unusual at first. But there's a powerful purpose to it. It helps you fully hear the words, believe what you're writing, and connect deeply with the choices you're making. When you hear it, you own it. And when you own it, you're far more likely to act on it.

> **"If you wish to know the mind of a woman, listen to her words."**
> – Johann Wolfgang von Goethe

Through self-assessments and powerful questions, you'll have the opportunity to express what you truly desire, what's important to you, and how you envision your

Future Self. Your role is to answer honestly, from your heart, and then to listen to your own words. When you hear yourself making the argument for change, it solidifies it in your mind. It becomes your voice, your ideas. This builds a strong connection to your needs, your reasons, and your desires for transformation.

This journey equips you with the language to harmonise your body and mind. As you hear yourself speak, you cultivate trust in your inner wisdom and develop vital Change Talk skills.

> Because when you hear it, you believe it.
> And when you believe it, it's more
> likely that you're going to do it.

Creating Your Sanctuary of Self-Discovery

I invite you to engage in this work in a private sanctuary, a space where you feel safe to be completely honest, free from judgement or shame. Here, you'll delve into your heart's deepest longings and the real reasons why change is vital to you. It's a profoundly practical way to reconnect with yourself.

At the heart of this journey is self-compassion. It's about treating yourself with kindness and discovering that inner voice that validates your experiences. It's learning to respond to yourself with love, gently quieting the inner critic, and holding your pain with acceptance.

Finally, this process is also about fostering your confidence, knowing you possess the power to make conscious choices, embrace your values, move forward authentically, and create the human experience you truly desire.

> So come, warm up that voice, my friend!

11. Motivational Change

Think About Your Current Situation
Why Do You Want to Change?

Ever feel like you completely lose yourself when something triggers you? Like you get so emotional, angry, upset, or depressed that you just can't function? Your brain feels foggy, and you're just going through the motions, often doing things that make you feel worse. It's okay; this happens to all of us! The Change Experience series is designed to help you change that.

To start, we'll examine and gain clarity on *why* change is important and the consequences of staying stuck. We'll also talk about that feeling of ambivalence, where you know you want to change but don't really want to do anything different. You're in. You're out. You're 50/50. It's normal, and we're going to normalise it!

It's like a wrestling match: the desire to change versus the comfort of staying the same. This internal conflict can keep you stuck. It's a common challenge.

> **"A sign of wisdom is not believing everything you think. A sign of emotional intelligence is not believing everything you feel. Thoughts and emotions are possibilities, not certainties to take for granted. Question them before you accept them."**
>
> **– Adam Grant, Organisational Psychologist**

You're here because you want to transform how your past is impacting you today, right? You want to stop self-medicating, automatically using food and/or alcohol as a coping mechanism when you feel overwhelmed, which means making some changes.

So, let's tackle the big question: *Why haven't you wanted to change in the past?*

Maybe you've felt like it's too hard, you don't have time, or your social scene makes it difficult. These are all excuses that keep us stuck.

Have you ever found yourself feeling or saying things like ...

"It's too hard. I've tried it before."

"I can't be bothered."

"It's too hard to change in my social scene."

"It's too hard to do anything differently in my relationship."

"This is what I'm given at home, so I have to eat this."

"I don't have time; I'm too busy, so I eat takeaway."

"I'm in a stressful job, so I drink."

"My partner really hurts me, so I drink and eat."

These are some of the reasons – excuses, really – why we don't make changes. These excuses become a sticky web that keeps us stuck.

But guess what? Change *is* possible, and I'm here to support you every step of the way. Let's break free from those excuses and create a life where you feel empowered and in control.

Ambivalence Is Really Normal

I know how challenging it is to be in that "comfortable/uncomfortable" place, where you're not sure how to change, and all those tricky things in your environment, relationships, home, and work feel so tangled.

I want to help you gain clarity and understand this, so you feel comfortable with it. It's such an important part of this work. I want you to know it's okay to feel back and forth. Give yourself a break, please. Don't be hard on yourself for that. It's completely normal. I will help you identify all the reasons you should change, and all the wonderful ways you can gently guide yourself out of that ambivalent, "stuck" feeling.

What you need are some strategies to help you transform those automatic patterns into conscious, thoughtful, and compassionate actions. None of this will happen overnight, and that's okay. You will slowly see progress if you just make a start. Acceptance of the fact that it takes time is vital. Throughout this journey together, I'll often refer to this as building a muscle, developing a skill.

If You Were to Stay the Same
Do You Know What the Costs Are to You?

Do you ever stop to really think about what it might cost you to keep going the way you are going with food and drink? What might life look like in the longer term if nothing changes? Have you ever let your mind wander to those "what if" scenarios about your health down the road if things stay the same? A bit scary, hey? So perhaps this is something you've been too afraid to even consider?

I know these can be tough questions to ask ourselves. But let's gently explore this idea together, shall we? It's okay to be curious and take a peek. Let's take a moment to reflect on what it might mean for you if you continue with your current patterns.

For instance, let's really look at what a dysfunctional relationship with food and drink might be costing you. Just some small examples:

> [?] Are you a moody cow during the day? Do you get angry easily if you haven't eaten?

> [?] How does your facial skin look? Bright, smooth, and radiant? Or dehydrated, tight, and rough?

How are you with hangovers? How do they affect your job, your relationships, your personal wellbeing, the way you feel about yourself, and the way you behave? Or the way you smell the next day?

Take a Deeper Look: What's the Cost, Sister?

What are all these things you're doing with food and drink costing you today? It's so important to be aware of these things, not to scare ourselves, but to truly understand how our choices can impact our wellbeing. Remember, knowledge is power, and making small, positive changes can have a huge ripple effect! So, let's take a closer look at some common issues I see a lot of women suffering from.

1. **Unwanted Weight Gain and Obesity**
   How is your weight? Is it where you want it to be? This one might seem obvious, but carrying excess weight can put a strain on your heart, joints, and overall body. It can also lead to other health issues.

2. **Fatigue and Low Energy**
   If you're not giving your body the nutrients it needs, you might find yourself feeling tired and sluggish all the time. It's amazing how much energy we can gain just by being conscious of what we are putting into our bodies.

3. **Joint Problems**
   Excess alcohol, coffee for some blood types, and highly acidic foods cause inflammation. Not to mention, carrying extra weight can put a lot of pressure on your joints, leading to pain and conditions like osteoarthritis. I can personally testify to this, having had a hip replacement myself, and horrible osteoarthritis from drinking excessively.

4. **Digestive Issues**
   Your microbiome is the defence force against viruses and infection. However, you can manifest a "scorched earth" effect in one binge

eating or drinking session and put yourself in a high-risk category for illness and infection. Also, overeating or eating foods low in fibre can lead to digestive problems like constipation and irritable bowel syndrome (IBS).

5. **Sleep Issues and Apnoea**

    How is your sleep? Do you wake up feeling refreshed, ready for anything, full of beans? Or do you wake up feeling sluggish, tired, and wishing the alarm hadn't gone off? Do you have broken sleep, waking up in the middle of the night, finding yourself ruminating over something, over and over again? Do you need to urinate many times during the night? What you have had to eat and drink each night can have an immediate impact on your sleep and prevent you from getting a solid eight hours. Also, being overweight or obese can increase your risk of sleep apnoea, a condition where your breathing repeatedly stops and starts during sleep. My friends, good sleep is so, so essential; you cannot take this for granted!

6. **Mood Swings, Imbalance in Your Emotions**

    How consistent are your moods? Do you find it hard to regulate your emotions after a good session of eating and drinking? How would you describe your moods? Are you happy, or not so? Be honest. There's a strong connection between our diet and our mental wellbeing. Unhealthy eating patterns can contribute to mood swings, anxiety, and depression. Nurturing our bodies with healthy food also nourishes our minds.

7. **Pre-Diabetes and Type 2 Diabetes**

    Have you had your blood work done recently and checked your glucose levels? Overeating, especially sugary foods, can lead to insulin resistance, which can develop into type 2 diabetes. Managing this can be challenging, and it can affect many areas of your life. This can creep up fast and get out of control very quickly, so please review this in your health chart.

8. **Heart Disease**
   Did your blood test check your cholesterol and heart? How is your blood pressure? Is it normal, or are you bordering on being hypertensive? Diets high in saturated and trans fats can raise cholesterol levels and increase the risk of heart disease. Our heart is so precious; we want to take good care of it. High blood pressure is one of the leading causes of strokes in women over forty. Heart attacks are now the leading cause of death in women globally – yet so many women have no idea that is the case!

9. **Certain Cancers**
   Cancer is now often called the "lifestyle disease". All those automatic behaviours of ours are being linked to certain types of cancer. Who wants to have the "Big C" chat with our doctors and have to undergo chemo and radiation therapy and lose all our bodily hair? Not me!

In your journal reflection, I'll ask you some specific questions to help you really consider these things. Please, I encourage you to be honest with yourself. When you see your words written down on paper, when you see those behaviours and their consequences laid out in front of you, that's the part of you we need to connect with and understand. Those words will be the key to making empowered decisions.

> **Ask Yourself:**
>
> "Is that really what I want for myself?"
>
> "Do I really want to sign up for all of that?"
>
> "How long am I going to keep doing this to myself?"
>
> "Can I, and will I, make an effort to change?"

So, now that you're bravely connecting with the ways food and drink are impacting you today, what happens next? Well, that's truly up to you. My friend, this is where we really dive into the challenges, the opposition, and

> **"Every day, do something that will inch you closer to a better tomorrow."**
>
> – Doug Firebaugh

the adversity that can arise when you're making changes. Ask yourself: What would your superhero do in these circumstances? Or, even better, what would your Future Self ask you to do?

This, my friend, is where the real growth begins. This is the sweet spot, those precious nuggets of gold where you'll find those small, but powerful, wins of transformation. Hold on tight, because I'm not going to leave you hanging. I'm here to support you every single step of the way, and I'll give you some really effective tools to help you make these changes.

> You've faced bigger things than this,
> and I know you have what it takes.

Normalising Mistakes
The Message Is in the Mess, My Friend!

When we're trying to bring about real change in our lives, it often goes hand-in-hand with learning something new. And when we step into the unknown – because that's what change truly is, doing things differently than before – it can feel a bit scary, can't it? It's like there might be a boogie monster lurking in the shadows. So, it's completely understandable that we might feel a lack of confidence, and, yes, mistakes are bound to happen. It's all part of being human. Let's be honest with ourselves: We all make mistakes, whether we're feeling brave or not. It's a natural part of life's journey. And it's time we embrace this and start to normalise those little stumbles.

You may be feeling like you have taken a wrong turn, or you're just not able to get things right. Relapse, falling off the wagon, feeling like you can't stick to a new routine, or struggling with a diet – trust me, you are not alone. We've all been there. In these moments, it's so easy to feel guilty, ashamed, or like we've failed. But you know what? You absolutely don't have to feel that way!

The most important thing in this whole process of change is to normalise those mistakes. If you mess up, if you stumble, if things seem to fall apart, that's okay. In fact, it's more than okay – it's actually great. The message is there in the mess. Why? Because you've learned something incredibly valuable. You've caught a glimpse of a part of yourself that's trying to communicate something important.

You've observed an aspect of yourself that you can now use to guide your next steps forward. My friend, there's a wellspring of wisdom within you, just waiting to help you learn from that mistake and that experience. It's about giving yourself permission to try again, with a little more insight this time.

Never, ever think a mistake is something terrible. Because, in reality, it's an amazing opportunity to learn and grow. And no matter the outcome, it's a step forward, a sign of progress.

> I truly believe that it's the "crunchy" little mistakes in life that often turn out to be the very best things for you. They add flavour, texture, colour, and depth to the bigger picture of your Change Experience journey.
>
> (When I say "crunchy", I mean, things that aren't smooth in life!)

12.
The Art of Change

Change Is an Experience
Simple Tools for Making It Last

I often get asked how to make changes that stick. You know, the kind of changes that don't just fizzle out after a few weeks. I've seen so many people struggle with this, feeling like they're constantly jumping from one thing to the next, never quite finding a way to make change work for them. So, I really wanted to share what's worked for me. And I can honestly say, hand on heart, that the changes I've made in my own life are lasting, sustainable, and have brought me so much peace and joy.

> **A SIDE NOTE FROM ME ...**
> What I'm about to share with you are the core things – the key ingredients – that I've found are helpful in any situation. And I want to be clear: I'm not here to tell you what to do. This is about giving you the tools to discover things for yourself. There's a big difference, right? As I've said, I know it's not always easy. All those little and big shifts we go through ... it can be tough. And it's easy to give up if you don't feel like you have the right support. So, I've put together these thoughts – my simple strategy for change ideas.

Throughout my book series, you'll see that I expand on all of these points. I weave them into the different topics I discuss, so I really hope you'll feel a sense of comfort and familiarity as we journey on together. And I like to think of these as gentle ideas, not strict rules. It's absolutely okay if you don't do them perfectly. We're all learning and growing. You might use some of these ideas, or you might use all of them – it's really up to you.

So, let's dive in, shall we?

My Strategy for Change Ideas

1. Journalling and Reflection: Getting to Know Ourselves Better

Journalling: I find it really useful to jot things down. Just how I'm feeling, what's happening, when certain things come up. It doesn't have to be anything fancy, just honest. It's like talking to myself on paper. But it gives me clarity on what's happening at that time for me. I tend to do this at night, but maybe mornings work better for you? Whatever feels right.

Identifying Triggers: We all have those things that trigger certain reactions, don't we? Situations, people, even social media sometimes. Just noticing what those triggers are can be a real help.

2. Challenging Old Beliefs: Questioning Our Thoughts

Writing Down the Negative Thoughts: When those "I can't" or "I'm not good enough" thoughts pop up, I try writing them down. Getting them out of my head and onto paper can make them feel less overwhelming.

Questioning the Evidence: Then, I take a closer look at those thoughts. "Is that really true?" "What's the evidence for that?" "Is there another way to look at this?" Sometimes, just questioning a thought can make a big difference to resolving its power over you.

Reframing with Kindness: Then, I try to reframe those thoughts in a kinder way. Instead of "I'm only worthy if ... ", maybe it's "I'm worthy, period." It takes practice, but it's worth it.

3. Focusing on What Really Matters: Your Values

Identifying Your Values: What's important to you? Like, really important? Get really clear on that. Authenticity, kindness, honesty? Or do you need to develop the value of "challenge", to challenge yourself to be more honest and to trust yourself more? When you know your values, it helps guide your choices and actions.

Aligning Actions with Values: Trying to live in line with those values can bring a real sense of peace and grounding.

Celebrating Your Authentic Self: Let's celebrate the unique person you are, not who you think you should be.

4. Being Kind to Yourself: Self-Compassion

Treating Yourself with Kindness: Honestly, this is something I have to remind myself of a lot. Speak to yourself as you would a good friend.

Acknowledging Imperfection: We're all imperfect. That's part of being human. And it's okay. (This was a big shift for me, someone who lived with the burden of perfectionism in order to be recognised. It was such a relief when I dropped this one off! Ahhhh, seriously, huge!)

Self-Forgiveness: If you make a mistake (and we all do), forgive yourself. Learn from it and keep going.

5. Being Present and Body Neutral: Mindfulness

Focusing on the Present: It's so easy to get caught up in the past or the future. But let's try to be here, now.

Mindful Eating: Just paying attention to our bodies' signals. No judgement, just listening.

Body Scan: Taking a moment to check in with our bodies.

Neutral Language: Describing our bodies without labels like "good" or "bad". "I have a body." "My body does amazing things."

Mindful Moments: Even a few minutes of quiet can make a difference.

6. Building Your Support Network

Supportive Relationships: Surrounding yourself with people who lift you up.

Trusted Friends or Family: Having someone you trust to talk to is so important.

It's Okay to Let Go: If a relationship feels draining, it's okay to take a step back. It's okay to let it go.

7. Setting Boundaries: Protecting Your Energy

Identifying Boundary Violations: Noticing when something doesn't feel right.

Practising Saying "No": It's a small word, but it can be powerful.

Communicating Your Needs: Being clear on what your needs are, and letting others know what you need.

8. Small, Steady Steps: Consistent Change

One Thing at a Time: No need to change everything at once.

Replacement Behaviours: Finding a healthier alternative.

Being Patient: It takes time. And that's perfectly okay.

9. Celebrating Your Wins: Acknowledging Progress

"Wins" List: Writing down the things you've accomplished, big or small.

Acknowledging Your Strengths: Remembering what you're good at.

10. Gratitude and Self-Love: Nurturing Yourself

Being Grateful: Before bed, say out loud the few things you're grateful for from the day.

A Little Self-Hug: It might sound silly, but it can feel good. I do this every night before I go to sleep.

Telling Yourself "I Love You": Because you deserve it. I also do this every night before I go to sleep.

These are just my personal experiences, and you can take what resonates and leave the rest. I hope this helps you in some way.

Changing Your Current Values
Getting to the Heart of Who You Want to Be

You know, if we want to change the direction of our lives – if we truly want to move towards that vision we have for ourselves – then we have to commit to the behaviours that will get us there. It's as simple, and as profound, as that. Our values? They're like our personal roadmap. They guide us, they show us where to go, they help us celebrate those little wins, and they offer us some relief from the chaos and challenges that life throws our way.

> **"Hold fast to dreams, for if dreams die, life is a broken-winged bird that cannot fly."**
> – Langston Hughes

In the next chapter, we're going to dive deep into this all-important step, of choosing your values for who you are today. This is where you consciously decide what behaviours you want to embrace, embody, and commit to in your life now, and for your Future Self. Because, honestly, that's what will allow you to live the life you truly desire – and, yes, that includes transforming your relationship with food and drink.

So, what are values anyway? Well, in my heart, I believe they're the deepest inclinations of who we are. They're the blueprint for how we want to behave and show up in the world. It's not about achievements or accolades; it's about how we want to act and treat ourselves, others, and our world on a daily basis.

Living by your values is a choice. It's a decision you make for yourself. Now, that might sound a bit basic, but when you're so used to running on autopilot – doing those automatic behaviours, when you don't even think before you act – reconnecting with that conscious choice is HUGE. It's life changing.

But first, let's take a little step back and look at where your current values – perhaps rooted in the past imprinting from your family of origin – have come from. You might have a set of "values" in your head that you've put on a pedestal, the version of yourself you want people to see, but honestly, your behaviours might be telling a totally different story, one of contradicting values and beliefs. It sounds complex, right? But it's not, really. I'll explain. It all goes back to that time when we were little – a time so many of us seem to forget or ignore. This part might be a bit eye-opening.

And then, we'll talk about what happens when we don't live by our value and those value-based behaviours. Think of it like a company. A company sets out its core values so employees are all working towards the same goals and behaving in a way that achieves those goals. If a company doesn't adhere to its mission and values, it's going to descend into chaos and likely fail. It's the same with us. We'll look at the consequences you'll face when you step away from what truly matters to you.

If you're like most people, you'll readily do things automatically, without much thought, most of the time. (And I'm not trying to be harsh here, but you might feel like you're on autopilot, which can feel a bit out of control.) But here's the wonderful news: I'm here to guide you as you discover how to make changes. It's all completely within your hands.

So, my friend, change doesn't happen unless you take the reins and responsibility for implementing the steps that will lead to the results you desire. If you did the things you are capable of, you would literally astound yourself. Show up and give it a go!

On that note:

Let's now connect with your Future Self before we dive into your values. This is such an important step, where we'll begin to see clearly the woman you're meant to be. We'll explore who she is at her core, how she lives her days, and what truly matters to her. It's also a beautiful chance to reflect on your values and perhaps choose new ones that will powerfully support your journey towards that Future Self.

Think of your Future Self as your guiding light, helping you understand and nurture your relationship with food and drink, and always put her needs first.

13.
Your Future Self

Who Is Your Future Self?
This Is Something that Only You Can Decide

Throughout this book, I am going to help you change the narrative you have created of yourself, relating to what has happened to you in your life. This is particularly relevant to how your trauma is held as a memory. You see, trauma is not just what happens to you; it is the perception of an experience you hold inside, often in the absence of an empathetic witness.

Connecting Your Future Self to Your Past

Why does working on your Future Self have anything to do with this? Well, it is another building block of change. When you have a clear vision of who you truly want to be and the life you want to live, you then work on the values you want to hold to achieve that life. This commitment to your new values – and the behaviours they embody – is a significant building block of change.

This vision of your future self is how you are breaking free from the past narrative, you see. You are no longer just a victim or someone who struggles with low self-worth and holds shame that doesn't belong to you. You are becoming the woman you were born to be, unburdened by a whole heap of mess from other people that once clouded your view.

> So, my dear friend, your Future Self can help you transform this story you created as your unconscious narrative of trauma.

Part One: Getting to Know Your Future Self

Remember when you were little and someone asked, "What do you want to be when you grow up?" I'm sure you had all sorts of ideas – maybe some came true, and some stayed in that fantasy world kids have. This is the same thing, but the adult version.

Have you ever thought about the woman you were before and the woman you are now? Have you ever talked with a friend, colleague, therapist, or loved one about your progress and how far you've come? Or have you ever made New Year's Eve resolutions that weren't fulfilled? Well, maybe those things weren't specific enough. Maybe you couldn't use the right resources and skills to make your wishes, hopes, desires, and dreams a reality.

This, my friends, is where we start building the skills to become who you want to be. This is where you move out of a victim state – that place where you constantly feel like "Why does this always happen to me?" – and into being an empowered woman. This is an important step, so please take it seriously and approach this exploration with compassion and honesty.

The Future Self exercise is something we'll do now and at the end of The Change Experience Series (in Book Three: *Liberated Connection*). This is where you get really clear about who you want to be in life – something that only you can decide.

> I loved doing this the first time with Doctor Benjamin Hardy. I got so much out of it that I'm teaching it to you now.

When you start to identify what your Future Self looks like, you can look at her characteristics, successes, failures, and wisdom. This Future Self can become your most incredible advisor along the way – if you let her. This is all about setting the pathway to becoming the person you want to be. It's about how you want to live your life, which is important when we talk about values, and what's important to you in life. It's also a great tool to find a mentor within yourself.

Let's be honest: Even when you want to change, finding the motivation to do it can be tricky. So, think of this as increased motivation to make the changes you've always dreamed of. Your Future Self can help you face your fears, develop creative solutions to overcome barriers, look at your worries head-on, and embrace change.

This is building your roadmap – making a pathway to becoming the person you want to be. The person you envisage is the person who will give you freedom to move on from where you are today.

This woman will become a mentor for your current self. She will help you step out of your comfort zone and expose you to a wider variety of scenarios and situations.

She will be the one who allows you to challenge yourself and embrace the possibility of change. She will be the one who inspires you to act. The lovely part about this is that it draws on your internal wisdom.

> Here is something for you to contemplate: This woman, your Future Self, is more influential to you than anyone else in your life. More than you can possibly realise right now … but will by the end of this!

The exercise starts below, where I will ask you a set of questions in order for you to start building the vision and picture in your mind. For me, I found it useful to draw this out on a piece of paper. Like a mind map of sorts, nice and visual, so I could see the bigger picture. Perhaps that may work for you too. I also took some time to really think about this deeply, so it wasn't just an "off-the-cuff" exercise; it had meaning and investment.

So, to help you prepare for this exercise:

I will initially ask you to start thinking about the people you admire or respect – in your life, community, or even on TV. Who do you look at and say, "Yeah, I would like to be a bit more like that person"? Think about why that is. What traits inspire you?

Once you've taken a moment to do that, write down five people who inspire you and two aspects of each that inspire you.

Looking at people who inspire you can help you identify some of the characteristics or successes you want for yourself. I want you to do that as a first step because sometimes we're just a bit uncertain about who we really want to be.

Next, I'd like you to think about a life legacy that you would feel proud of. This doesn't have to be some amazing life achievement that makes you famous. It can be as simple as the compassion and kindness you showed one person you encountered. If this is a little challenging, start here: What do you want people to be talking about in your eightieth birthday speech?

Then, take some time to think about what your Future Self looks like. How do you show up in the world? As you imagine, apply self-compassion and love to everything you decide and the imagery you create in your mind. Think about her with inspiration. Think about her as someone who will be your mentor.

MY TIP: If at any time you find yourself seeking a spark of inspiration as you explore these questions, consider this: Think for a moment about the women who truly inspire you – perhaps someone in your community whose kindness shines, a figure on TV whose strength resonates, a colleague whose dedication you admire, or a dear friend whose authenticity you cherish. Who comes to mind? What is it about them that stirs something within you? What are two specific qualities they possess that you feel would beautifully enhance your own journey?

I invite you to contemplate and look at this with real optimism about what your future holds, because this person will give you the freedom you're looking for today. You will come to see how this part of your roadmap will tie in nicely and help you establish the values and behaviours you will align with in the coming pages.

> **"The greatest discovery of all time is that a person can change her future by merely changing her attitude."**
> – Oprah Winfrey

Questions to Ask Yourself

Remember: Read your answers aloud so you hear yourself speak the words – so you believe what you say.

Who Is She?

1. Imagine the woman you are becoming – the woman who has embraced growth, navigated challenges, and blossomed through transformation. What does she look like? How is she showing up in the world? What is her overall presence? What energy does she carry?

2. Envision the environment in which your Future Self lives. Describe the area, her home – is it a cozy sanctuary, a vibrant space filled with life? What are the immediate surroundings like?

3. Take a moment to consider her sensory world. What subtle scents do you associate with your Future Self? Is it a familiar perfume, the invigorating freshness of nature, the comforting warmth of her home? What does her personal atmosphere evoke?

4. Observe your Future Self moving through her day. And as you picture her, what does her physical presence tell you? What is her posture like? How does she carry herself – with confidence, grace, ease? What details do you notice about her

appearance – her hair, her style, the light in her eyes? What kind of energy emanates from her physical presence?

5. Envision the tapestry of connections your Future Self nurtures. What are her relationships like at home, perhaps with beloved fur babies who bring her joy? How does she connect with colleagues in her professional life? What is the depth and quality of her friendships? How does she engage with her wider community?

6. What kind of love beautifully weaves through your Future Self's life? Consider all its forms – romantic love, the cherished bonds of family and friends, and the unconditional affection from her fur babies, if she has them.

7. How does your Future Self cherish her own company? What are her favourite ways to relax, recharge her spirit, and enjoy the peacefulness of her personal space?

8. Consider the moments when your Future Self is completely herself, behind closed doors, without pretence. What brings her private joy and allows her authentic self to shine when no one else is watching?

Her Journey

1. What fulfilling path has your Future Self chosen for her work or life's dedication? What ignites her passion and brings her a deep sense of purpose in how she contributes her unique gifts to the world?

2. Reflect on the milestones your Future Self has celebrated, both the grand achievements and the quiet personal victories. What accomplishments fill her with a sense of pride and validation?

3. Envision your Future Self embracing challenges with a "mistakes are good" mindset. How does she approach each misstep not as a negative but as an opportunity for deeper

understanding? How does she glean wisdom and use these experiences to propel her forward? What is her resilient attitude towards imperfection?

4. Even the most luminous journeys include moments of learning. What setbacks or perceived "failures" has your Future Self navigated? And more importantly, what profound wisdom and invaluable growth has she extracted from those experiences? Remember, these are powerful stepping stones on her path.

Her Evolution

1. Tune into the inner dialogue of your Future Self. What kind and empowering conversations does she have with herself? What are her go-to affirmations or self-supporting beliefs? What is the tone of her inner voice – is it consistently kind, warm, and deeply encouraging, allowing her authenticity to be honoured?

2. Picture your Future Self navigating her emotional world with self-awareness and grace. How does she listen to the messages her emotions offer and communicate to her? How does she understand and regulate her emotions, without being overwhelmed by echoes of the past? How does she create a safe inner space to soothe herself and respond to challenging situations with calm clarity?

3. Imagine your Future Self moving through her life anchored in unwavering self-trust. What does this deep knowing look like in her decisions and actions? How does she intuitively listen to and honour her gut feelings? What is the profound sense of security that comes with this self-trust?

4. Envision your Future Self moving through her life completely free from the grip of guilt and the influence of manipulation. What does she look like when her choices are genuinely her own, no longer driven by a sense of obligation to fulfil others' needs at her own expense? How does she carry herself when

she is no longer acting out of a deep-seated feeling of not being "good enough" and instead acts from a place of inherent worth and self-respect? What is the feeling of this newfound autonomy and self-assuredness?

5. Envision your Future Self living with healthy boundaries that lovingly protect her energy and consciously prioritise her own needs and balance. What does this look like in her daily interactions and the choices she makes? How does she communicate these boundaries with both confidence and grace?

Her Wisdom

1. Imagine your Future Self looking back at her journey with profound empathy and deep understanding for all she has navigated. What does it look like for her to truly see and acknowledge her own pain and the weight of the difficult circumstances she faced? How has she extended forgiveness to herself for any shame she carried and for the choices she made while navigating past life challenges and trauma? What is the feeling of profound self-compassion and self-forgiveness that flows from her?

2. Envision your Future Self radiating a deep sense of inner security and self-validation. What does it feel like for her to no longer seek external approval or validation from others? What is the liberating sense of self-acceptance and inherent worth that shines from within her as she confidently values herself and lives authentically?

3. Imagine your Future Self having embraced her past with acceptance. What does it look like for her to acknowledge her experiences without the weight of resentment or lingering pain? How does she carry her history with wisdom rather than viewing it as a burden? How has she found peace with her story and cultivated enduring joy in her present?

Her Truth

1. Picture your Future Self immersed in a moment of pure, unadulterated joy. What is she doing that makes her heart sing? Who is she sharing this moment with? What are the specific details – the sights, sounds, and feelings – that illuminate her from the inside out? What does joy physically feel like within her body?

2. Imagine your Future Self living in a state of gentle inner and outer peace. How does she show up in the world, and what does this feel like in her everyday existence? What shifts in perspective or circumstances have cultivated this profound sense of peace? How does she navigate life's inevitable challenges while maintaining this gentle state?

3. What does it truly mean for your Future Self to deeply and unconditionally love herself? What are the tangible ways she demonstrates this self-love in her thoughts, actions, and the choices she makes? What does the deeply nourishing feeling of self-love feel like for her?

4. Then, imagine your Future Self embracing that profound beauty of self-love and confidently meeting her own needs. What does it feel like for her to be fully capable of nurturing and caring for herself, without relying on others to fill that space? What is the experience of being alone, yet feeling completely whole and at peace within her own company, free from the pang of loneliness? What does this self-contained sense of love and belonging feel like?

Her Messages to You

1. Looking back with the clear wisdom of your Future Self, what message of unconditional love, profound understanding, and gentle healing would she offer to the younger version of you (your former self or inner child) who experienced such deep

hurt? What kind words of compassion and essential truths would she want her to know and embrace?

2. Imagine your wise and compassionate Future Self sitting right in front of you in this present moment. What gentle yet powerful words of wisdom does she have to share about your Change Experience? What would she say to offer reassurance, provide guidance, and illuminate your path forward from where you are right now?

> The vision you are creating here
> is you; this is all in you.

If you allow your inner voice to speak to you, you will truly connect to who this woman is. I suggest sitting with this for a while. Through this process, you'll begin to understand how to make some small, sustainable steps towards your desired life.

When I did this, I had a heartfelt conversation with the woman I wanted to be – my Future Self. I had a clear picture of her, where she'd be, her house, her relationships – and I have that now. This is manifesting. It's powerful. I've created everything I set out to create when I had this conversation a few years ago because I set my intention. You can do the same.

You will appreciate the value of making changes, so you are no longer trapped by automatic coping mechanisms to numb pain or distract yourself from what's bubbling away inside. And appreciate that everything is a process of small steps of change. You simply just need to start.

Part Two: Your Former Self Meets Your Future Self

These exercises allow your Future Self to validate your past self. It's a way to start the process of healing your trauma with self-compassion and acceptance. If you lean into this, it can be powerful.

> To give you context, the former self is the person who has gone through pain and trauma, while the Future Self is the woman who has healed from that trauma and achieved her desired outcomes in life.

I invite you to find your safe space, your personal little spot where you feel good. Get cozy, close your eyes, and prepare yourself to imagine the conversation between these two.

First, take a moment to think about your former self. Gently picture what she looks like in your mind. Remember, she might be a little different from who you are today. Now, imagine your Future Self sitting down with your past self.

 What would they chat about? How would your Future Self support your past self? What kind, loving, and comforting words would your Future Self offer? Ask yourself, "What would my Future Self say to my past self?"

There is no doubt this might feel a bit strange at first (well, it did for me initially, but then it all started to flow), so bear with me and just allow the flow to happen. If you sit quietly, without distractions, your mind will give you the answers. As the words come to you, say them out loud to yourself.

 A LITTLE NOTE: You may have heard the expression "connecting to your higher self". Well, this is about allowing your inner voice to come through. Giving yourself the space and place of quiet to hear the words that are innately in you.

Then, as you say the words, gently touch a part of your body – your knee, arm, or heart. Feel a sense of connection and touch. It may be helpful to write about this in your journal, so you can capture the natural expression that comes from doing this exercise and experience. And take a pause. Explore this in your safe space.

When you connect with your higher self, the answers will come. The wisdom comes because that's the power we all have within ourselves. We all have our own higher intelligence that knows what we need.

If you've ever felt your gut telling you something, that's it – that's the part that knows the words you need to hear but sometimes ignore.

In my experience, the answer always comes when I sit quietly and ask my higher self. It comes when I am grounded, present, and connected. Otherwise, my ego can step in and change the conversation.

When you allow yourself to do this, without distraction, you will start to feel a deeper connection with yourself. Slowly, with practice, and self-belief, you will start to speak, write, and communicate again, from the source of your inner voice. This, my friend, is you finding your superpower.

> **"Do not go where the path may lead; go instead where there is no path and leave a trail."**
> – Ralph Waldo Emerson

I'm asking you to do these exercises now because they're all about becoming aware of your automatic behaviours. When you understand your Future Self, you'll understand the behaviours you need to adopt to become her. Then you can recognise the automatic behaviours that are holding you back now. It's those automatic, contrary behaviours that keep us stuck. So, take the time to do this and think about it.

Questions to Ask Yourself

Remember: Read your answers aloud so you hear yourself speak the words – so you believe what you say.

Now, try the process again. Close your eyes and find your comfortable place. Take some deep breaths to ground yourself in the present moment. Ask again: What are the words?

1. As you witness your Future Self connecting with your former self, what are the first words of understanding and validation that flow between them? How does your Future Self lovingly acknowledge the pain and experiences of your past self?

2. As your former self receives these kind and validating words from her healed and empowered future, what emotions begin to stir within her? What sensations might she feel in her body as she experiences this acceptance?

3. Looking ahead, what might your envisioned Future Self feel or experience if you were to remain in your current patterns, without embracing the growth and healing you are capable of? What might she long for or regret?

4. Imagine your Future Self gently holding the hand of your former self. What is the feeling that passes between them in this moment of connection? What unspoken understanding is shared?

5. What is one message of hope or encouragement that your Future Self whispers to your former self about the journey ahead? What reassurance can your healed self offer to the part of you that has carried pain for so long?

Sit with this for a while. Let it percolate in your mind. See what comes up for you in the days that follow.

> Remember: Everything you intend, you will create!

14.
Your Progress, Your Reward

Celebrate Every Part of Your Journey
Every Little Step (Forward or Back) Is Growth

You are almost halfway through this book now. Superb effort! None of this is light reading, I know! I would like to say, my friend, that through these pages you have consumed so far, you've already progressed, you've learned new things, and you've gotten some insights that will potentially motivate you to take some steps forward. That's progress. I mean, look at you; you've stuck with this, and you're here, continuing with this work because, deep down, you see how valuable it is for you. I want to acknowledge that genuinely – because I know, none of this is easy stuff. (Warm hugs.)

Okay, I also want to be real with you here. This journey will never be a straight line. It can't be! That's not how we learn, evolve, and rewire our brains. Struggle and discomfort are temporary, but it's also where change is born from. And it takes bravery and commitment to keep going. So, remember that. Every little pain point you face is temporary. Say to yourself, "This too shall pass."

> I heard this great saying once: "The Universe makes us uncomfortable, so we move."
> It sure does, but it always works out.

This one is an interesting one. We should always reward progress, as when you feel a sense of achievement through that reward, it promotes even more interest and willingness to keep progressing, wrapped up in those warm and fuzzy feelings of "Go me!". So, every time you do something well, every time you learn a new skill, I want you to praise and reward yourself from the Top Ten List of Rewards you're about to create. AND... make sure you applaud yourself for showing up here. This is VERY important.

I'm sure you're always showing gratitude to everyone around you, consciously and unconsciously (it's a common trait among us people-pleasers). Now, it's time to give some of that back to yourself for the energy and effort you're putting into your growth as you do this work. If you've never really done this before, this is a must-have life skill you need to build. Non-negotiable, got it?

You get to choose what gives you that little pick-me-up and motivates you to continue your progress.

> Learning something new after a mistake or a stumble is a reward in itself. In fact, that is the most powerful kind of progress.

The Reward-Yourself List

Take some time to create your Top Ten List of Rewards – a wonderfully compassionate expression of your needs today. What rewards are perfect for you to acknowledge your progress each week? Think of it as your little "pick-me-up" to motivate you to continue. How will you feel when you enjoy the reward? Describe why.

Put a note in your journal of what the reward was and why you gave it to yourself. Keep score each week, and at the end of the book series, I want you to tally how many rewards you've given yourself. Question: Do you think you can commit to doing that?

These rewards don't have to be material things (like a new dress or handbag); they can be about your time, space, or personal needs. For example, how about those two hours of that "you time" you never allow yourself? The much-desired manicure/pedicure you've been putting off? Or just that movie you've always wanted to watch, with no interruptions? See how it feels to be reminded each week that you are progressing and moving forward! These rewards are a great way of making yourself feel good without the use of quick fix stimulants you have previously relied on.

> **"It's not how far you fall, but how high you bounce that counts."**
> – Zig Ziglar

Embrace all the lessons, make space for all the mistakes, and remember that every time you practise something or decide to do something intended to help you move forward, it is all progress.

> No matter what happens, no matter what the outcome, it is all progress.

For deeper clarity:

In your journal, I ask you to describe how you feel when you receive the reward. This is an essential part of the process, especially if you've never rewarded yourself before. Writing down how you feel when you accept each reward is important, as it creates a positive connection in your brain. You're telling the pleasure centre of your brain to get ready to feel good about what is coming!

15.
My Trauma Experience

I Was Groomed at Fifteen
This Is What Happened to Me that I Denied for Years

When I was younger, I wanted to be an actor and a singer. However, because of my dyslexia, I could never read the scripts, I could not manage the audition process, and I was always such a hot mess. I would have to learn and memorise lines to pull it off. I had enough bravado (thanks to my false self) to see me through. I was never a leading lady, but I managed to get small but fun roles in the plays at school and loved them. One in particular was my Year 10 play, Pippin; I was Big Bertha. The character needed a big voice and to command the stage, which I thought was perfect for me.

A couple of family members came to see the play, with a close family friend, in support of me. When all the parents left after the show, the two males of the group took me to a bar. I was fifteen. Risky, yes – but it seemed like a lot of fun, so why wouldn't I go? I was with family and a close friend, so yeah, okay! The short story here is that we drank a lot of beer. They bought the drinks. I got pretty drunk, I've got to say, unsurprisingly.

The family friend was someone who visited us quite a lot. This person was friendly and nice to me; he would go out of his way to do things for me. Make me laugh and always sit next to me at the dinner table when he came for a meal. This would be called grooming in today's terminology.

He would do me favours. He would treat me like I was a special person. He would sneak me alcohol. And he would feed me his wine or beer, you know, if we were having a family lunch. He was hilarious. He was so funny. There was a lot of trust there. I would go as far as to say he would flirt with me. I was being groomed.

So, I was in this state of being totally plastered (inebriated). It was like the lights were on and no one was home, I guess. When the family member wanted to leave, the family friend wanted to stay with me at the bar longer. He convinced me that I needed to stay with him. Then (I don't know how this happened to this day), he persuaded my very conservative family member that I was safe with him and that he could return home to his college dorm.

I was underage. I was fifteen. In real terms, my family member was nineteen and responsible for me. But he left me there. Seemingly assured I was safe with his friend, who was six years older than me.

After my family member left, I didn't feel all that comfortable. I knew this was wrong, so I pleaded for a cab. Agreeing that the hour was late, he took me home in a taxi shortly after, being charming and funny as always. In the cab, he asked me to return to his college room with him. I said, "No. I need to go home." I recall the feeling of anxiety at that point. I know I moved closer to my door and hugged the handle.

When we finally got home, he asked me again to come back to where he lived and talk. And I said, "No. I need to go inside." Still persisting, he asked if he could get out and take me for a walk in the park next to my mother's house. He was insistent that we should talk. I was terrified and very intimidated. His tone was firm, as was his body language and his stronghold on my arm.

I felt like I had no choice, as his grip was pretty tight on me. He walked me into the park. There was a bench seat ahead, where he pushed me forward, bending me over it, and he raped me.

He then took me back to my mother's house, knocked on the door, and left. Leaving me standing in freeze mode, in the cold, half undressed, bleeding, and in shock.

My mother let me in, saw my state, put me in a shower, and washed me down. The following day, she told me I would be taking the week off school as if it were a confirmed arrangement. I remember she said it in a way that made it sound like I needed to take a break from school. I didn't question it. She knew.

This family friend came back during that week, knocked on the door, let himself in, and I froze. And he did it again. And I remember he used the words, "This is what love is." And I just froze.

Afterward, he took me into the front sitting room and sat with me on the green velvet sofa. I remember sitting in the pristine room with several silver photo frames of family and friends and all this quiet. Then, out of nowhere, I started throwing the frames at him and screaming for him to get out and go away. Which he did. I never saw him again. He never visited. He never came to a lunch. We never spoke his name. We never talked about it or what happened to me; it was like it never happened.

I stopped eating. I was at boarding school, and when they noticed I wasn't eating … I wouldn't say they forced me to eat, but they ensured I was eating. So then I started to make myself throw up. First, only dinner, then everything I ate every day.

My behaviour was erratic. I suppressed the whole memory; I didn't remember or couldn't connect to any of it. With the enormity of this trauma, my psyche went into overdrive, building walls, and my false self became even more magnified. To hide from the pain, I became more and more outwardly fabulous.

I became hell-bent on winning every athletic game, being the best at netball, pretty much trying to be the best in every circumstance. I'd be extremely confident and cheeky in social situations, and, at times, I engaged in some pretty risky behaviour too. Venturing out to the pub underage, dressing up in clothes that were way too mature for me, and being very provocative. I was still at school, and we were sneaking out of the boarding house and going to nightclubs on a Thursday night. This went on for two years.

In my final year of school, at age seventeen, the girls and I in the boarding house would watch movies together for study breaks. On one particular occasion, it was *The Accused*, where Jodie Foster was raped by five men on a pinball machine. Boom. That did it. That little box inside my head where this horrific memory had been stored was blown right open. The movie triggered everything for me, and I lost the plot.

I had a massive anxiety attack. You would call it a panic attack these days. I was crying, and all I wanted to do was break everything I could get my hands on and lash out. But I couldn't; I was a boarder at my mother's school, and more shame would be attached to me if I did that, so I had to pull my head in.

To my best friend, I admitted what had happened to me. Saying the words didn't even feel real to me at the time. I was never validated as a kid growing up, so I always felt insecure about speaking my truth. Regardless, the cat was out of the bag with my nervous system, and things just steamrolled. I was having panic attacks and fainting at school, and I was still trying to be fabulous, all while attempting to hide the fact I was throwing up. I ran a million miles an hour and had nothing in my system.

I was full-blown bulimic. Every meal I ate, I threw up. After a while, I could throw up without even putting my fingers down my throat. But I couldn't tell anybody about it. Everybody knew because I would stink of vomit. And people could hear me making myself sick. Yet, I was still in denial.

Even though I was avoidant of the effects of what was going on, the boarding house mistress could no longer avoid taking action. They called my mother, and I was sent to a psychiatrist.

I saw the psychiatrist, and it was on the second visit that I admitted what had happened to me, that I had been raped. Today, legally, when there is a sexual violence crime, at the point of learning about it, the doctor has to inform the parents and the authorities. The law was not as strict back then, but they did have to notify the family. My psychiatrist shared the details of my case with my mother and father, with little response from them. However, a very clear action was that they stopped paying the psychiatrist's bills without informing me.

Unaware, I turned up for my next session only to be turned away because of non-payment from my parents. I felt ashamed about this. I felt like this was my fault. That I was an embarrassment to my family, and this is why we didn't talk about it, because of the shame it would bring to our family.

I rang my mother, who immediately blamed my father for not paying. This was her usual manipulation, blaming my father for everything. She gushed at how terrible it was, but in her poshest voice, she delivered her usual invalidating speech. "You have the strength to get through. Courage and quiet mind, darling, and you'll be fine." And she ended the call.

The rape was never discussed. My food disorder was never addressed. The fact I was throwing up every meal – it was never discussed. I was just told to have courage and a quiet goddamn mind.

I lived with that shame, and I suppressed it, deep inside. I made myself sick for years. My poor, frail, invalidated former self. She endured so much pain in silence.

A Mask and a Memoir

When a child experiences profound trauma, as I did – physical violation by multiple people, multiple times – it's simply too much for the psyche to bear. It's too hard. Too painful. Too extreme. As I have outlined previously, the mind does what it must to survive: It suppresses the memories and creates a false self, a protective persona. This persona is imbued with an almost impervious quality, seemingly unaffected by most things. It becomes a suit of armour, a shield to protect the inner child from the overwhelming trauma she endured.

So, then came another layer of protection. I conjured up "Fleur Jazz Hands" – an image of a fun, flamboyant young woman with the world at her feet. I transformed again into this untouchable character. It was a world where I felt safe, and maintained the fantasy that everything was okay. "Fleur Jazz Hands". It sounds playful, doesn't it? It was more of a throwaway line, a label I used for those moments when I felt fabulous or, let's be honest, fabulously cringeworthy. Deep down, my insecure self worried others might think I was a bit "over-the-top", and I probably seemed that way! But no one could get to me. How could I be made to feel not enough if I was fabulous?

But the creation of "Fleur Jazz Hands" was so much more than a bit of frivolity. She was an untouchable persona, a carefully constructed unconscious mask to hide the deep, gnawing pain of what had happened to me – a way to protect the delicate, deeply traumatised little girl I wouldn't truly connect with until my late forties.

Behind this mask, even though I knew what had happened to me when I was fifteen, I totally dismissed how serious being raped actually was. The feelings of violation just weren't real to me. There was nothing wrong with me. The family motto, "Courage and a quiet mind", meant no emotional words or feelings were allowed, so they simply didn't exist. The rape didn't exist, and neither did my bulimia. After all, Mum knew I was raped and didn't say a thing. She saw the look on my face in that shower. She washed the blood from between my legs, wrapped me in a towel, and put me to bed. She took my blood-stained undies and washed them. Telling me to take five days off school was just a way to protect the family, to distance me from anyone who might see me, and to keep up the pretence. "This never happened".

Essentially, she refused to support me through that ordeal, as she would not acknowledge such shame within our family. Another dark secret we kept. She knew I was chronically making myself sick and did nothing. The inaction was an outward statement that there was nothing to worry about, so how could it have meaning or validity? How could I have ever held the belief there was something seriously wrong to deal with? Her lack of actions normalised hiding my bulimia, keeping it swept under the carpet. I didn't know how to support myself and validate my own feelings. Seeking professional help was already shamed in their refusal to pay those bills, so I wouldn't ever dare venture back there again. Denial of pain and consequences was what I was taught. This was the only lesson I learned. So, "Fleur Jazz Hands" helped me pretend that everything was fine. Because it honestly felt like that horrible night didn't happen.

Each time I put my fingers down my throat, it was as if for a moment I could hate everything about all this mess, an outlet to detest the chaos surrounding me, to punish myself for the assault and the isolation it caused. Then, I would wipe my mouth, furiously wash my fingers so they wouldn't smell, and pretend everything was fine and dandy, and skip along as though this wasn't happening either.

Looking back now, after all that buried trauma, I can see I ended up with a whole bunch of misguided values that were completely at odds with what I truly needed deep down. On the outside, I was dedicated to being fabulous, the best at everything, constantly happy, and overly generous – it was all a carefully crafted facade. But underneath it all, the truth was I didn't trust myself, I didn't respect my own body, and I really couldn't put my own needs or my health first. Instead, I valued validation from others more than anything, desperate for even a tiny bit of attention to feel loved.

Generosity – another "loaded" value I learnt from my parents. I was generous to a fault. While it felt lovely to be so giving, in reality, it was a manipulation, a bid to garner attention, love, and adoration from others. I'd cook up lavish dinners, be first to the bar for rounds (and then some!), and cover expenses most wouldn't dream of. What inevitably transpired was an unspoken expectation from these people for a perpetual free ride, with no return favour, gesture, or even an offer. I recall a specific night, hanging back from the bar, purposefully not buying that first round. And did any of those mates offer to buy me a drink? Not one. I had taught them they didn't need to. Two-way relationships were foreign to me. All of these trauma-driven habits left me feeling resentful, quietly fuming, or utterly annoyed. It created the exact opposite of what I craved; I'd end up feeling rejected, unworthy, and just not good enough. As I grew more aware of these tendencies, I'd often say, "I made monsters out of people" – being overly generous out of a sheer desperation for connection, then silently lambasting them for never reciprocating. Was it their fault? Heavens no; the responsibility was squarely on my shoulders.

When things triggered me, I'd either spend money for a quick fix, a temporary high, or get absolutely blotto because I just couldn't handle the emotional storms raging inside me that came from feeling invalidated. When I think of all the money I poured into others, trying to fill that void within me, it makes me shudder. I could've bought a house with all that coin! Generosity, putting others before myself, with no boundaries – that was a tough pattern to break and I traded my worth on it for years. I'll admit, sometimes even now, I slip into old habits, but thankfully, I quickly realise what I'm doing. The friends I have now are rooted in reciprocity, which is a truly refreshing experience, I have to say. As for the old buddies, well, it won't surprise you to hear that 98% of them didn't stick around.

My sense of worth was also deeply entangled with male approval, and I felt a constant craving for validation from men, often after intimate moments. I have clarity now that I genuinely didn't know, and wasn't taught, how to value my authentic self at all.

My upbringing had taught me to relentlessly deny the ugly truth, to squash down my emotions, and to prioritise "keeping up appearances" above everything else. While I was taught the importance of family loyalty, for us, this translated into an unspoken rule: Never discuss what truly happened behind closed doors; protect all those shameful secrets. Indulgence was also highly valued – my family knew absolutely no limits when it came to food and alcohol. A perfectly reinforced message, a fuel for all those messed-up patterns I had.

I was taught the virtues of resilience and strength: to stick it out, not to break down, to keep going no matter what, and to remain stoic. So showing vulnerability, expressing emotions, or communicating your needs simply weren't part of our family's value system at all. Displaying emotions, I learned, meant I wouldn't be accepted; I'd be labelled a "drama queen" and dismissed.

Boundaries were non-existent in our family. Nothing private in your life was safe; while genuine "dirty secrets" were kept locked away, you couldn't share anything personal without it being twisted into ammunition, fodder used to put you down, or weaponised for control. And finally, I was comprehensively taught the value of perfectionism, or perhaps more accurately, the value of shame. If you weren't the best, if you had flaws, you simply weren't good enough – and you certainly weren't worthy.

Honestly, how could I have been real about any of my past trauma when I was living with all those ingrained family beliefs? I grew up in such a chaotic place, full of mixed messages, feeling constantly invalidated and swamped with toxic shame, where everyone was keeping secrets. How could anyone be seen or truly heal in that sort of environment?

So, when my therapist first asked me what I actually valued, what really mattered to me, it was so tough to find an honest answer. It felt like I needed a crowbar to crack open that question and get to the heart of it. I knew I had to heal myself before I could even begin to figure it all out.

This is my truth. This is my story. It's a story of resilience, healing, and, ultimately, using the tools that would enable me to find my peace in acceptance.

My Inner Child: A Journey of Healing

My story has unfolded in layers, some of which I've shared with you before. But there are depths yet to be revealed, moments where I felt utterly vulnerable and alone, with no one to witness my pain or validate its reality. My inner child carried the heavy burden of feeling "not enough", "unworthy", and fundamentally unable to trust. In those times, I used my body as a currency, engaging in risky and transactional behaviours. And, as I've openly shared, food and alcohol became my tools for distraction and self-medication. That young part of me desperately needed a lifeline, a connection, and an empathetic hand to help me rewrite my beliefs and values.

The work I've done to reclaim my inner child has been transformative. It's reshaped my mental landscape and how I hold onto old fears. This truly is my life's work – a journey of struggle and ultimate recovery. I started this path to validate my own experiences and become my own empathetic witness, and it changed my life and removed so many triggers that I used to have quick, automatic emotional reactions to. Everything I share in this journey comes from the heart of my own lived experience.

With the guidance of my therapist, I bravely delved into inner child work (I will teach you these in Book Two: *A New Perspective*. Through meditations, I revisited those difficult times and spoke directly to my younger self, offering her the words of comfort and validation she so desperately needed to hear – words she never received then. I've returned to her many times throughout my life, enfolding her in my arms, pouring out the love and support she needed then and still needs now. I reassured her that she was okay, that her mistakes and those wild, impulsive, risk-taking behaviours were understandable, born of pain and a need for survival.

For years, I carried a heavy cloak of shame for those behaviours. I even tried to deny they ever happened. I was deeply ashamed of the extreme ways I used food and alcohol to cope.

But today, I find peace with my past. I've distanced myself from associating with those painful experiences. I choose to accept what happened and to create space for that pain when it arises. I no longer run from it. I lean into it. I deal with it.

This is the core of my life's work. I am a survivor of abuse and the debilitating effects of complex trauma. Now, at fifty-one years young, I can hold that truth with strength, make space for it in my heart, and normalise the chaotic aftermath of what I endured. I have become my own unwavering empathetic witness, supporter, and validator. A huge part of this journey has been about reconnecting with the inner child I had buried so deep, hidden beneath the layers of trauma. I've written extensively about this, and I will delve deeper as we go. It's been a profound journey of rediscovering the girl I was before the abuse, the essence of her spirit – and allowing that beautiful part of my personality to emerge once more.

I've opened my heart and allowed that part of my soul, that gentle, soft, vulnerable woman within, to step forward and dissolve the false persona I created for protection. I no longer need to hide behind anything. What a beautiful thing it is to embrace the whole woman within me, the woman who always yearned to be seen and accepted.

I am immensely proud of the woman I have become. And I truly, deeply love the woman I am today. The power of acceptance work is extraordinary; it has given me so much clarity on who I am and what happened to me. I have found so much peace in acceptance. I no longer struggle with denial or the shame of what happened to me and the consequences of suffering from a food disorder. I no longer carry that hefty backpack.

Thank you for taking the time to read and appreciate what has happened in my past, and what has coloured my story.

> I have done a lot of work on accepting all that was and allowing myself to sit and ground myself when I experience an emotional trigger or emotional storm. These triggers don't scare me anymore because I am not fighting against them!

A LITTLE SIDE NOTE: My own profound healing through inner-child work and embracing acceptance as a way to break free from the past became another powerful motivator to study psychology and specialise in Acceptance and Commitment Therapy (ACT). The goal was to gain professional expertise in these skills, so I could help other women, just like me, find their voice and no longer suffer in silence.

Your Values

16.
Life Is Automatic

Are You Okay There, My Friend?
Or Are You Stuck in the Comfortable Place of Discomfort?

Sometimes, life can feel like we're just going through the motions. We have our routines, the things we do to make things "work" at home, in our jobs, in our relationships, and in our communities. We might speak a certain way to fit in, eat certain foods because it's "right", dress a certain way, style our hair, drive a particular car – all habits we've been conditioned to adopt. And … we do all of this stuff automatically. We have been conditioned to adapt to our environment, to be accepted. However, what we are not so conscious of is that these automatic reactions to our life circumstances also become a weird, moulded set of values to cope with the world around us.

But these external factors can become traps. They can make us feel stuck, mechanical, and inflexible. The average person often resists change, because they believe to change would mean they have to experience discomfort. They stick to those automatic behaviours, and that becomes their existence.

Many of us fall into this. We live the same patterns, over and over, until the end. We do the same things, go to the same places, see the same people, voice the same complaints, and stay in the same jobs. We tell the same stories, the same jokes, day in and day out.

Perhaps you grew up with parents or grandparents who carried their own traumas – fear, resentment, pain, or guilt. When our caregivers act from these places, it shapes our family system and our own biological

> "To make sacrifices in big things is easy, but to make sacrifices in little things is what we are seldom capable of."
> – Johann Wolfgang von Goethe

and emotional makeup. And because we often feel obligated to respect our elders, their traumas, pains, and fears become ingrained in us. Their fear-based values, automatic behaviours, and limiting beliefs become ours.

Letting go of something you've held onto for a long time is incredibly difficult. But if you want more out of life – more energy, more awareness – you have to release the baggage you've been carrying. You have to let go. Some traditions refer to this as a symbolic "death" or shedding of old skin to allow for rebirth.

What we avoid often controls us. If you avoid failure, your growth will suffer. If you avoid an uncomfortable conversation, that might just be the very thing you need to face in order to move forward. Messiness comes from avoidance.

Humans can be so reactive. We react based on our conditioning. If someone treats us well, we're happier. If someone compliments our appearance, we feel validated. If someone says something hurtful, we crumble. We let others become the authors of our story. We depend on them for our emotional wellbeing instead of taking responsibility for our choices, finding acceptance within ourselves, and writing our own narrative. When we make mistakes, we need to own them, learn from them, and not wait for someone else to tell us it's okay.

Right. If you truly want to change, you have to be willing to embrace a little discomfort. Don't be afraid of that, okay? If you desire a different outcome, if you're tired of asking, "Why does this keep happening to me?" and feeling stuck, you have to be willing to walk a different path.

The question I would like you to ask yourself now: Are you truly willing to change, or are you finding yourself stuck in a pattern, feeling like a victim of circumstance?

Those Automatic Behaviours
What Is Your Distraction Technique for Coping?

Like many of us, you probably have a "conscious" list of values that sound good and feel good to say. We often desire to be loving, supportive, fun, trustworthy, honest, reliable, and compassionate. But let's be real – why do we sometimes act in ways that feel the complete opposite?

Why do we spiral into self-loathing, that awful negative self-talk, judge ourselves so harshly, become totally unfun, lie to hide our chaos, and let people down because we just feel completely overwhelmed? Can you see any alignment with those values in those behaviours? No, me neither.

> **"Until you make the unconscious conscious, it will direct your life, and you will call it fate!"**
> – Carl Jung

A trigger happens – something creates discomfort, pain, a challenge, or heartache – and suddenly, we're doing anything we can to take our mind off it. We might eat, drink, binge-watch Netflix, endlessly scroll on social media, punish ourselves, work out to exhaustion, project our feelings onto others, deny ourselves what we truly need, party way too hard, or neglect our sleep. The cycle continues. I know you understand exactly what I'm talking about here.

> This might be hard to hear, but please ask yourself honestly, "Are these the characteristics I want to hold onto when I'm choosing my values now, at this stage of my life?"

This has become our norm, our comfort zone. We automatically do these things every time we don't feel great about ourselves, every time someone or something makes us feel bad. It might feel familiar, but that doesn't mean it's what we truly want. It's where we hide, and it's where we end up feeling stuck and missing out on life.

This distraction from ourselves is so detrimental to our emotional balance and wellbeing, our mental and physical health, and our energy levels. It's the stuff that just doesn't serve us, plain and simple. Distracting ourselves has become a coping mechanism, so our brain often thinks it's just the way things are. As a result, we might not even realise that these behaviours aren't in line with our values at all.

As such, you might feel controlled by past traumas and triggers, and I understand that deeply – I've been there too.

When you're triggered, your body responds as your nervous system reacts to feeling ignored, denied, or invalidated; there are countless ways past pain is awakened in the present.

> But here's the thing, my friend: There's that space between that trigger and your response. In that tiny moment, there's potential. That's where your power lies. That's where you can learn to emotionally regulate yourself.

To gain real clarity, self-awareness is key. It's how you move beyond what's keeping you stuck in the past and break free from old emotional patterns. Our worlds can feel so programmed, almost predictable. But you don't have to be predictable. You have free will, a voice, a heart full of desires, and a brilliant mind. Together, they can help you achieve so much more than you might have thought possible.

> I hope this resonates with you, my friend, and gets you thinking about what is important to you, and how you want to start fostering self-love through your values!

17.
The Roots of Your Truth

Where Your Values Truly Began
Unravelling Old Beliefs to Now Choose Your Own

Our "family of origin" – it's such a meaningful term, isn't it? It really gets to the heart of where we come from. Essentially, your family of origin (or FoO, as some call it) refers to the main caregivers and siblings you grew up with. Think of it as that very first social group you belonged to, the place where your story began and evolved from. Most often, this is our biological family, but it can also be an adoptive family.

The Influence of the Family of Origin

This is where our values were first shaped, where we had our first experiences with relationships, and especially that relationship with food and drink. It's where our global picture of our body was formed – how our weight fluctuates, how it responds to stress, and how we perceive our body image. Does that resonate with you? I bet you'll discover some real insights here about where some of your automatic behaviours originated.

Now, I know this can be a sensitive area. For many of us, it's where we feel like things got a bit ... complicated. You might have very positive feelings about your family, or perhaps it's a mix of both positive and negative. It's vital to understand where we've come from in order to move forward.

Let's have an open and gentle chat about your family of origin. This is a huge influence in your life, your original "imprinting", where your belief patterns started. This is where you observed, learned, and adopted the common ways of living within your household's dynamics.

Were Your Needs Met as a Child?

When a child grows up in a home where their needs aren't met or in an unsafe environment, they often develop a set of beliefs and values that are, at their core, falsehoods. These beliefs stem from what we've now comfortably defined as their complex trauma – their perception of reality shaped by difficult experiences.

For example, as I discussed in Chapter 5, a child might not value authenticity because they feel, "If people see the real me, they'll reject me." So, they create a "fake" persona. This "fake self" then chases connection, as they believe pleasing people is the way to be accepted. And so, being a "people-pleaser" becomes a core value.

If a child experiences abandonment, criticism, or being put down, they might grow up believing, "I am a failure and don't deserve much out of life." This can lead them to believe their own needs don't matter and they must be subservient to others. They start thinking, "I don't matter as much as other people do."

Another point I should add, along with the "I'm not good enough" belief, is that a person might believe they can never be angry or upset. They think that showing any negative emotion proves they're not good enough, proves they are a bad person.

Another value stemming from this lack of authenticity is the idea that "I must be perfect to get acceptance and love." Therefore, perfectionism becomes the driving force. (Can you see the pattern? These values often lead to negative or destructive behaviours, especially with food and drink.)

Or, perhaps, their worth becomes tied to their body, brain, or accomplishments (this relates to the image attachments I discussed in Chapter 5).

They become an overachiever, pursuing accomplishments with incredible commitment and focus. The subconscious belief is that "People only want me if they can use me for something or see me as something special." And on top of this, they might feel, "People will only be interested in a relationship with me if they want something from me; I can't have a relationship with no strings attached." They believe they need these "trophies" to be wanted and desired. Or they deeply believe they'll only be respected for their status, position, or possessions, not for who they truly are.

They might also believe, "My needs are not valid, and I should never ask for help. People will resent me, see me as a burden, and think I'm selfish and shame me for it." This is how people become fiercely independent, self-sufficient, or even outwardly detached. (When, in reality, they cry behind closed doors and have a deep sense of loneliness.)

Trust often becomes a challenge. When trust is broken in so many forms in the home environment, a child grows up believing, "People will always let me down and break my trust. People will always talk behind my back. I can't trust that their intentions are real." This can cause significant pain and isolation, a big contributing factor to the cycles of unhealthy behaviours of using food and drink to numb and escape the discomfort.

So, are you starting to get a clearer picture now of how the values of your past, linked to these past experiences, can hinder living a healthy life in the present? Can you see how these values and beliefs are not serving you today? And can you see that potentially there is room to ask yourself what values you would like to adopt consciously and authentically today?

> **"Values are like fingerprints. Nobody's are the same, but you leave them all over everything you do."**
> – Elvis Presley

Acknowledge that if you have experienced such challenges in life, your perception of the world can lead to seeing the wrong things as values, because they are, in reality, not your truth. This is how a confused state of consciousness is born from your past hurts. Recognising this is a MASSIVE first step. Huge.

Ugly, uncomfortable – okay, yes, I know; I am with you here – but this is the reality of trauma. It's the story we create in our minds based on what happened to us when we were vulnerable and suffering. The child forms a strong attachment to these internal stories, so letting go isn't easy. I know this firsthand. But if I can do this – and there were times I thought I'd always be stuck – I truly believe you can too. You can. You just need to try.

This is why it's SO crucial to establish a NEW AND TRUE set of values for who you are today, how you WANT to show up in the world, and how you truly want others to treat you.

This is why you need to discover the real truth of your authentic self. This is where the real work of change begins – the manual effort to reprogram your brain with what is important to you now.

> I am here with you, holding your hand.

Family of Origin Values

Taking a moment to understand your family's values is like tracing the roots of a tree. It's crucial – you have to know where those roots go to truly understand how the tree grows. In the same way, to make lasting changes in our own lives, we need to see the "umbilical cords" that connect us to our past. This way, we can make conscious choices about what we want to keep and what we want to lovingly release.

Our families, the people we grew up with, had such a profound influence on us during our formative years, didn't they? The dynamics of that immediate household environment shaped so much – how we see the world, how we form relationships, and, crucially, our behaviours. It's those day-to-day experiences, interactions, and specific behaviours we observed and absorbed that have now translated into the values we hold today.

In the kindest possible way, I want you to know this: for our work to be most effective, you need to connect with what really happened behind closed doors. This isn't about pretending everything was fabulous. It's about courageously finding where the hurt began, okay? So, please be real with yourself. Whatever you've been hiding away, now is the time to gently bring it into the light and let it breathe. No one else is here right now; this is just you.

It's time to be honest, be real, and remember, this is all about connection and your own self-awareness. Please, take your time with this.

Questions to Ask Yourself

Okay, first off, children primarily learn their values by watching their parents' behaviour. So, what were the values your family was most proud of? For example, respect, love, humility, responsibility, trust, spirituality – can you specifically identify them?

Remember: As you write your answers in your journal, read them aloud so you hear yourself speak the words – so you believe what you say.

Now, let's delve into the examples that were set for you growing up:

1. Love and compassion for one another. How did each of your parents (or caregivers) characterise acts of kindness or empathy towards others?

2. What were your parents' examples of taking personal responsibility for their behaviour in conflict or challenging situations?

3. What were your parents' examples of helping you make sound and solid decisions in your life (having discernment)?

4. What were your parents' examples of acting with honesty and integrity in all areas of their lives? (You can also detail it if they lacked honesty or integrity in particular circumstances.)

5. What were your parents' examples of acting with acceptance? (Accepting that good and difficult things will happen and making room for challenging thoughts and feelings that may

come with these situations.) And how did they teach you to be open to acceptance in your life?

6. What were your parents' examples of teaching what a healthy, balanced lifestyle looks like?

7. What were your parents' examples of helping you become an independent person who can make the right choices and decisions for your wellbeing?

8. What were your parents' examples of forgiveness and teaching you to be forgiving towards yourself and others?

9. What were your parents' examples of how to be a good communicator and express your thoughts and emotions when required?

10. What were your parents' examples of teaching you to challenge yourself to learn, keep improving, and grow as an individual?

11. What were your parents' examples of behaving with reciprocity in relationships? How did they teach you to build relationships with a fair balance of giving and taking?

12. What were your parents' examples of behaving with self-awareness? How did they teach you to be aware of your own feelings, thoughts, and actions?

13. What were your parents' examples of building trust?

14. How did they teach you to be trustworthy, loyal, faithful, sincere, and reliable?

15. What were your parents' examples of expressing and demonstrating romance?

16. How did they teach you to be romantic, to display and express love or strong affection?

17. What were the more challenging aspects of the contradictions between your parents' behaviours and their values?

18. What are some of the examples of how your parents deviated from their values when they were triggered by an emotional storm?

I know that some of these questions might take time and deep thought, and that's perfectly okay. It's a good thing to pause and contemplate.

Again, I want to emphasise that this is all about connection and your own awareness. So now, I'd like you to reflect on these questions:

1. What can you relate to or see in yourself within these answers? Have you been behaving similarly to your parents?

2. Can you see any link between your automatic behaviours and some of their values?

3. And ask yourself: Are their values what you want to live by now? Are these behaviours what you want to keep?

As we go through this process, you'll start to recognise these influential factors and how you may have been automatically behaving because of them.

> My friend, this can be a lot to take in and process. So let this flow through you for a little while. If you find this exploration process difficult or triggering, please reach out for professional help. Talking to a mental health professional can provide a safe space to explore these feelings.

As we move through this chapter, it may become clear what you would like to do – keep those old patterns, or make some changes and choose values and behaviours that truly resonate with your heart's desires? Hmm, let's see how you go in the next section. **There is absolutely no judgement if you want to keep or remove any of these behaviours. It's entirely your choice.** Use your reflection journal to write down what you want to do.

This is where the magic happens
and where lasting change takes hold.

18.
Living Your Truth

Your Values Are the Language of Self-Love
Tuning In: How Your Values Give You Clarity

Exploring the values that resonate with you today can be a liberating, sometimes challenging, but ultimately beautiful journey. Solidifying these core values is like discovering a nugget of gold; it will empower you to become the beautiful vision of your Future Self – a person with unwavering self-love and authenticity. The values you choose are the deepest, most authentic inclinations of your heart.

They serve as your blueprint for how you want to behave and show up in the world. They aren't about achievements, but rather about how you choose to act and live each day. This includes how you treat yourself, others, and the world around you.

When you're aligned with your values, self-love flows more naturally. You experience less inner conflict between what your heart desires and your automatic responses. This is where you truly connect with your authentic self. Think of your values as a language that helps you connect to self-love. Trauma can sometimes disrupt this beautiful, natural flow of self-love and connection. It can leave us feeling adrift, unsure of where we belong, and disconnected from who we truly are. In these times, we might cling to others and their values as a lifeline.

Loving yourself is a choice, one that stems from living authentically. Similarly, choosing to live by your values is a conscious decision that creates space for authenticity to flourish. It's a commitment you make to yourself. This might sound simple, but when we're accustomed to acting on autopilot, becoming aware of and consciously making that choice is incredibly important.

If you desire a change in your current direction, commit to the behaviours that will move you towards the life you envision.

This is your opportunity to discover what true self-love feels like. This is your time – perhaps the most honest time ever – to make a genuine connection with what is truly important to you, and only you. How wonderful is that?

What Is Most Important to You Today?

This journey of self-discovery, of choosing your values, might feel a bit challenging at first. It's not uncommon to struggle with it. Sometimes, we reach for values that we *think* we should have, values that sound impressive or that others expect of us.

Perhaps you've been wearing a mask, trying to be someone you think others want you to be. Perhaps you've been carrying burdens that aren't yours to carry. Now is the time to gently set those things down, to shed those layers, and to reveal the beautiful, genuine soul that you are.

But I want you to dig deeper. I want you to find *your* values, the ones that resonate with your heart.

That's why I've placed this chapter here. It's meant to be a starting point, a catalyst for your thinking. You might find that as you read through the series, as you learn and grow, you'll want to come back and revisit these values. That's absolutely okay; in fact, I encourage it!

All the education, knowledge-sharing, and assessments in this series are designed

> **"A value is a way of being or believing that we hold most important. Living into our values means that we do more than profess our values, we practice them."**
> – Brené Brown

to help you cultivate a deeper awareness and more clarity of who you truly are and the patterns that guide your actions. That awareness of your "self", of those automatic behaviours, is key. The closer you get to understanding yourself, the clearer your values will become. You'll begin to see what *you* truly want for your life and what those values look like in action.

And when life throws its inevitable curveballs – when you feel triggered, pushed, stressed out, and the world feels noisy – you can pause, take a breath, and ask yourself, "Are my actions moving me towards the woman I want to be, or are they pushing me away?"

Once you can see those patterns, once you can identify the event, behaviour, and consequence cycle, you can start to understand when and how it all happens. This, my friend, is all part of understanding your emotional model, which we'll dive deeper into in Book Two.

But please hear this, from my heart to yours: When you're aware of your values, when you know what behaviours align with them, and when you can create that space to choose in the moment, you begin to reclaim control. You slowly shift those automatic behaviours and start making conscious, intentional choices. Knowing your values is, in essence, learning how to direct your life.

Building Self-Confidence and Taking Back Control

Choosing your values for the woman you are today is truly about stepping back into the driver's seat of your life. It's about gently taking control of your needs, one small, simple step at a time. With clarity.

Now, confidence isn't about getting everything perfectly right and gloriously conquering all – no, that's more about skill and experience. True confidence comes from the willingness to step out and try. That's what confidence really means: It means giving something a go. Because, let's be honest, everything we truly desire but don't yet have lies just outside our comfort zone. And when you're willing to take that step forward, there are always trade-offs. You might need to let go of people-pleasing or putting others' needs before your own. So, the question is, what's the trade-off you're willing to make?

To honour your values, you'll need to be willing to set boundaries. When you do this – and we'll explore this in more detail in Book Three: *Liberated Connection* – something wonderful happens.

You begin to feel more grounded in your choices, which fuels your confidence and willingness to try again. You'll start to trust yourself more deeply, and that inner critic begins to quiet down. The tendency to reach for numbing agents, distractions, or a messy relationship with either food or drink starts to shift. Your dependency changes, your health improves, and you're finally able to connect with your true needs and desires.

You begin to make choices that feel right, that resonate with your soul. You start to say, "Right, this is for me. This feels good. Because it aligns with *my* values."

> My friend, it's really as simple as this: You're taking control of the "it" (that thing or automatic behaviour you have that you couldn't quite articulate before), instead of the "it" controlling you.

Making Room for Your Thoughts and Feelings

This journey is also about practising acceptance – accepting your thoughts and feelings, just as they are. This isn't about condoning what caused you pain in the past, not at all. It's about gently acknowledging your emotions, without judgement or resistance.

Another key objective is to help you learn how to sit with your pain and feel comfortable with your emotions. In Book Two: *A New Perspective*, I'll share simple, approachable strategies to manage those challenging emotions. These tools will help you allow those feelings to flow in and out of your life, rather than trying to suppress or change them. Acceptance is about recognising your thoughts and feelings as they are, even when they're uncomfortable. And your values? They play a big role in how you navigate this.

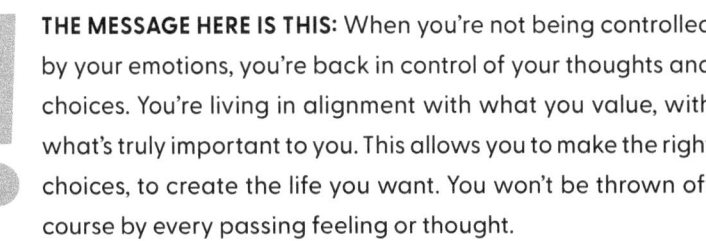

THE MESSAGE HERE IS THIS: When you're not being controlled by your emotions, you're back in control of your thoughts and choices. You're living in alignment with what you value, with what's truly important to you. This allows you to make the right choices, to create the life you want. You won't be thrown off course by every passing feeling or thought.

Setting Beautiful Boundaries

As a heads-up, we'll dive deep into setting boundaries in Book Three: *Liberated Connection*. But I must emphasise right now: Honouring your values means honouring your boundaries. Setting boundaries is a must-have life skill, and you'll learn to protect those boundaries with love and conviction. Part of this is learning to listen to your gut, to really tune in to what your body is telling you.

When you know your values, you also learn to identify your needs. And when you honour both, you step into your power.

Another wonderful thing about staying true to your values? You truly own who you are. I want to help you see and embrace that. For instance, if people-pleasing, letting others cross your boundaries, and having your energy drained don't align with your values, we address that. Putting others before yourself becomes a thing of the past.

So, an essential part of this journey is speaking out loud about what *you* need and what *you* want from life.

> Sing out loud what your values are, lady!
> They are your life support system.

Choosing Your Values: The Essential Building Blocks

Throughout this book series, I'll refer to building blocks and the building of new muscles for change. It's important to remember that this isn't a quick fix. Wouldn't that be amazing! But think of this like building a house. You

> "Authenticity is a collection of choices that we make every day. It's about the choice to show up and be real. The choice to be honest. The choice to let our true selves be seen."
>
> – Brené Brown

need a solid foundation and beautiful walls around your sacred pool of serenity, right? It's the same here.

Don't be afraid, my friend. You have time. You have my encouragement to revisit and reflect as needed. You'll discover that each of these building blocks is designed to help you transform your relationship with yourself, own your role in life, make empowered choices, and put food and drink in its proper place – to nourish you, not control you.

This Is Your Safe Space

This next exercise is for *you*. Just you. This is between you and me, and I want you to know you're in a safe space here.

May I offer some advice? When you dive into this, create a little bubble for yourself. Find the space and time to truly focus. This is 100% yours.

No one needs to know what you're saying or doing. You don't need to share this with anyone. These values are yours, and yours alone. Don't let anyone else influence them. This is about you choosing how *you* want to live your life, taking care of your Future Self.

🔍 Revisiting and Refining Your Values Over Time

- **Personal Growth and Evolution:** As you learn, grow, and experience life, your perspectives and priorities may shift. What was important to you five years ago might not hold the same significance today. Revisiting your values allows you to align them with your current self.

- **Increased Self-Awareness:** Reflecting on your values helps you understand yourself better. You gain clarity about what truly matters to you, which can guide your decisions and actions.

- **Adaptability to Change:** Life is full of changes, and external circumstances can influence your values. Revisiting them allows you to adapt and ensure they still resonate with your life situation.

- **Living Authentically:** When your actions align with your values, you live a more authentic and fulfilling life. Regularly refining your values ensures that you stay true to yourself.

- **Improved Decision-Making:** Clear values provide a framework for making choices. When you know what's important, it's easier to make decisions that align with your priorities.

- **Enhanced Emotional Wellbeing:** Living in accordance with your values can reduce stress and increase overall happiness and wellbeing. When you revisit and refine them, you strengthen that alignment.

In essence, revisiting and refining your values is an ongoing process that supports your personal development and helps you live a more purposeful life.

Getting the Most Out of This

Creating a safe and comfortable environment for reflecting on your values is key to truly connecting with yourself and doing this important inner work. Here are some suggestions to help you create that space.

Choose a Private and Quiet Space: Find a place where you won't be disturbed. This could be a comfy spot in your bedroom, a quiet room in your house, a garden bench, or even a park. The key is to find somewhere you feel at peace and can think clearly.

Set the Mood: Create an atmosphere that feels relaxing and conducive to introspection. This might involve:

- Lighting candles or using aromatherapy.
- Playing soft, instrumental music. Or music that soothes your soul.
- Decluttering the space to minimise distractions.
- Having a warm drink that warms your heart.
- Start off by wrapping your arms around your shoulders to give yourself a hug. (The brain can't tell the difference whether it's another person or you – and naturally it will release oxytocin, which is called the "cuddle hormone". This helps promote feelings of calmness and relaxation.

Schedule Dedicated Time: Carve out specific time for your values reflection. Treat it as an appointment with yourself. This makes it a priority and helps ensure you won't be interrupted.

Remove Distractions: Turn off your phone, close your laptop, and let others know you need some quiet time. This is your time to disconnect from the outside world and tune into your inner world.

Gather Your Supplies: Grab your journal, and have it ready to record your thoughts. You might also want pens, markers, sticky notes, or anything else that makes you feel prepared.

Start with a Ritual: Begin your reflection time with a small ritual to signal that this is a special time. Start by setting your intention for choosing your values (will it be effortless?). Then, perhaps, take a few deep breaths, or close your eyes in meditation for a few minutes, and just be still. Whatever works for you.

Practise Self-Compassion: Remind yourself that there are no right or wrong answers. This is about exploration, not judgement. Be gentle with yourself and your thoughts as they come in and out of your mind. Then return to focusing on the task of choosing your values.

This may all seem like quite a process, so if it's not for you, don't worry; that is okay. You can skip all this and move straight into the nitty gritty. Remember, the choice is yours.

I suggest all of this as a way to help you be conscious of your energy and the space around you. By creating a safe and comfortable environment, you'll be able to explore your values more openly and honestly, with clarity, leading to greater self-awareness and personal growth.

• • •

19.
Choosing Your New Values

Step One: Your Time to Choose
Review the List of Values Below

This is, to me, the sowing of the seeds. This is the heart and soul of how you're going to start to affect real change in your life.

You'll see a list of values here for you to spend some time considering. Are these really right for you today? See what truly resonates with you as the incredible woman you are right now and for the woman you're becoming – your Future Self.

The Task

You can look at this holistically, globally, for your entire life, or you could pick a specific area or part of your life that you want to improve – family, relationships, work, physical/mental health, or exercise. Read through the list below and write a letter next to each value. Use this key:

"M" - Most Important
"V" - Very Important
"S" - Somewhat Important
"N" - Not Important (to me right now)

Once you've marked each value as M, V, S, or N, go through all the Ms and make a shortlist. Choose your **Top Twenty** Most Important Values from this list.

Then select the **Top Three** that are most important to you for where you are in your life today. The first three things that you want to master, the first things you want to build skill in.

These are your values that you're going to work on in your daily life, until you are super comfortable with them and feel like they've become automatic.

Choose the three most pertinent to you for what is happening in your life right now. Practise building those skills until they become automatic. Then, choose another three to work on and repeat the process.

From here, your focus is taking small steps towards looking at ways to commit to these behaviours in your life – so you can live a life guided by your values.

Here, you have the opportunity to decide the values that you're going to live your life by. Here, you look at the behaviours you need to hold onto in order to have the life you want to live.

You may have a clear view, inspired by what we've already talked about, for what values you want and what you can choose to work on to promote a healthier, happier life. Or you may come back to this after some time and space to reflect – and that's totally okay too!

This is where you start to do that manual change, taking things from automatic reaction to deliberate action. Taking back your power, having conscious thought and control over your choices.

I know this was one of the big, big links in my chain. It helped me connect the dots and work out how I could avoid the destructive behaviour I was stuck in.

There are many values out there, but I've chosen the most common ones for you to review. (Some may even be irrelevant to you, which is also okay.) Each of these words

> **"One of the most vital goals in life is to be consistently inspired to be flexible to change, so that we can easily take on different strategies until we arrive at the desired destination."**
>
> – Dr. Jacinta Mpalyenkana, PhD, MBA

describes the types of behaviours you want to hold – your role here is to make sure you process what each one is and what it means to you.

My Tip

If you find that there's something missing that's important to you, please add that! But I've chosen the most common values that are out there today.

- Take some time to digest these. Please make sure you read them out loud, see how they feel. What does it do to you when you say aloud what that particular value is?

- When you make your list of values, there are a few pointers for you to consider that I found helpful.

- Taking time to process this is going to ensure these are valid and accurate to your needs.

    For example: You could take an hour to walk away from it and then come back. Or leave it overnight, which is what I did.

- When you return, read your list again, out loud, and ensure the values still resonate with you. Sense-check. What does it feel like? What's going to be different? Does it excite you? Does it feel good? Does it feel uncomfortable? Does it feel like something you need? Does it feel like something you want?

Every sailor needs a compass so they don't get lost in a storm, and that's how your values will guide you. They are the compass you'll return to, so you don't get lost in an emotional storm.

> Remember: There are no "right'" or "wrong" choices. Your answers are purely what you decide is suitable for you and the future you envision for yourself. And they will help you identify what is important for you RIGHT NOW!

My Process for Choosing My New Values

The first three values I chose to work on were **honesty, acceptance, and challenge.**

I wanted to be really **honest** with everyone in my life because I'd been keeping up appearances for so long. I wanted to **accept** where I was in my life because I was having health issues, and I needed to accept that and deal with it, rather than trying to fight it. I had to learn to lean into it. I wanted to **challenge** myself to keep moving forward and keep growing.

At the time I did this, things were not great for me. I was hiding away and desperately trying to find myself again. Ironically, this was perfect because these three nuggets of gold shone a massive light on a path for me to walk forward on. I grabbed hold of them with both arms. This was a commitment – perhaps even a life raft. I decided what all the behaviours were that went with holding those three values, and I didn't waver. At certain points, maybe I was a little bit extreme, sure. I had to learn how to turn the taps to the right temperature. Soon enough, I got there, and they became my automatic behaviours. Food and drink were only my nourishment, my energy, my enjoyment.

> **SO, MY MESSAGE HERE TO YOU IS THIS:** Even if the landscape is looking a bit bumpy, there is a way forward. I'll leave this with you. Go and do the work. See how it feels. Try it on for size. And then we'll carry on.

I hope you enjoy the process.

Your Values List

- ○ **Acceptance:** To be open to and accepting of myself, others, life, etc.
- ○ **Adventure:** To be adventurous; to actively seek, create, or explore novel or stimulating experiences.
- ○ **Accuracy:** To state accurately my opinions and beliefs.
- ○ **Achievement:** To have important accomplishments.
- ○ **Art:** To appreciate or express myself in or through art or in some artistic way.
- ○ **Assertiveness:** To respectfully stand up for my rights and request what I want.
- ○ **Authenticity:** To be authentic, genuine, and true to myself.
- ○ **Autonomy:** To be self-determined and independent.
- ○ **Beauty:** To appreciate, create, nurture, or cultivate beauty in myself, others, the environment, etc.
- ○ **Belonging:** To have a sense of belonging, being part of something.
- ○ **Caring:** To be caring towards myself, others, the environment, etc.
- ○ **Challenge:** To keep challenging myself to grow, learn, and improve.
- ○ **Compassion:** To act with kindness towards those who are suffering.
- ○ **Comfort:** To have a pleasant and comfortable life.
- ○ **Compromise:** To be willing to give and take in reaching agreements.
- ○ **Connection:** To fully engage in whatever I am doing and be present with others.

○ **Contribution:** To contribute, help, assist, or make a positive difference to myself and others.

○ **Conformity:** To be respectful and obedient to rules and obligations.

○ **Cooperation:** To be cooperative and collaborative with others.

○ **Courage:** To be courageous or brave; to persist in the face of fear, threat, or difficulty.

○ **Creativity:** To be creative or innovative.

○ **Curiosity:** To be curious, open-minded, and interested; to explore and discover.

○ **Encouragement:** To encourage and reward behaviour that I value in myself or others.

○ **Dependability:** To be reliable and trustworthy.

○ **Diligence:** To be thorough and conscientious in whatever I do.

○ **Equality:** To treat others as equal to myself and vice versa.

○ **Excitement:** To seek, create, and engage in activities that are exciting, stimulating, or thrilling.

○ **Faithfulness:** To be loyal and true in my relationships.

○ **Fairness:** To be fair to myself and others.

○ **Fitness:** To maintain or improve my fitness; to look after my physical and mental health and wellbeing.

○ **Flexibility:** To adjust and adapt readily to changing circumstances.

○ **Freedom:** To live freely; to choose how I live and behave, and help others do likewise.

○ **Friendliness:** To be friendly, companionable, and agreeable towards others.

- ○ **Forgiveness:** To be forgiving towards myself and others.
- ○ **Fun:** To be fun-loving; to seek, create, and engage in fun-filled activities.
- ○ **Generosity:** To be generous, sharing, and giving to myself and others.
- ○ **Genuineness:** To act in a manner that is true to who I am.
- ○ **Gratitude:** To be grateful for and appreciative of the positive aspects of myself, others, and life.
- ○ **Growth:** To keep changing and growing as a person.
- ○ **Honesty:** To be honest, truthful, and sincere with myself and others.
- ○ **Health:** To be physically well and healthy.
- ○ **Hope:** To maintain a positive and optimistic outlook in everything I do.
- ○ **Humour:** To see and appreciate the humorous side of life.
- ○ **Humility:** To be humble or modest; to let my achievements speak for themselves.
- ○ **Imagination:** To have dreams and see possibilities.
- ○ **Industry**: To be industrious, hard-working, and dedicated.
- ○ **Independence:** To be self-supportive and choose my own way of doing things.
- ○ **Inner Peace**: To experience personal peace.
- ○ **Intimacy:** To open up, reveal, and share myself – emotionally or physically in my close personal relationships.
- ○ **Justice:** To uphold justice and fairness.

- ⚪ **Kindness:** To be kind, compassionate, considerate, nurturing, and caring towards myself and others.
- ⚪ **Knowledge:** To learn and contribute valuable knowledge.
- ⚪ **Leadership:** To inspire and guide others.
- ⚪ **Love:** To act lovingly or affectionately towards myself and others.
- ⚪ **Mindfulness:** To be conscious of, open to, and curious about my here-and-now experience.
- ⚪ **Moderation:** To avoid excesses and find a middle ground.
- ⚪ **Monogamy:** To have one close, loving relationship.
- ⚪ **Music:** To express myself in music.
- ⚪ **Non-conformity:** To question and challenge authority and norms.
- ⚪ **Nurturance:** To encourage and support others.
- ⚪ **Order:** To be orderly and organised.
- ⚪ **Open-mindedness:** To think things through, see things from others' points of view, and weigh the evidence fairly.
- ⚪ **Patience:** To wait calmly for what I want.
- ⚪ **Passion:** To have deep feelings about ideas, activities, and people.
- ⚪ **Persistence:** To continue resolutely despite problems or difficulties.
- ⚪ **Pleasure:** To create and give pleasure to myself and others.
- ⚪ **Power:** To strongly influence or wield authority over others, e.g., taking charge, leading, and organising with kindness and compassion.
- ⚪ **Practicality:** To focus on what is practical, prudent, and sensible.
- ⚪ **Protect:** To protect and keep safe those I love.

- ○ **Purpose:** To have meaning and direction in my life.
- ○ **Rationality:** To be guided by reason, logic, and evidence.
- ○ **Realism:** To see and act realistically and practically.
- ○ **Reciprocity:** To build relationships with a fair balance of giving and taking.
- ○ **Respect:** To be respectful towards myself and others; to be polite, considerate, and show positive regard.
- ○ **Responsibility:** To be responsible and accountable for my actions.
- ○ **Risk:** To take risks and chances.
- ○ **Romance:** To be romantic; to display and express love or strong affection.
- ○ **Safety:** To secure, protect, or ensure the safety of myself and others.
- ○ **Self-acceptance:** To accept myself as I am.
- ○ **Self-awareness:** To be aware of my own thoughts, feelings, and actions.
- ○ **Self-care:** To look after my health and wellbeing and meet my needs.
- ○ **Self-control:** To act in accordance with my own ideals.
- ○ **Self-development:** To keep growing, advancing, or improving in knowledge, skills, character, or life experience.
- ○ **Self-esteem:** To feel good about myself.
- ○ **Sensuality:** To create, explore, and enjoy experiences that stimulate the five senses.
- ○ **Sexuality:** To explore or express my sexuality.

○ **Simplicity:** To live life simply, with minimal needs.

○ **Skilfulness:** To continually practise and improve my skills and apply myself fully when using them.

○ **Solitude:** To have time and space where I can be apart from others.

○ **Spirituality:** To connect with things bigger than myself.

○ **Supportiveness:** To be supportive, helpful, encouraging, and available to myself and others.

○ **Stability:** To have a life that stays fairly consistent.

○ **Tolerance:** To accept and respect those who are different from me.

○ **Tradition:** To follow respected patterns of the past.

○ **Trust:** To be trustworthy; to be loyal, faithful, sincere, and reliable.

○ **Virtue:** To live a morally pure life.

In your journal, you will be able to write out the Top Twenty values, and then circle your Top Three. To gain even more clarity, you can write out the behaviours that are more relevant to you, and what function those behaviours serve in your life.

• • •

Step Two: Understand the Function of Your Values
Can You Connect with How They Affect Your Life?

Your values form a significant part of your personal identity. They shape you into your authentic self and give you a sense of purpose and meaning, driving your personality, goal setting, and how you lead your life. Your values also give you a better understanding of who you are. The values you choose will have a direct impact on how you react when you are triggered, feeling unbalanced or tempted by those unhealthy coping mechanisms.

When I talk about the function of a behaviour, I'm essentially asking: What effect does this behaviour have on the life you want to lead? How does this work for you? How does it help you show up in the world and live the life you've designed or set out to achieve for yourself?

Okay, so, let's look at this another way, shall we? You see, first, there's the form of the behaviour. That's what we can see with our eyes. Like, let's say you're playing netball, and you're losing. You're under pressure, and you start to behave poorly. Maybe you lose focus and just give up. Or you might get angry and start accusing your teammates of not pulling their weight. Now, if you value being inclusive and compassionate – truly value it, deep down – is this behaviour really in line with that?

The function of the behaviour, on the other hand, is the why. Why are you getting so angry when you know, in your heart, that they're trying their best? That anger, it's not just random. It's telling you something's going on inside you. And that's where we need to ask those all-important questions. Why am I reacting this way? Are you angry because you drank too much the night before and you're feeling tired, hungover, and just plain grumpy? Are you angry because you felt like you gave your power away in a recent situation, maybe because your boss was, well, a bit of a jerk that day? There are so, so many reasons.

But here's the big question, my friend, the one only you can answer: Whatever those reasons are, are they worth acting in a way that goes against your values? Is it worth it to betray who you want to be because of a temporary feeling or situation? Take a moment, breathe, and really think about that.

Why is this important? Because understanding this will help you see that having values isn't always about warm and fuzzy, positive feelings. It's not about the quick high, the adrenaline rush, or simply trying to get rid of your pain and suppress it – none of that. It's about you working out the best way to live a full, rich, and meaningful life of integrity, with all its ups and downs. A complete, rich, and meaningful life includes both good times and bad. There's pain and sunshine, and we must learn how to make room for both.

If you're constantly chasing that adrenaline rush or that dopamine high – woah, watch out! That's not reality. What goes up must come down.

This isn't something easy to do straight away. It's something that, over time, you'll become more aware of. I have an exercise coming up where you'll write down what you do in two settings: public and private. This exercise is designed to help you harness a holistic view of how these behaviours affect your life.

This is going to be your new superpower. You will transform from someone who behaves mindlessly (automatically) to someone who acts mindfully, considerately, and gracefully. You'll be acting more skilfully, more resourcefully, and more in the present because you're choosing the behaviours you want to have every time you show up. You're choosing who you want to be because of the values you want to live by. There's a big difference.

Private and Public Behaviours

Now, I want to help you do some work around connecting you with the private behaviours you have – the thoughts, the feelings, and the emotions you experience behind closed doors. Then, we'll deal with your public behaviour – how you present yourself in front of others. This is also a consolidation of your commitment to your values.

These are the things that I'm going to help you become conscious of along this journey, because I know it's something that I stumbled over myself. Think about it.

When you reflect on a situation from an outward perspective, you shift your accountability and power to something or someone else. But when you practise the skill of inward reflection with honesty and vulnerability, you empower yourself to unlock your full potential. This is your opportunity to do just that.

Digging Deeper: Public vs. Private

Now, something I really want you to consider, and it's so important, is this: When you think about how you behave in public, remember that your outer world is often a mirror reflecting what's going on inside. So, ask yourself what that reflection is telling you. What's happening beneath the surface?

When you're choosing your values and behaviours, you've got to think about this holistically. How are you showing up not just for the world to see but in those private moments too? You need to choose what's right for the long game, not just what feels good in the short-term. And, hey, I'm the first to admit I lived that dopamine-high life for years. Especially with food and drink, there was always that rush, that high, that quick pleasure … but it always led to long-term pain. Thankfully, I've learned that those quick highs just aren't important anymore. They're not the long game for me, and I know they won't be for you either.

"Behaviour is the mirror in which everyone shows their image."
– Johann Wolfgang von Goethe

So, let's dive into these two deceptively simple questions. They might look easy, but I want you to really think deeply about them. They're designed to help you create a much deeper connection to who you are today and who you want to become.

Questions to Ask Yourself

Remember: Read your answers aloud so you hear yourself speak the words – so you believe what you say.

1. What are your public behaviours?

- The stuff you do to keep up appearances.

- The stuff you do to gain acceptance from others.

- The stuff you do to hide your pain or mask your true feelings.

2. What are your private behaviours?

- The stuff you do behind closed doors when no one is watching. How do you treat yourself in those moments?

- How can you empower yourself to move through fear-based emotions and behave in a way that's truly aligned with your truth?

- How can you be fully present in this life you're creating for yourself?

Keep focused on being present in the moment. Allow your thoughts to come and go, without judgement. Discern which thoughts you want to acknowledge and process, and which ones you need to let pass. Lean in, listen to the messages your inner self is giving you. You are, after all, your own best chaperone as you journey towards becoming your Future Self.

> I really encourage you to embrace this process of connecting with your inner wisdom. I know it might feel a bit uncomfortable at first, this digging deep, this self-examination. But trust me, it's the key to forging your own path forward.

Step Three: Having Flexibility with Your Values
Get Excited. You Are Learning New Skills!

When we are learning new skills, it takes time to get things spot on, don't you agree? Implementing these new values into your life is just that, a new skill. So, if and when you fall over or make a mistake, please don't judge yourself. Pick yourself up, give yourself a hug (yes, literally!), and be right there in the moment with yourself. Tell your brain, "It's okay. I'm alright. This little hiccup is okay." We all need to be flexible when learning. Sometimes, you may not always get it right when developing these values, which is absolutely okay! Let's normalise that.

Please embrace the fact that, like all of us, you will fall over sometimes. You might stumble, and you may even go back to old patterns. That's perfectly alright. Forgive yourself for that. Or you may feel a little ambivalent, a bit unsure. That's okay too.

SO, THE MESSAGE IS: It's more than okay to make mistakes. In fact, let's normalise them and give that inner critic a well-deserved break. I actually champion those little blips because that's how we learn and understand ourselves better. When you observe what you're doing, you can catch yourself the next time. With each experience, you'll also learn to be a bit gentler with yourself, and trust me, that's a beautiful thing.

Here are some common challenges people face when identifying their core values, which I've learned from processing and understanding vast amounts of text and human communication.

It gets confusing socially, and at home: People often adopt the values of their families, cultures, or societies without consciously questioning whether these align with their own inner beliefs. Disentangling these external influences from personal values can be tricky.

You may struggle to connect within at first: Identifying core values requires introspection and self-awareness, which can be challenging, and for most people is also a new skill. It involves asking yourself those tough questions about what truly matters and what you want to prioritise in life. So, take your time.

Your values can change over time: As we get older, and evolve and grow, it is completely normal for our core values to shift as we experience life in a different light. What was once a top priority might change as circumstances and perspectives change. This means the process of identifying values isn't static but ongoing, which can feel a bit overwhelming sometimes. Feel good about that.

What to Work on First

Prioritising Values: Even after identifying the three values that are most important to work on, it can be hard to prioritise them or move on from there. Deciding which values are most fundamental and which are secondary requires some consideration. Often, they will naturally fall into place as your life unfolds. Give it a chance to percolate.

Fear of Judgement: This is a common one. Sometimes, we might suppress our true values due to fear of judgement from others. It takes courage to embrace and live authentically and by your values, especially if they differ from those of the people around you.

Lack of Clarity: Sometimes, we might struggle to articulate our values or may not have the precise vocabulary to describe what's truly important to us. Finding the right words to express our core values can be part of the journey. Sit with this, in your quiet moments, and ask yourself the question; the words will come to you. You will connect to your own internal wisdom if you allow it.

When you feel like you are not the only one growing through these challenges, it makes it easy to feel normal. You can approach the

> **"Stay committed to your decisions. Stay flexible to your approach."**
> – Tony Robbins

process of identifying your core values with more awareness, patience, and a whole lot of self-compassion. And, with less fear, right?

> **If I were sitting in front of you right now, I would hold your hand and compassionately say this:**
> My friend, a big part of your success with implementing new values and behaviours in your life is flexibility. Flexibility combined with a truckload of self-compassion. Mistakes are good. Make no mistake about it. Mistakes are good. Are you hearing me?

Step Four: Think About Your Legacy
How Will Your Values Create Life Outcomes?

What do you want your legacy to be? And how do you envision yourself exiting this world? Take a moment, right now, to really think about that. I know I've talked a lot about the importance of cementing your values, and that's because it's absolutely critical for setting up a smooth, balanced human experience and, ultimately, achieving your life goals.

A strategy I personally found incredibly helpful, when I wanted to really nail down what my values were, was to think about my legacy. What did I want to be remembered for when it was my time to say goodbye? How did I want to exit? Healthy, happy, and wise? Or … as someone else entirely?

> For me, when I contemplated this, it came down to the fulfilling relationships I've had. The exploration of life and the things I've done. The integrity of self, the choices I make, the health I nurture, the peace that I find, and the way that I will exit – being peaceful, content, and knowing that I've done everything I could to have the best human experience for me.

To achieve this vision, I realised I needed a plan, a path to follow on my map of life to get me there. Where I lived, who my friends were, removing chaos from my life, the way I ate, the way I drank, and the way I consumed the stimulants in my life (and, yes, they are stimulants; you'll see why I say this in the book) all played such a big part.

For example, one major element for me was this: I soon realised that if I continued to eat sugar the way I was, I'd be heading down the path to diabetes, just like both my parents. And that's a path I did not want to follow. My father left this world with gangrene in his foot because of his diabetes. It was horrible to watch him suffer through that.

If I continued to drink regularly and in large amounts, I'd be on the road to horrible arthritis in all my joints and other health issues, just like my parents. Again, a path I wanted to avoid.

If I continued with that destructive binge eating, it would lead to nothing but ill health, ill health, ill health. And there's absolutely no way my exit would be the graceful vision I have for myself – you know, sniffing the proverbial roses, with peace and contentment. Not a chance, sister.

Now, I don't mean to be a party pooper or boring, as one of my more hedonistic friends jokingly called me. Certainly not! But it was a wise choice – my wise choice – to look at the bigger picture and decide what was right for me. What was going to serve my Future Self?

I concluded that if I bravely addressed some friendships that had no boundaries and were very chaotic (I'll talk about this more in Book Three), I would create space to call in people with the same values as me.

Another element I looked at was this: What did I want my professional legacy to be? I wanted to be remembered as someone who had a loving, kind, compassionate spirit. A woman who was passionate about helping others have a better human experience. I wanted to be remembered for my warm smile. And for the way I inspired you to reach out and grab what's right there in front of you.

What is your legacy? What is right for you? What does having clarity about your big picture look like to you? And how are you seeing yourself exit this beautiful world of ours?

> **"Perhaps the most significant thing a person can know about herself is to understand her own system of values. Almost everything we do is a reflection of our own personal value system. What do we mean by values? Our values are what we want out of life."**
>
> – Jacque Fresco

Remember: Your values all play a part in creating this map. Do you see that? They are the guide to your Future Self.

> When you remove all the cloudy, messy noise from the stuff that keeps you stuck in a lower vibration state, it gets a lot easier to see what's really there in front of you.

A Simple Question to Ask Yourself

Remember: Read your answers aloud so you hear yourself speak the words – so you believe what you say.

1. What do you want your legacy to be?

Sit with that for a while, as it may take some time to connect to. Then, write your thoughts out in your journal.

20.
My Values Experience

These Changed My Life Forever
It's Amazing How Important These Values Became to Me

Well, let me tell you, my new values – they saved my life. Honestly. Having to be brutally honest with myself was exactly what I needed to do to break free and climb out of the hole I was in. It wasn't easy, but it was necessary.

In my relationship with food and drink, that honesty was non-negotiable. I had to really challenge myself, look in the mirror, and accept that my relationship with food and drink was, well … pretty dire. At the time, it was all about binge eating chocolate. I had this back injury, I was stuck at home, I was suffering from depression, and I was in a truly terrible place. I was reaching for that chocolate, or some kind of sugary treat, every single day.

And I had to be honest about the physical stuff too. My heart rate was elevated. My blood sugar was creeping up to a pre-diabetic level (how scary is that?) – and I needed to face that truth. All those repetitive trips to the fridge? That was me avoiding the reality of it all. And something had to change. I had to admit that I was in bad shape because I was no longer in control of those trips to the fridge.

So, I had to challenge myself. I had to ask myself, "What's really important to me? What do I truly value?" And the answer was clear: my health. I had to accept that I'd just been through a few years of chronic health problems, which was incredibly lonely. Did I want that to repeat itself?

> "Watch your thoughts, for they become words. Watch your words, for they become actions. Watch your actions, for they become habits. Watch your habits, for they become character. Watch your character, for it becomes your destiny."
>
> – Lao Tzu

Or, worse, turn it into a downward spiral of metabolic syndrome? Good grief, was I seriously inviting diabetes into my life too?

This is what I mean when I keep talking about coming to terms with your emotional model and being conscious of your behaviours. It all links up, you see.

I needed to slow down that walk to the fridge. To take a breath. To ask myself, at each step, what truly mattered. So, when I got there, was that white-chocolate Easter egg, or that piece of caramel chocolate, really more important to me than the healthy, happy, kick-ass life I had envisioned for myself? Was it?

I had to ask myself out loud, "Do I really want to be diabetic?" Guess what the answer was? Nope. Not a chance.

Next question was, "Do I want to have a heart attack?" Absolutely not. Not on your life!

My mind was ticking away: "Alright, let's back up. Beep, beep, beep. Reverse! Okay, sister, you are going to put the kettle on, pop some mint in that hot water, and sip that. If I'm actually hungry, I'll have some blueberries or a protein shake." I worked out what my challenges and routine needs were; for example, I loved the hand-to-mouth thing (the sensation of putting things in my mouth, to put it plainly). So, soothing myself with something else – replacing the bad with the good – that was the key. And we will definitely discuss crowding out the bad stuff with the good later.

Leaning into the true meaning of those first three values stopped that walk to the fridge. And you know what? I still slow down my walk to the refrigerator today. Because, yes, I still want that chocolate sometimes. That temptation can still raise its ugly head. But my need to live by those values, to honour myself, has grown so much stronger than that old need for avoidance.

When you choose your values, I truly hope my story can help illustrate the importance of this work. Because it is work. No shadow of a doubt. But it's so worth it.

> We all can choke on our truth at times, but it is not so scary when you see what it is telling you!

21. Living By Your Values

Creating the New Automatic
This Is About Getting Comfortable with Your New Set of Values

If, like me, you have chosen a whole set of shiny new values to implement, work on, and challenge yourself to live by on a daily basis, my friend, this takes work. Not to put you off – you just need to practise the new soft skills you are learning here, combined with your new evolution of thought and connection.

When I say it's work, what I mean is, you are manually changing that automatic behaviour. Think about living by your new values as your guard-rail, your boundary-setting tool, and the motivation to stop self-medicating and engaging in acts of distraction when you experience difficult thoughts and feelings.

When you start to practise implementing your values in your life, you will quickly realise they truly are your ticket to living out the life of your heart's desire (and leaving all the messy crap behind you).

Coupled with all this great work you are doing to envisage your Future Self, your values will get you there, no doubt. These are what determine how you behave in your everyday life. These are the qualities of character that you aspire to have. Does this all make sense to you? If it does, please say, "Yes, I am on board with this!" out loud to yourself.

Living By Your Values Strategies: Steps to Help You Move Forward

Here is a summary of the essential ingredients and steps to take when practising these skills. In your journal, you can write down an action plan on how each of these steps might work for you in your daily life. It will help you gain more clarity.

 1. Deep Dive into Your Values

Review and Refine: We've talked about this before, but it's worth revisiting. Make a list of your core values. Now, go deeper. For each value, write a few sentences about what it really means to you. How do you want to live that value each day?

Rate Your Alignment: On a scale of 1 to 10, how well do you think you're currently living each value? This will highlight areas where you might want to focus.

Visualise Your Values: Create a vision board, a journal entry, or a piece of art that represents each of your core values. This helps make them more tangible and keeps them at the forefront of your mind.

 2. Everyday Actions

Small Choices, Big Impact: Start small. Choose one value to focus on each week. How can you incorporate that value into your daily life? For example, if you value "kindness", make an extra effort to be kind to everyone you encounter.

Decision Filter: When faced with a decision, big or small, ask yourself, "Does this align with my values?" This simple question can help you make choices that are true to yourself.

Reflect at Day's End: Before bed, take a few minutes to reflect on your day. Did you live in alignment with your values? What could you do differently tomorrow?

 3. Relationship Check-In

Value Alignment with Others: Consider the people in your life. Do they share your values? Do they support you in living your values? It's okay if not everyone does, but it's important to be aware of these dynamics.

Communicate Your Values: Share your values with the people closest to you. This can deepen your connections and help others understand you better.

Set Boundaries: If someone consistently disrespects your values, it might be time to set some boundaries or re-evaluate the relationship.

 4. Future Self Vision

Planning: Keep thinking about your Future Self and your legacy. How do your values contribute to the person you want to be remembered as? This long-term vision can guide your actions today.

Goals with Values: When you set goals, make sure they are in alignment with your values. This will make them more meaningful and increase your motivation.

Regular Check-ins: Schedule regular check-ins with yourself (monthly or quarterly) to review your values and how you're living them. Life changes, and your values might evolve too.

 5. Self-Compassion Is Key

No Perfection Needed: Remember, it's a journey, not a destination. You won't always be perfectly aligned with your values, and that's okay. Be kind to yourself.

Learn from Misalignment: When you notice a misalignment, don't beat yourself up. Instead, ask yourself, "What can I learn from this? How can I do things differently next time?"

Celebrate Progress: Celebrate every step you take towards living in alignment with your values, no matter how small. This positive reinforcement will keep you motivated.

By taking these practical steps, my friend, you can intentionally create a life that reflects your deepest values and brings you closer to the human experience you desire. It's a beautiful journey, and I'm cheering you on every step of the way.

Your New Soft Skills

As you journey through this book series, I will give you some new soft skills, which are your building blocks. It is then up to you to practise them and work at the implementation part in your everyday life. In this section, I will cover with you:

- How to set boundaries.
- How to navigate and what to do when you encounter conflicts that challenge your values.
- How to connect with your Choice Point, the small moment of time before you react.

Setting Boundaries: Your "Must-Have" Life Tool!

When you are trying to establish new behaviours, especially those aligned with your newfound values, your boundary skills are going to come in handy. Setting boundaries allows you to create a space to realise your needs and feel respected and safe. Boundaries let others know what is and what is not okay/acceptable. Equally, they will help you live by your values and maintain the behaviours to which you commit.

To help you stay on track with the life you envision – maintaining and upholding your values so that you stop reaching for those quick fix stimulations, or ways to numb the emotional struggles you are feeling inside – I want to talk to you about setting boundaries. This is a muscle and a skill that is one of those must-have-in-life, important things to master. Why? Often, the behaviours that throw us around and trigger us are created when people cross boundaries or when we don't instil a boundary in certain areas of our lives.

If you weren't taught how to set boundaries in your family of origin, it can be a little intimidating at first. As I said, it's a muscle to build; it takes a bit of practice, but I can assure you that once you learn how to do this, life starts to change for the better.

> **Let's find out if you set boundaries or not:**
> I will highlight some things that indicate whether you have boundaries or not. It may not necessarily be something that you're aware of, but that's okay. Or perhaps you are aware that a lack of boundaries is causing problems in your life. Let's find out.
>
> **❓ Can you say no to people?**
> You might have a problem saying no to people.
>
> You might have a problem with overcommitting your time to help other people and leaving yourself short of time, creating internal chaos.
>
> **❓ Do you overextend yourself?**
> You might have a feeling that sometimes you are being a bit used, and you do it anyway. You're giving a lot to somebody who's not necessarily giving you much back in return.
>
> You might feel that you're constantly putting other people's needs ahead of your own, but you don't know why.

❓ Do you listen to your friend's problems all the time?
You may feel a sense of being overwhelmed, exhausted, and tired. Are you in a cycle of taking on someone else's problems and being responsible for solving problems? You end up living someone's problems.

❓ Are you able to ask for what you want, and what you really need?
Do you have a problem putting your needs first?

If you said yes to any of these or all of them, you have no boundaries or need better/stronger boundaries in your life.

When you learn how to set a healthy boundary and maintain this beautiful, proverbial fence around yourself, you stop that cycle of feeling like you're being exploited; you stop that cycle of people taking from you. The ugly truth here, I am sorry to say, is that people keep taking from you because you allow them to do it. There is no point at which you're setting a boundary to communicate what your needs are.

A healthy boundary will give you that beautiful space to take back your time. You can choose yourself first. You can have time for the things that are important to you – your family, your loved ones, your physical and mental health. You can find this lovely balance in your life again – or for the first time.

> **"The first step to getting what you want is to have the courage to get rid of what you don't."**
> – Zig Ziglar

At first, you might feel guilty, you might feel a bit weird, and trust me, there will be people who will get really shady because you set a boundary. They are so used to you not having one, they might get a bit aggressive, they might be a bit rude, they might be pushy, or call you stubborn and selfish. You might lose a friendship; trust me, I've lost a few when I set my boundaries. But that's okay.

All I want you to do is notice, observe, and give it a name when that happens. But don't let it throw you around. Just know that this stuff might happen. Because the long game here is for you to be able to live towards your values. It's for you to be able to have the choices that you want. It's for you to be able to choose when you want to eat, what you want to eat, and why your choice of food and alcohol is the right thing for you at that moment, not because of some automatic behaviour that's going to throw you off course and put you back on square one.

This is something to practise. It's a new muscle. It's a new skill. You can think about applying what you are learning here to your life and practise it.

> Remember: This is a must-have life skill. No doubt about it.

Navigating Values Conflicts

You know, there's something I find myself saying quite often: "Life is never a straight line." It's a phrase that really resonates with me, because isn't it true? Life is full of twists, turns, and sometimes those really challenging moments when our deepest values seem to clash with the beliefs or actions of others. These "values conflicts", as we call them, can feel incredibly personal, and honestly, they can knock you around a bit. It's not always the big, obvious things like lying or cheating either. Often, it's the subtle stuff – expectations or requests that might push us to compromise our health, ignore that gut feeling, or leave us feeling like we're being dumped on with constant negativity and complaining. Or even just a subtle little feeling of disrespect towards ourselves or others.

> And let's be real. Standing up for what we believe in can be just as tough. When we act in line with our values – like sticking up for someone who's being treated unfairly or reaching out to befriend the "outsider" – it can sometimes feel like we're going against the flow.

These conflicts pop up everywhere, don't they? At work, maybe your boss asks you to do something that doesn't quite sit right with your values, but you also know it's important for the company's success. What do you do then? Or in your community, when new rules clash with what you believe is right and fair. And, oh goodness, within our friendship circles, where the desire to fit in and be accepted can make us question our own values! Do we go along with the crowd just to belong, or do we stay true to what's important to us, even if it means we risk being rejected? It's a tough spot to be in.

So, what happens when these conflicts arise? What do we do? Being honest about this means you are being prepared. You know, getting your skills ready for when life throws one of those curveballs, and you need to stand your ground.

And let's be gentle with ourselves, okay? We don't always get this "new skill" thing right the first time, and that is perfectly, absolutely okay. Building new skills takes time, and you might stumble a few times. Trust me, I know I have! It's all about figuring out what works for you. We all mess up sometimes –

> **"If you don't like something, change it. If you can't change it, change your attitude. Don't complain."**
> – Maya Angelou

it's part of being human. Understanding and accepting conflict is part of that journey too. There will always be things that challenge your values, try to knock you off course, or that little voice that whispers, "Let's go back to the old ways." But just remind yourself that mistakes are normal. Take a deep breath and centre yourself in what you know is your truth.

Strategies for Resolving Conflict

A Gentle Guide to Finding Your Way

I think we can agree that we all run into conflict sometimes, right? It's just part of being human. And while it can feel overwhelming or tough, I truly believe we can learn to navigate these moments with grace and compassion. So, I've put together a little step-by-step guide to help you through those times when conflict shows up in your life, with more clarity. Think of it as a gentle hand to hold as you find your way.

Steps for Resolving Automatic Behaviour in Conflict

Step 1: Acceptance

When issues pop up, the most empowering thing we can do is accept what's happened. If something is beyond your control, what can you do but simply accept it?

Acknowledge your feelings. Recognise that this conflict is causing you pain. It's okay to feel that. Hold yourself through it without judgement.

Let go of the fight. Fighting against something you can't control just drains your energy. It leaves you feeling defeated and cheated. And, in that struggle, there are always consequences.

> Ask yourself: "Can I make room for this reality?"

Step 2: Costs and Benefits

Weighing up the costs (the downsides) and the benefits (what will work for you) is always a helpful way to find a resolution.

Make a list. Create a list with two columns: "Cost" and "Benefit". Write down what you see relating to your conflict in each column.

Don't be afraid to ask for help. This can be a challenging process, and feeling a bit stuck is okay. Discussing it with a friend might make it easier to identify each point.

Choosing the easy option, the path of least resistance, is very typical. Ask yourself, "Why is this happening, and what am I supposed to learn from it?" You might discover different answers than you initially thought.

> Remember: Objectivity is key. Every situation is like a mirror, showing you something.

Step 3: Accept There Is No Perfect Solution

Conflicts arise to encourage us to make choices. Most of us dislike change, so conflicts often come along to give us a little nudge to move forward. To learn from and evolve.

The path forward from conflict can often feel clunky and imperfect. And that's perfectly okay and expected. Normalise that.

Embrace the imperfection. With imperfection comes anxiety – this is normal. Try not to worry about making the "wrong" decision. Just allow yourself to flow through the process.

Don't wait for perfect. Waiting for the perfect moment might mean waiting forever. Encourage yourself to seize the "now".

> Trust that you will find your path,
> and another door will open, where
> before there were always walls.

Step 4: Take Committed Action

If the conflict is forcing you to take action, you need to decide to move forward and lean into it or resolve it.

> Remember:
> Not making a decision is a decision.

Step 5: Acknowledge the Choices You Make

This ties into the step above. Trust what your gut is telling you, and honour that.

Be kind to yourself. You're making choices based on relevant information to you, and the place you are currently in.

Step 6: Back Yourself

Conflicts can sometimes come back to haunt us. So, stand by the choice you made at that moment. Be loyal to your decision-making process. That's what honouring yourself truly means.

It's okay to change your mind. If your choice turns out to have results you don't like, that's okay.

You can reassess and make a new decision based on your unique circumstances and your values.

Step 7: Reflect on Your Role

It's always helpful to take a step back after experiencing conflict to reflect on your role in the situation.

Build self-awareness. Taking time to understand your responsibility in the conflict is a valuable self-awareness skill.

Focus on what you can control. You can't control other people or places; you can only control and influence your own actions. When you see how you contributed or how you could have done things differently, you can create clearer pathways forward.

> You have a choice. You can change your behaviour so that you don't experience that conflict again.

Step 8: Normalise and Breathe

Having strong emotions and anxiety from conflict is very normal. If you accept that this is expected, the struggle and inner fight tend to stop.

Practise the 4-7-8 Breathing exercise to help ground yourself and make room for those feelings:

Breathe in for 4 counts. Hold for a count of 7. Release for a count of 8.

Repeat at least three times. Do more if it helps you feel centred.

Acknowledge your anxiety. Remind yourself that it's okay and normal. Allow yourself time to sit with it.

> The feelings might not entirely go away, but the powerlessness you feel will lessen.

Step 9: Compassion, Compassion, Compassion

Have compassion in everything you do. For yourself, your body, your mind, your health, your emotions, your mistakes, your anxiety, your habits, your self-talk, and your automatic behaviours.

- **Validate Yourself:** Remind yourself that conflict is complex, challenging, and makes you uncomfortable.

- **Be Human:** Validate yourself for being human and having these emotions and hurt feelings.

- **Nourish Yourself:** Treat yourself with compassion in your choices of food and drink. Ask yourself what your body needs right now.

- **Practise Self-Care:** What will nurture your body, mind, and spirit? Not what will feed the ego or pain, or make you want to numb yourself or push away the conflict. Treat yourself with self-care by doing things you love.

Movement, music, singing, or dancing are beautiful ways to offer compassion to your body and mind – they lift your vibration and soothe your nervous system.

> Practise these steps. Use your wise mind to create space to think through them each time you have a challenge or conflict that you know can be triggering.

As you build skills, they will become automatic – shifting and changing the chaos and conflict you previously experienced. You now have the tools, choices, and reasons to change your role in these situations.

> I hope this helps you, my friend!

The Choice Point
That Small Moment Before You React

Do you remember how I talked about that tiny space between feeling triggered and reacting? That's where the Choice Point lives. That split second where you decide who you're going to be and what you're going to do. In that blink-of-an-eye moment, your Choice Point determines if you'll live by your values or go against them.

There's a moment when we choose the life we truly desire, and another when we risk turning away from it. That pivotal moment – that's your Choice Point. It might sound a bit formal, but trust me on this.

Some days, making choices is a breeze. Other days? We're hit with triggers, conflicts, and challenges that really test us. Sometimes, decisions are made in a heartbeat. Other times, we need to sit with ourselves and truly consider what's best for us. And then life throws those curveballs, those unexpected things that throw us off balance. What will you do then? I'm asking you to be aware of that exact point – the point where your Future Self is relying on you, right now. Will you slip back into old habits, or will you courageously choose to create lasting change, even when it's hard?

Those difficult thoughts, those triggers, the things that hook you, the people and places that influence you, those automatic behaviours – those are where your conscious choice matters most. That's the Choice Point. It's where you become aware of the decision at hand and ask yourself, "What am I going to do here?"

Trust me, I know how uncomfortable those places can be – for all of us, myself included. It's so tempting when that little voice whispers, "I want, I want, I want." It's easier to go back to what you know, to slip into that familiar discomfort. It's worked to block the pain before. It's helped you to retreat into the person you used to be, even if it didn't make you happy.

> "If you do what you've always done, you'll get what you've always gotten."
> – Tony Robbins

Change is hard; that's a truth we all have to embrace. In those moments, we have to find our strength and step up. Because I promise you, it's so much brighter and more peaceful on the other side of that wall you have resisted climbing.

Your Role to Impact Change

Lean into the Choice Point. When those old patterns come up, meet yourself with compassion. It's okay. Mistakes are part of the process. Slow down and notice those automatic behaviours. Choose to switch to manual control. Lean into that. This is your moment to take charge.

Think about what truly matters to you. Go back to those values you chose and the behaviours that align with them.

If you need to revisit what each value means, do it. Gently unhook from those old thoughts and fear stories, and remember you have the power to act now. This moment is the only time when action happens. You can't change the past or act in the future – only in the here and now.

When you feel anxiety rising, tell yourself, "This is okay." I am going to teach you some really effective grounding techniques. One is **Dropping Anchor**, to anchor yourself in an emotional storm and bring yourself back to centre. Another is **Name and Tame** is a super-easy skill to stop the whirling thoughts running around your head. And, well, this one is very easy but incredibly useful and effective: **4-7-8 Breathing** – a simple breathing exercise.

 **NOTE:** When I talk about "changing manually", I mean consciously deciding not to follow the automatic behaviour. Remember, my friend, you're not alone in this. Many people feel overwhelmed when making the right decision. It's okay. With practice and self-compassion, you can develop the skills of effective grounding skills and navigate these situations with more ease.

To help illustrate the meaning and flow of where the Choice Point sits with you, I've created a diagram.

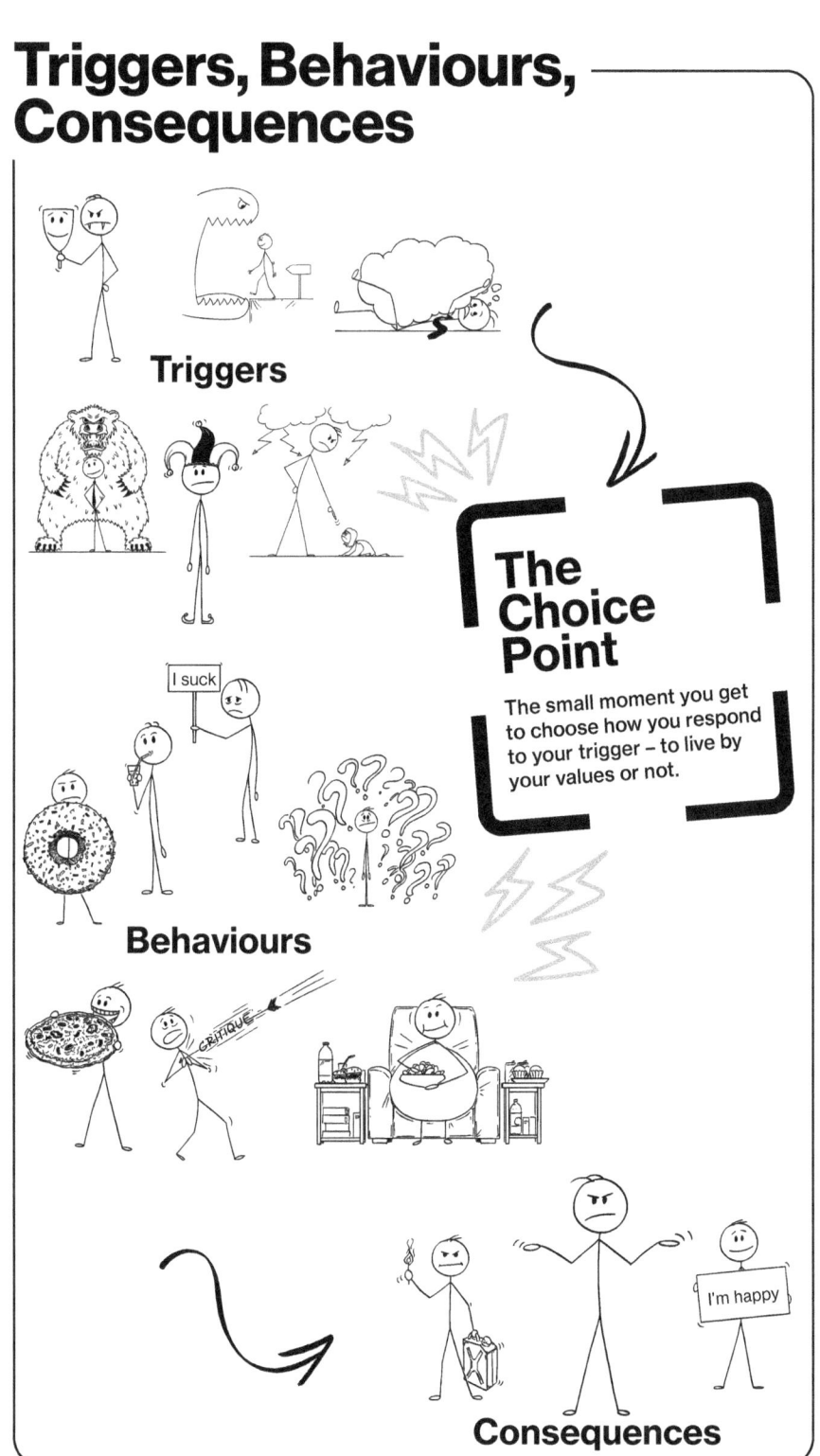

Skill Building for Staying Grounded at a Choice Point

Dropping Anchor: A Gentle Pause for Conscious Decisions

At your "Choice Point", when you feel overwhelmed and are about to react emotionally, "dropping anchor" can be invaluable. It allows you to pause, ground yourself, and regain control.

1. **Acknowledge (with a Warm Embrace):** In that crucial moment, notice what's happening inside. Think to yourself: "Okay, this is my Choice Point. I'm feeling [name the emotion] right now." Acknowledge the feeling without judgement, creating space for a thoughtful response.

2. **Connect with Your Body (Your Safe Haven):** Immediately, bring your awareness to your physical self. Feel your feet on the ground, your hands resting. Take a deep breath. This anchors you in the present, slowing down the emotional rush.

3. **Notice Your Surroundings (Your Present Moment):** Quickly scan your environment. Name five things you see, and three things you hear. This pulls your attention away from the emotional trigger and back to reality, creating space for a choice.

4. **Check In (with Compassion):** After these steps, ask yourself: "How am I feeling now? Do I have more clarity to choose my response?" By creating this pause, you gain the ability to choose a calm and considered action instead of an automatic reaction.

By intentionally dropping anchor at your Choice Point, you are actively preventing an automatic, emotional response. This technique offers clarity, allowing you to gain a better understanding of your current state and empowering you to make conscious decisions rather than just reacting. You're giving yourself the gift of calm and control precisely when you need it most.

Name and Tame Technique: Finding Calm at the Choice Point

There are moments in our day when emotions rise, and we reach a Choice Point – that moment when we can either react instinctively or make a conscious decision. The Name and Tame technique can be a gentle anchor during these times, offering clarity and calm.

1. **Notice It (with Kindness):** As a thought or feeling begins to surface, pause. Take a gentle breath and simply notice it without judgement. This is your Choice Point. Acknowledge what's happening with kindness.

   > Imagine saying to yourself: "Ah, I can feel some anxious thoughts stirring right now. This is where I pause."

2. **Name It (with a Smile):** Give that thought or feeling a light-hearted name. This act of naming helps create a little distance, offering you clarity at your Choice Point. It removes some of the immediate emotional charge, allowing you to choose how to respond.

   > You might think: "Oh, hello there, 'Sultan of Silliness' thought! I see you, and I have a choice in how I proceed," or "Here comes 'Grand Poohbah of judgement again! Let me breathe and see what this really is."

3. **Validate It (with Compassion):** At this Choice Point, remind yourself that whatever you're feeling is valid. It's okay to feel it. These feelings are a natural part of being human. Give yourself permission to experience them without needing to react immediately. This self-compassion brings clarity and allows you to make a more conscious decision.

   > Whisper to yourself: "It's completely all right to have these thoughts, dear heart. They're just thoughts, and I'm here at my Choice Point to choose wisely."

4. **Thank Your Amazing Brain (and Breathe):** Your brain is always trying to help. At this Choice Point, after noticing, naming, and validating, thank your brain. Let it know, "You tried to alert me, and now I'm consciously aware and I can make a choice." Then, let a soft smile spread across your face.

> A gentle thought: "Thank you, brain, for always trying to help me. Now I can choose with clarity and calm."

By using these steps at your Choice Point, you'll find those challenging thoughts lose their power. You'll discover a beautiful sense of calm and clarity, allowing you to respond rather than react.

The 4-7-8 Breathing: A Simple Path to Better Choices

This incredibly simple breathing technique can be a powerful tool to connect to your authentic self when you need to the most. It helps you slow down your reactions and creates a moment to pause and consider how you want to respond. This technique is excellent for quieting racing thoughts, easing nerves, and providing space to make thoughtful choices.

1. **Breathe In (for 4):** Gently inhale through your nose for a slow, silent count of four. Feel your lungs fill with air.

2. **Hold It (for 7):** Hold your breath gently for a quiet count of seven. Simply experience the stillness.

3. **Breathe Out (for 8):** Slowly and smoothly exhale through your mouth for a count of eight. You can make a soft "whoosh" sound, which can help release tension.

4. **Repeat:** Repeat this cycle three to four times.

Focusing on your breath can quickly offer your mind a moment of clarity and help you transition from feeling reactive to making thoughtful decisions. You'll likely find yourself feeling more peaceful and grounded after just a few breaths. It's a wonderful practice to incorporate into your daily life, not just when faced with a difficult choice.

> These strategies empower you to become more aware of your choices and respond with greater intention. In Book Two – A New Perspective, I delve deeper into skill-building with these techniques, offering you further opportunities to practise and develop mastery in managing your emotions and triggers. I'm always here, by your side. You've got this.

From Me to You, With Grace

By embracing these gentle grounding techniques, you'll truly feel empowered. You'll start to notice a beautiful shift – a newfound sense of calm and resilience, especially in moments that once felt overwhelming. Just imagine: In that tiny Choice Point – that fleeting moment when you need to decide – you'll have the clarity to pause, breathe, and choose consciously, instead of reacting blindly from emotion.

This isn't simply about managing a moment or making one good choice; it's about breaking free from those old, automatic patterns that just didn't work for you. It's about stepping into your own power and intentionally creating the life, the results, and the peace you truly desire and absolutely deserve, my friend. Life is far too valuable to spend stuck in cycles that don't serve you. Now is the time to truly show up for yourself and claim the calm, clarity, and control that's waiting for you. These simple practices have helped countless others make lasting, beautiful changes, and I truly believe they can do the same for you.

Please – Practise, Practise, Practise: Like any skill, grounding takes practice. Try these techniques when you're not feeling overwhelmed, so they're easier to access when you need them.

Make Them Your Own: What works for one person might not work for another. Experiment, tweak them a little, and find the techniques that resonate with you.

Please Be Kind to Yourself: If you're struggling, it's okay. Grounding is not about perfection; it's about finding moments of calm in the midst of chaos.

The choice now is yours!

Three Key Reminders to Help You

We face choices every single day. That moment when you can go one way or the other. What will you choose next time?

1. **Do What Matters:** Reconnect with your values and the behaviours that support them. Unhook from old thoughts and fear stories. Reaffirm your commitment to be the authentic you and make some brave changes.

2. **Lean In:** Be aware of your past patterns, with self-compassion. Normalise making mistakes. Slow down – be conscious of automatic behaviours and choose manual changes.

3. **Be Present:** When you feel discomfort, ground yourself and connect to the present. Use grounding techniques, e.g., 4-7-8 Breathing, Dropping Anchor, or Name and Tame.

4. **Read this aloud to yourself:** "I'm committed to standing by my values, my integrity, being honest, and acting with reciprocity in my relationship with my body. I'm ready to challenge myself. I'm going to stand firm and step forward."

22. Reflection Time

Questions to Help You Connect to What's Important

Let's really chat about this ... you know, our values? They're like the heartbeat of who we are. They whisper to us from our deepest selves, telling us how we want to live, how we want to treat ourselves, others, and the world around us. So, let's take a moment to really tune in, shall we?

Your values need to be about what truly matters to your heart. What's that quiet voice inside longing for? Give yourself permission to untangle any knots or restrictions you've been carrying. It's time to listen to that inner wisdom.

> **"The privilege of a lifetime is to become who you truly are."**
> – Carl Jung

Values aren't just big, fancy goals. They're about the day-to-day choices. How do you want to be? How do you want to treat yourself and those around you?

Remember: Read your answers aloud, so you hear yourself. It makes it all the more real, and so much more powerful!

Let's Begin

Take a gentle moment to reflect on your life as it is today – the challenges you're navigating, the dreams you hold close for yourself, and the gentle guidance of your intuition.

1. What gentle nudges have you been feeling inside that you might have been overlooking? What might you need to lean into with a little more courage?

2. Could you open your heart to the possibility that perhaps, without even realising it, you've been living by values that aren't truly yours? What if you've been echoing someone else's song?

3. When life throws its inevitable curves, and the urge for comfort in food or drink arises, how do you truly want to respond, guided by your deepest self?

4. Looking at the values we've explored, and the ones that resonated most with you, what are the first three that feel most alive and important to focus on and nurture in your life right now?

5. What are some small, everyday actions where you can begin to actively embody these values? What would it look and feel like to live these values in simple ways?

6. As you begin to align with these values, what's one gentle shift you sense might start to unfold in your life?

7. How can these core values become your allies in gently approaching that thing you've been hesitant to face?

8. In what tender ways can these values reshape your relationship with food and alcohol, so they become sources of nourishment and joy rather than a way to escape?

9. With these three guiding values lighting your way, how can you open yourself with gentle curiosity to the beautiful possibilities of change?

10. What feelings arise as you simply consider the idea of releasing past fears and that inner critic's negative chatter? Can you sense a glimmer of possibility?

11. Let's tune into your current self-talk. How can these three values help you cultivate a stronger sense of self-worth and establish loving boundaries? Is there another value that specifically whispers strength and confidence to you?

12. If you could gently shift your current mindset, even just a little, what new doors might open for you? What would you feel empowered to do more of?

13. What small, loving steps can you take to release any negative attitudes or limiting beliefs that might be holding you back from fully embracing and living by your chosen values?

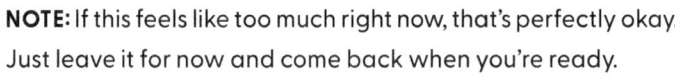

> **NOTE:** If this feels like too much right now, that's perfectly okay. Just leave it for now and come back when you're ready.

Next Step: Advanced

When you're feeling comfortable with your initial top three values, you can dive a little deeper and explore the top three values for different areas of your life: relationships, career/work, mental health/physical health and exercise practice. *You can simply write down the value word itself.*

1. Let's gently explore the values that illuminate the path of how you wish to show up in your beautiful life. Take a moment to consider how you believe others experience your presence. What is the essence, the personal warmth, you want to be known for? Perhaps reflect on your spiritual practices, those moments of

connection that nourish your soul. And listen to the whispers of your innermost desires, that radiant inner goddess yearning to be seen and expressed. What are the top three values that resonate most deeply with this vision of yourself?

2. Now, let's turn to your significant relationships, those precious connections that enrich your life. What are the top three values that guide these bonds? Why do these particular values hold such importance for you? What loving actions can you commit to, to nurture and strengthen these values within your relationships?

3. Considering your working life or vocation, that space where you contribute your unique gifts, what are the top three values that feel most authentic to you? Why are these values important in this area of your life? What mindful actions can you commit to that will bring these values to life in your work?

4. Let's also gently consider your physical and mental wellbeing, the foundations of your vitality. What are your top three values concerning your health? Why do these hold such significance for you? What nurturing actions can you commit to that will honour and support these values?

5. And when it comes to movement and exercise, activities that invigorate your body and spirit, what are your top three values? Why are these important to you in this aspect of your life? What joyful actions can you commit to that will weave these values into your movement practices?

...

Your Reflection

While you're doing this work, please remember to be kind and patient with yourself. Be grateful for the changes you're making. This alignment is a sign that you're willing to give yourself what you truly need from your heart.

Taking these steps to set and commit to your values is a powerful act of self-love. It's the beginning of rewiring those automatic behaviours.

> Now, it's up to you to nurture that connection with your inner voice, your intuition, and trust the messages there.

A Note on 'Food and Drink':

My friend, I want to take a moment to talk about a phrase you'll see me use a lot in this book: food and drink. I use this as a general label to keep things simple. However, I would like to acknowledge that indeed it's not.

I recognise that not everyone reading this may have a tendency to use both food and alcohol when feeling triggered, overwhelmed, or pushed around in an emotional storm. It may be that you have a vulnerable relationship with food, for example, but alcohol isn't your jam. Or, conversely, you may be totally happy and healthy with your food choices, but grabbing that beer or glass of wine every night is more your area of need and support.

I don't want anyone to feel like they aren't seen. I see you, and your personal experience is valid. So, if a food chapter isn't for you, please feel free to flip on to the next one. Or, if the alcohol chapter doesn't resonate, then by all means, skip it.

This book is a journey for you, and you can take it at your own pace. Just know that no matter what your personal relationship with food and drink is, you are in a safe place here with me.

Your Relationship with Food and Drink

23. The Hidden Language of Desire

Why You Reach for Comfort
Connecting Your Past to Your Plate and Glass

Welcome, dear friend, to this chapter – a heartfelt exploration of your unique relationship with food and drink. This isn't just about calories or diets; it's about you – your genetics, your history, your emotions, and how they all intertwine with what you put into your body. We'll gently unravel why those "one-size-fits-all" approaches often miss the mark and delve into how past experiences, even traumas, can shape our eating habits.

Together, we'll look at the powerful effects of stress and sleep on our choices, understanding that there's no room for judgement here, only compassion. We'll discover practical strategies – crowding out less nourishing options with vibrant, life-giving foods, tuning into our body's signals, and mindful portion control. We'll also have an honest conversation about alcohol, its impact on our health, and how awareness can empower us to make conscious choices.

At the end of this chapter is an invitation to reflect. What comes up for you? What feels "louder" in your mind? Do you see how

> **"When diet is wrong, medicine is of no use. When diet is correct, medicine is of no need."**
> **– Ayurvedic Proverb**

your food and drink choices connect to your values? Let's take a deep breath, settle in, and explore these beautiful, sometimes "crunchy" imperfections together (... *remember, the things in life that are not smooth!*). This is a journey of self-discovery, and I'm so glad you're here.

"I Want, I Want, I Want": The Relationship Between Food, Drink, and Trauma

We've touched on some reasons why we develop automatic behaviours, and now I want us to dive a little deeper into why this drives our choices around food and drink. It's also important to explore why those drinking and eating irregularities have such a direct connection to the impact of our challenging life experiences.

To truly understand this, we need to look at what's happening within our mind-body connection. It's so common for anyone who has experienced trauma, with a whirlwind of complex thoughts and feelings constantly swirling, to feel like their brain is in overdrive. You might feel weak, oversensitive, not normal, even worthless. But please remember this: Your brain's fundamental job is to protect you, to keep you safe and free from harm – it's all about preserving life. So, I want to revisit the "fight, flight, freeze, and fawn" responses, and connect them to what might be happening with you and your automatic tendency to reach for food and drink as a crutch. (In Book Two: *A New Perspective*, I delve deeper into why the brain sends us recurring thoughts, and how to tame them, so keep an eye out for that!)

Fight, Flight, Freeze, and Fawn

From the brief introduction in Chapter 7, you should be somewhat familiar with the term "fight or flight". It's our body's instinctive response to a perceived threat, preparing us to fight back, resist, or run away. This is our automatic pilot, governed by the intricate connection between our brain and our autonomic nervous system. There are other elements of this system that I think you'll find incredibly insightful as you start to understand how you react when triggered or threatened.

Our autonomic nervous system is the conductor of our body's internal functions. It has two main parts: the sympathetic nervous system, which revs things up and gets our heart pumping, and the parasympathetic nervous system, which is all about rest, digestion, and calmness. When a recurring, troubling thought enters our mind, our body can perceive it as a threat. That's when our sympathetic nervous system kicks in, releasing that rush of adrenaline.

> **NOTE:** The vagus nerve carries signals between your brain, heart, and digestive system. The vagus nerve is the main nerve of our parasympathetic nervous system. It's like the control centre for our body functions, including digestion, heart rate, and immune system. It's at the helm during fight, flight, or freeze.

When our brain senses danger (this is the same as when we are triggered by a memory that takes us back to a painful time), our body goes into what we know as "fight-or-flight" mode – that is, our body prepares to flee or fight. Our muscles tense, our heart races, cortisol floods our system, and our blood glucose levels rise. Along with these physical changes, a whirlwind of emotions like fear, anxiety, isolation, irritation, sadness, rage, and confusion can arise. It can be incredibly unsettling because there's often no actual fighting or fleeing to be done. There's no physical outlet for those intense feelings. And, you see, for those of you who have suffered more intense complex trauma, it is common for your fight-or-flight switch to be always on. We call this hypervigilance, meaning you are constantly looking for ways to numb that buzz you feel inside. I will explain more in the next section.

How many times have you been triggered, panicked, scared, vulnerable, felt that icky discomfort and immediately reached for something to make it stop? It's hard to keep count, isn't it? This is often when those automatic behaviours with food and drink begin – to numb the feelings, to avoid them, to self-medicate.

And then there's the "freeze" response, when the fight-or-flight mechanism doesn't quite work. The signals from your brain become so intense that your vagus nerve goes into emergency shutdown, and you feel unable to move, frozen or paralysed. Your heart rate slows, blood pressure drops, and non-essential bodily functions cease. You might not even be able to stand or sit up. It's like you're in a state of shock. If your experience with trauma was originally a situation that caused you to freeze, then it is likely that when you get triggered by something as an adult, you will experience that same freeze response. This is how the brain works, as I explained in Chapter 7.

It's hard, I know, right? When you experience something like this, it is all incredibly overwhelming, and I don't blame you (or myself) for wanting to avoid those feelings. But you know – and this is why you are here – that it is not entirely healthy for you or your Future Self. That's exactly why we'll be exploring strategies of change together.

"Fawn" means to please. In the face of danger, a child or adolescent might fawn, or become a people-pleaser, when a caregiver is neglectful, absent, has mental health issues (or is mentally challenged), or is abusive or violent. Or, as I discussed earlier, they may fawn to get their unmet needs met. As adults, we then find ourselves stuck in that people-pleasing pattern, unable to set boundaries, constantly neglecting our own needs, values, and pain – all to seek approval.

So whether you experienced a form of neglect, lived through conflict in the home, had an alcoholic parent, manipulative mother, scapegoating siblings, suffered from gaslighting, or were subjected to verbal, physical, or sexual abuse – all of which is so common (like it was for me) – you are likely to have some complex dependencies on food, alcohol, or substances to get you through the rough times, or just to keep you on an even keel. These experiences often lead to patterns: overeating, binge eating, strict eating rules, not eating enough, purging, control issues with over-exercising, and body image struggles. We all know that the mirror can feel like a dangerous place. These cycles, triggered by our emotions, can spiral into self-loathing. You are certainly not living an empowered life full of self-love, joy, and peace.

If you are a survivor of sexual violence or abuse, like I was, you may have some deeper patterns that you have developed as a coping mechanism. I want to normalise that for you too. Beyond what you are learning and working on here, collaborating with a licensed therapist can be a great way to help you build the tools for stability in your recovery.

A LITTLE NOTE: If any of this talk makes you feel low or exhausted, please take a break, put the book down, and go do something that gives you joy. Come back when you feel more ready to approach this again.

It can be difficult to face this stuff and say to yourself out loud, "This is what's happening to me." Getting stuck in those cycles of numb-yourself eating and drinking can be a very lonely and dark place. It's tough to break free. I acknowledge that feeling. I really do. I want to validate your experiences because I know many of you have been there. For me, it was a daily pattern, a daily routine of denial. What has it been like for you? Can you talk about it out loud?

Here is something I would like you to do now. Take a seat, put your feet on the floor, push your toes against the floor, roll back to your heels, then take a deep breath in and out. Quieten your mind. And then:

> Can you say this out loud: "Right now, I am doing this ... " and then finish that sentence for yourself? Describe what you are doing when you feel overwhelmed, anxious, or triggered in some way – even if it feels a bit like a guilty pleasure, or something you "shouldn't" be doing. Really connect to the action. And if you can, try repeating this exercise a few times a week, or even once a month. If you're up for a real challenge, make it a daily practice. Honestly, just connecting to what you're actually doing is such a huge, powerful step forward.

I invite you to write down what came up for you then. You can use your journal. Take note of this. Because by the end of this work we are doing together, I want to be able to gauge how far you have come.

How did that feel?
I'm holding your hand. You're not alone.

Sexual Abuse: Making It Okay to Talk About

Did you know that intimate partner violence is one of the most prevalent forms of violence against women globally? This includes physical, sexual, and psychological harm, verbal aggression, coercion, gaslighting, and controlling behaviours. So much of this goes unseen, and it really is very frightening. It can happen in any postcode or any pay grade. Frankly, I think it is a humanitarian crisis. The impact on individuals, their families, and society is immeasurable.

While more groups are working to support women, it's still not enough. We live in a society in which talking about pain is uncomfortable and not the norm, and this is especially true for abuse.

> **"Self-kindness involves extending understanding, patience, and benevolence to the self, especially in difficult times."**
>
> **– Russ Harris, Medical Practitioner, Psychotherapist, and Psychologist**

Without a safe space to openly talk about what we've been through, loneliness sets in, which can fuel those unwanted behaviours with food and drink. It can lead to depression, and another destructive pattern emerges. We become hypersensitive and hypervigilant, living in a constant state of anxiety. And you guessed it – that fuels more unwanted behaviour. We become so vulnerable to triggers.

So, if any of this resonates deep within you, please know, my friend, that I'm gently trying to share a truth: There's a beautiful, understandable reason why you might find yourself caught in these cycles. You are absolutely not unworthy; you are not abnormal. Far from it.

May I Ask You Gently?

If your past holds a harrowing experience – something that shook your world to its core – it's incredibly common, with magnificent strength, to have tucked it all away. Sometimes, even from yourself. These painful memories can be buried so deep within, perhaps locked in a glass box to which only *you* hold the key. The tender truth is, though, that the key to healing this wound can feel impossibly out of reach when you're still stuck in the narratives of that past darkness. This is precisely where we need to find that path of gentle connection, that way back to yourself.

Perhaps you've tried to reach for it before, or maybe those buried feelings are surfacing in ways that feel overwhelming, even frightening. It's completely natural for your brilliant defence and protection mechanisms to kick in – to numb the discomfort, to distract yourself from those murky, insistent, shameful whispers of pain saying, "I'm not worthy." Perhaps you find yourself reaching for a drink, acting out, eating to soothe, getting angry, meticulously crafting a life that appears perfect, or enclosing your world in the tightest of control, simply to keep it from spilling out.

What happens for you in these moments? Take a soft breath. This is your gentle invitation to reflect: When does this happen, what do you find yourself doing, what are you doing it with, and how does it play out?

I know, truly, this can feel incredibly scary. I get it. Every fibre of my being understands. But, please, my friend, don't worry. I am here with you, beside you every step of the way. My deepest desire is to help you find some peaceful clarity on how to tenderly work through this, together.

> So, please, hang in there. I will keep reinforcing that I'm holding your hand, and you are, absolutely, not alone.

The Sustainability of Diets: Do They Really Work in the Long Run?

I'm guessing you might have tried a few different diets over the years. And if you're anything like me, that initial burst of enthusiasm often gives way to ... well, slipping back into those old eating habits. It's such a common experience, truly. You're definitely not alone in that. But have you ever stopped to wonder why diets so often fail us? Why does sticking to a new way of eating feel so incredibly difficult? Let's have an honest chat about that, just you and me.

It's a journey so many of us take, isn't it? We often come from a place where our eating habits were, shall we say, a little messy, maybe even chaotic, especially if there's been trauma in our lives. And then, that moment hits. "Right, that's it. I'm going to change this!" We dive headfirst into a super-strict, rigid diet, with all those rules and steps, hoping for that "magnificent change" and, of course, that weight loss. Let's be real, for so many of us, that weight loss is a really important goal. There's absolutely no shame in admitting that.

So, what usually happens next? Well, we start to see some progress. The scale moves, a few kilos drop, and our brain lights up. "Wow, this is working!" We get that little hit of dopamine, those lovely feel-good hormones. There's a bit of a placebo effect too, isn't there? We get swept up in the excitement of "It worked for her. Maybe it'll work for me!" We think we've found that magic bullet, that quick fix to looking and feeling amazing. And that initial high, that motivation, it's incredibly powerful. We lose a bit more weight, maybe even start to see the transformation we've been dreaming of.

But life throws us curveballs, as it so often does. We get triggered. An emotional storm hits, and suddenly, that strict structure feels like a cage. All those difficult thoughts and feelings we've been trying to keep at bay come flooding back, and that old, automatic behaviour kicks in. The diet starts to feel painful, like another form of self-denial, and that just makes us crave what we're trying to resist even more.

> Denial does create desire. And then the cycle starts again. The diet didn't "work", all because we didn't address the real stuff, the root of it all.

That inner voice starts getting louder, doesn't it? The one that screams, "I want, I want, I want!" It often drowns out that quiet voice inside that really does want to stick to the plan. The rebel inside comes out, and we might swing to extreme behaviours – bingeing, restricting, reaching for the bottle. Whatever we find challenging in our relationship with food or alcohol just intensifies.

And then, the emotional turmoil sets in. That awful self-loathing starts creeping in, the cycle spins faster and faster, and that internal battle of "Gosh, I'm such a failure; I'm never going to lose weight; I'm never going to change" just makes us feel even worse. We end up punishing ourselves for "messing up", and that's just so heartbreaking, isn't it?

So, here's the question I really want you to ask yourself, and say it out loud.

 "Is this latest popular diet really in line with my values? Can I honestly see myself sustaining this way of eating for more than 12 months without falling back into those old habits?"

My absolute goal here is to give you the information and the tools you need to find an eating and drinking style that's tailored to your unique needs. I'm not about giving you a rigid diet plan to follow. Instead, I want to give you strategies and advice for creating sustainable eating and drinking practices, inside a reasonable change process that works for you. That is incredibly important to me. With this approach, you are in the driver's seat, making choices within the framework of healthy eating, rather than blindly following someone else's rules.

But first, we need to gain a little more clarity around your history so you can reach a greater internal connection with yourself. Next, we will delve into how your childhood experiences with your family values concerning food might be affecting you now. Were there any food restrictions, emotional eating patterns, or conflicts around food in your family? Perhaps your body image issues stem from beliefs that were bestowed upon you in your family environment.

JOURNAL NOTES: You will be asked a set of questions to consider soon about your family history and how you see your relationship with either food or drink. But while you are reading through this next section, or at any time, in fact, start to write down in your journal what is coming up for you. Can you express how your emotions are responding? Or how they relate to your eating habits? When you crave certain foods, what emotions are you feeling? Are you stressed, sad, bored, or lonely? Write it down.

You Are a Bio-Individual: One Person's Fuel Is Another's Poison

Isn't it amazing to think about? You are a bio-individual. Honestly, I love that term. It sounds a little fancy, but what it really means is something so beautifully simple: You are you. Your genetics, your ancestry, your blood type, the values you grew up with in your family of origin, and your stress responses – all of it is completely and utterly unique to you. That means the food and drink that brings you joy and makes you thrive might be totally different from what works for someone else.

Let me break it down a bit more. You are your own person, you are one of a kind. Why does this matter? Because it means the way you eat – the food you choose, how your body processes it, how it turns it into energy or stores it as fat, or even how it transforms it into something vital or, yes, harmful – is incredibly specific to you. It's a personal journey. Remember when we talked about why diets often don't work? Well, here's another big reason. All those trendy, one-size-fits-all diets are designed for a general type of person, not the singular person you are.

What's good for you, what gives you pleasure, what makes you bounce out of bed in the morning, sleep soundly, feel truly vital, energised, and alert might actually be someone else's downfall. It might make someone else wake up at three in the morning with brain fog and feel utterly drained. Your whole makeup, your body's genetics, your blood type, the way you handle stress, and even how your body retains water – it's all entirely different from the person sitting right next to you.

So instead of getting caught up in what everyone else is doing, let's focus on you. Let's get to know you. Listen to your body and truly love it. Your body is the most amazing, intelligent, sophisticated system on this planet. It tells you when it's hungry or thirsty. It tells you when it needs to sleep and when it's had enough rest. Your heart beats on its own; you breathe without having to think about it. It can tell you when something is wrong. You sweat to eliminate toxins and cool the system. It's fabulous, absolutely fabulous, and you just need to get better at listening to it and trusting the messages it's sending you. This is about having a relationship with your body first, before you worry about everyone else.

Bio-Individuality with Genetics, cultural background and blood types

My friend, if this idea of your unique biotype has sparked your curiosity, I have something for you.

On my blog, I delve much more deeply into genetics, ancestral types, and cultural backgrounds – all the things that make you uniquely you. The blood-type stuff is not necessarily for everyone, but I do encourage you to take a look at it. Find out your blood type and make up your own mind, as it's fascinating to learn how differently our bodies process foods based on our type.

To explore all of this in much more detail, head over to my blog page at **www.fleurelizabeth.com**

Before we go any further, I think it's important to take a little trip back in time, to your past. It's there, in your family of origin, that you can often find the roots of your eating habits, the values and beliefs that were imprinted on you. And that can help you understand those automatic behaviours you might have, those behaviours that maybe don't quite align with your new values and the life you're now envisioning for yourself.

If you look at yourself from a bio-individual perspective, you can appreciate how interesting being unique actually is, right? Again, this is all about giving you information to understand your unique bio-individual type, so you know how to create a plan that works for you moving forward.

Exploring Your Family of Origin and Its Influence on Food and Drink

I know diving into family history can sometimes feel a bit daunting, but trust me, it's such a powerful journey. We're going to gently explore how your family's values, behaviours, and interactions around food and drink might have shaped your automatic behaviours today.

As we go through these questions, please take your time. There's no rush at all. It might feel like a task at first, but I promise, as you sit with these questions, things will start to bubble up. You might begin to see those little threads connecting your past to your present, and how they've influenced your relationship with food and drink.

This is about gaining a deeper understanding of yourself, my friend, and giving yourself permission to choose the path that feels truly right for you. Imagine we're looking at a beautiful tapestry of your life, with all its light and shade, and we're simply noticing the patterns. It's all about connection and gentle self-discovery.

Questions to Ask Yourself

Grab your journal and get comfy somewhere you can jot down your thoughts easily. Let's begin, shall we?

Let's Talk About Your Family's Food Story

1. When you think about your parents, what comes to mind about their overall approach to food and a healthy lifestyle? How

would you describe their understanding of nutrition, their cooking habits, and even how they looked at food labels?

2. What did your parents truly believe a healthy diet looked like, and what were their personal health goals around food? Take a moment to reflect honestly here.

3. We all pick up habits along the way. What were some of your parents' less healthy habits when it came to food and drink?

4. Looking back, how did the money spent on food and drink in your household seem to impact the quality and types of food that were available to your family?

5. What were home-cooked meals like in your family? Were they focused on nutrition? Were they exciting, simple, or perhaps something else entirely?

6. What was it like for your family to get enough good food on the table? How did factors like your budget, where you lived, or even just time, shape what your family ate and how you made daily food choices?

7. What kind of "treasures" (or perhaps not-so-treasured items!) were often hiding in your family's pantry and fridge?

Your Family Food Story, Unpacked

1. Thinking about your family's beliefs, their access to food, and the overall "food story" you grew up with, what underlying messages about eating do you now realise you've carried into your adult life? How might these unspoken rules or inherited perspectives be shaping your daily eating habits and your overall wellbeing right now?

2. After exploring your family's food history, from their habits to the "treasures" (or guilty pleasures) in the pantry, what echoes do you notice in your own life today? Are there specific food

choices, cravings, or even subtle feelings about your body that feel directly connected to those early patterns – for better or for worse?

Now, Let's Chat About Your Parents' Food and Drink Legacy

1. Beyond just what they ate, what were your parents' true eating styles and patterns? What silent (or not-so-silent) lessons did they pass on to you about how to eat, when to eat, and how to approach food and drink in general?

2. Were there any unspoken "food rules" or firm boundaries in your childhood home that shaped what, when, or how you ate when your parents were at home?

3. Did your parents ever control or restrict what you could or couldn't eat? If so, how did those restrictions make you feel then, and how might they still influence your choices now?

4. When you were home alone, what were the "unwritten rules" around food? Were there specific times or types of foods that were off-limits, or perhaps suddenly allowed?

5. How did your parents' relationship with alcohol play out in the home, especially when they might have had "too much to drink"?

6. Beyond their actions, how did your parents talk to you about alcohol and drinking responsibly? What messages did you internalise?

7. Let's talk about the sweet stuff. What was the family dynamic around soda, sugary drinks, and treats like slushies? What messages did you get about them?

Their Legacy – Your Adult Food Blueprint

1. Looking back at the exploration of your parents' eating styles, rules, and messages about food and drink, what specific reactions or habits do you notice in your own eating now that feel almost automatic? Can you see where these reactions came from now? And how could understanding this help you feel more in control of your food choices today?

2. Thinking about the big picture of how your family dealt with food – the restrictions, the treats, their beliefs about health, and how they used alcohol – what "way of eating or drinking" do you think you've unconsciously picked up and followed as an adult? How does developing clarity around these patterns open up possibilities for you to make more intentional and fulfilling choices about food and wellbeing now?

Let's Explore The Emotional Heart of Your Food Story

1. Thinking about your parents, were there any significant emotional patterns or mental health challenges in your household? How might these deeper currents have subtly shaped the atmosphere around food and drink in your home?

2. What were the prevailing emotions in your household? Did you notice food or drink being used as a way to cope with feelings – whether it was stress, sadness, joy, or even boredom?

3. Beyond just meals, how was food discussed and perceived in your family? Was it often a source of celebration, a neutral necessity, a point of tension, or something else entirely?

4. How would you describe your parents' overall relationship with food enjoyment? Were they passionate "foodies" who savoured every bite, more "eating to live" types, or did food evoke a mix of pleasure, duty, or even stress?

Reflecting on Your Emotional Connection to Food

1. Take a gentle breath, my friend. As you reflect on these emotional and mental insights, what echoes do you sense in your own relationship with food today? Is there anything you've uncovered that you now feel a gentle pull to understand or adjust in your own life?

2. If so, remembering to be kind and patient with yourself, what's one small, compassionate step you could take to begin shifting that pattern?

Now, Let's Unpack the Influences on Your Eating Habits

I hope this is offering you some clarity around the many threads that weave together to create your unique approach to food and drink, from what your parents or caregivers understood about nutrition, to the atmosphere in your childhood home, and even the broader culture around you. Let's take this a step further now.

1. Beyond rules or restrictions, how did your parents or caregivers guide you towards a way of eating that they believed supported wellbeing? What subtle cues or direct teachings did you receive about how to approach food for health?

2. What kind of language surrounded food and eating in your home? Can you recall instances where you were praised or criticised in connection with your eating habits?

3. And crucially, how did they talk about your body size and shape? Was their language affirming and loving, neutral and accepting, or did it lean towards shaming or negative comments? How did that make you feel?

Reflecting on Your Inherited Habits

1. Take a moment to let these reflections settle. As you consider these early influences, what connections are you now making to your own automatic eating behaviours and self-perception today? Is there anything that truly stands out, perhaps something you now feel ready to explore or approach differently for yourself?

2. If so, remembering to meet yourself with deep self-compassion and kindness, what's one gentle, actionable step you could take to begin cultivating a new, more aligned habit?

Let's Get Clarity on the Lasting Impact of Your Caretakers' Eating Habits

Family patterns can be tricky, can't they? They're so deeply ingrained and tied to who we are and how we see the world.

1. Thinking back to your earliest memories, how did your parents or caregivers typically respond when you expressed hunger? Were you fed right away, or did you often have to wait?

2. Was food easily available in your home, allowing you to eat when your body signalled a need, or were there times when access felt limited?

3. Did you ever experience feelings of guilt or shame for being hungry or for wanting more food?

4. How did your caregivers use food or drinks to "reward" you? Can you recall examples where treats or special foods were tied to good behaviour, achievements, or comfort?

5. On the flip side, how was food or drink used to "deny" you, perhaps as a form of discipline or as a privilege taken away? If comfortable, what are some examples that come to mind?

6. Was there a clear difference in food experiences between special occasions like birthdays and just regular, everyday meals? How did that shape your perception of food's role?

7. Beyond your immediate family, what cultural norms or traditions surrounding food were present in your upbringing? How might these broader influences have shaped your eating habits?

8. Did your family typically eat meals together, or was eating often a more solitary experience, perhaps with siblings but without parents or caregivers?

Reflecting on Your Deepest Food Roots

1. As you connect these early experiences with your caregivers' responses to hunger and their use of food, what fundamental beliefs or automatic reactions about food and your body do you recognise in yourself today? How might these "food roots" still influence your hunger cues, your relationship with pleasure from food, or even how you treat yourself?

2. Considering everything we've explored, what's one powerful insight you've gained about the true origins of your current eating patterns? How might this deeper understanding empower you to approach food and your wellbeing with newfound clarity and compassion?

> So, how did that feel, my friend?
> Just take a moment to sit with it.

The patterns we've been exploring together are learned behaviours, ingrained in you over time – the beautiful thing is, they're not set in stone. You have the power to make changes, to rewrite your story around food.

I know how deeply food can be tied to our emotions, but please know that this, too, can shift. We will get to that part, and I'll be right here with you. Gently exploring these influences is a gift you give yourself – the gift of deeper self-understanding and clarity. You're paving the way for conscious choices that truly honour your health and wellbeing.

> **"There is nothing rarer, nor more beautiful, than a woman being unapologetically herself, comfortable in her perfect imperfection. To me, that is the true essence of beauty."**
>
> –Steve Maraboli

Find solace in your truth and comfort in your evolution. What you're unfolding is your authentic self. Trust that journey. I'm holding your hand.

24. My Trauma Experience

Blindly Fed, Unintelligently Shamed
The Day My Body Became a Problem

To put it bluntly, I was fat-shamed as a child by the very people responsible for feeding me. I know this might be triggering for some, so please be aware that the language and descriptions in this story reflect how I was spoken to at the time.

My mum was a chef, so I practically grew up in the kitchen. My early memories are filled with the sights and smells of her cooking school in our small country town, Bacchus Marsh, in regional Victoria. I'd sit at the end of the bench, watching as she taught local women how to make a perfect beef bourguignon. I can still make that recipe with my eyes closed; it's etched in my brain.

Years later, we moved to Albury, on the boarder of New South Wales and Victoria, where she opened a restaurant, and after school, I'd rush there to watch the action in the kitchen while she worked her magic. She was famous for her rich, decadent, gourmet delights, and her patrons particularly loved her flourless chocolate cake – oh my goodness, it was divine! Each week, Mum would bring home food from the restaurant for our dinners, including an array of different cakes and always her infamous flourless chocolate cake. Yum, yum, yum! We were never allowed to leave the table until our dinners were all eaten and the plates were cleared. And let me tell you, my mother's servings were extremely voluptuous. My childhood was one of pure, super-size-me gourmet delight. (And a nutritional health coach's worst nightmare! Let's be honest.)

A vital ingredient in those cakes was her high-quality Belgian chocolate. Next to the staff bathroom was the foodstuff storeroom. I'd sneak in there, pretending to go to the bathroom, and pay a visit to the massive bag of chocolate buds that stood as tall as I was. Coming back into the restaurant with buds spilling out of my pockets, and the warmed, smeared evidence on my hands, nothing was said to me. It seemed okay to Mum, or it was just ignored. I didn't get in trouble for it. Mum always giggled when she saw me with chocolate around my mouth, looking delightfully guilty, my pockets bursting. Really?!

For dinner, we'd have beef stroganoff, potato dauphinoise, lasagna, beautifully crumbed veal cutlets, chicken and mango salad loaded with mayonnaise, or rich, creamy egg and bacon pies with flaky, buttery pastry. Every night was a culinary adventure – a vibrant, full-calorie, full-strength, gourmet extravagance! No exaggeration.

So, guess what happened? I became a little bit tubby (no kidding!). I was ten, and I will never forget the day my mother came home from the restaurant, all worked up. She came flying into my room. I didn't know what was wrong; I was terrified of getting into trouble. She looked at me and said, "I'm very worried about you. I'm very, very worried about you. If you are fat now, you'll be fat forever." She bleated on about how I was about to hit puberty, which meant that the extra weight I carried now would be imprinted as my fat life sentence.

Soon after, she picked me up from school – which was unusual as normally I had to walk to the restaurant – and I was taken to the family doctor. Mum was again in this weird, angry, flapping, irritated state, which frightened me. This seemed important, as though there were a medical emergency and something seriously wrong with me. What? I had no idea. I was naturally very nervous about her chaotic behaviour. The world seemed fine where I was sitting. We went in to find a very serious-looking doctor, sitting in his high-backed, black-leather swivel chair. This was to be an experience that would scar me for life.

Sitting there, fawning, I listened to my mother complain about my eating habits and my size, saying she was very worried that I'd become this "very tubby", overweight child and that I was out of control. She wanted the doctor's help to bring me into line because she thought I was too fat. I felt like I was shrinking into the chair, trying to shy away from a once-loving parent who suddenly was demonising me for how she fed me.

The doctor asked me to pull up my t-shirt, then lean to the right, and count out loud how many rolls of fat I could see. Then lean to the left and count aloud again. Counting my fat rolls, "1, 2, 3", with a broken, frail voice, was utterly humiliating. My eyes welled with tears.

"Now, young lady," the doctor instructed, as if I were mature enough for such a title and this type of consult, "lean forward and grab your stomach. Squeeze the tyre and tell me how that feels." Holding my little Buddha belly, I burst into tears. I was completely and utterly ashamed. A vulnerable, exposed girl, hit by this body image attack. It was horrible. I can tell you something else; my tears were not met with any comfort or compassion – no, not at all. (See, there was the lack of the empathetic witness from someone I hoped would be one, sitting right next to me.) Instead, the two adults in the room just mirrored each other, shaking their heads. No offers to cradle my pain, no soothing words, no physical touch. No tissue. I wiped the snot from my nose on my school jumper, pulled my clothing back down, and adjusted myself. That was it.

My mother, I remember, had this look of disgust and horror on her face. She was ashamed of me. These rolls, magnificently cultivated by her food and abundantly rich meals, were the result of her provision of my daily nutritional intake. Yet she sat there, not offering a shred of compassion or taking any responsibility, but so easily damning me with her disapproval as if it were all my fault. All the while, she had a stomach of her own and a very tubby figure. "You'll have to do something about this, my girl," she said, shaking her head at me, then looking at the doctor for his approval. He nodded in agreement. It was horrible, just horrible, demeaning behaviour.

Did the food she provided ever change after that? No. At no point was there any discussion about my mother's food choices. There was no question about the beef stroganoff or the carrot cake with lashings of cream-cheese frosting in our fridge each week. We could never criticise her delicious potato dauphinoise. Good God, no! We were to be fed the best food, and in her eyes, that was restaurant food. It didn't matter that at such a young age, I couldn't choose or pay for healthy food myself. The weight and the shame it brought to my mother were made to be my fault. I was responsible for the "rolls of fat" they claimed were my downfall.

And Dad, bless his heart, he loved his food too. He had what I affectionately call a "basketball stomach". Not helping matters, he'd bring home sweet treats – vanilla slices, coffee scrolls – a few times a week. Weekends were for doughnuts, maybe three at a time. Looking back, it's clear I was swimming against the tide, isn't it?

It took me a long time, a real journey, to unravel the tangled mess of all that and how it shaped my adult life. The constant stream of negative self-talk, the dark emotions, the entire narrative of trauma that followed me. It stemmed from those moments with my mother and the doctor. That constant criticism? It burrowed deep into my very belief system. "I'm not enough" became a mantra, an unrelenting inner critic. "I'm disgusting." "I'm unlovable." Every glance in the mirror felt like confirmation of my flaws, fuelling this toxic cycle of self-hatred and punishing exercise. "My body is ugly" – those thoughts became ingrained, colouring how I saw myself and the world. I carried this gnawing sense of shame, this feeling that my body was fundamentally wrong, almost a betrayal.

That constant fear of judgement and the deep-seated shame? It led to ongoing, sometimes crippling, anxiety. There were times I withdrew, isolating myself to avoid the scrutiny, the constant reminder of my perceived inadequacies. And forming healthy attachments? That was always a struggle. The betrayal by my mother, the very person who was supposed to protect me, shattered my trust. Fear of rejection loomed large, so often I'd reject people before they could reject me. Intimate relationships? They were tricky, sometimes terrifying if we got too close. I was always waiting for the judgement, the criticism of my body to be laid bare, just like it was by my mother.

Perhaps the hardest, most heartbreaking realisation was the torture I endured from what I now recognise as toxic love. It's crucial to understand the unique cruelty of this type of abuse. It wasn't just the words, but the source. My mother, who provided sustenance, who *should* have offered unconditional love, became the source of my deepest pain. That betrayal created such profound confusion and helplessness, making it so much harder to heal. And my "Buddha belly", well, it became a symbol of my trauma, a constant reminder of love being weaponised against me. It became a body of evidence, a way for me never to forget.

And so, whenever I was triggered, food became my refuge, a way to bury the shame that threatened to consume me. I'd crave the rich, familiar foods she'd cooked, seeking that fleeting sense of comfort, a moment of reprieve from the relentless self-criticism. It was as if food became a friend, a silent companion that understood the pain I couldn't voice. I'd recreate the cycle of indulgence, seeking solace in the nostalgic tastes and textures, then be consumed by self-loathing afterward. I'd travel to cities and visit restaurants, eating massive amounts of rich food. Then I'd judge myself for the "indignity of the results" – a larger stomach, back fat, lack of cheekbones, whatever. Of course, this meant I wasn't good enough. Every sign of fat, every perceived flaw, became a trigger for those humiliating moments, a constant reminder of my mother's disapproval and my own perceived inadequacy. I was trapped in a cycle of seeking comfort and then self-destruction until I finally began to understand that I deserved kindness, especially from myself.

This whole repetitive process was incredibly normal for me. I hated it, but I couldn't stop it. It was a complete cycle I couldn't break free from. I didn't understand it as a pattern because it was all so automatic – it was how I operated. It was how I was fed, and what was normal in my family of origin. It wasn't until I did a lot of inner work that I realised this automatic behaviour was something I could put the brakes on, and I could change the narrative I held in my head about this. I retrained as a nutritional health coach and guided myself back into what would become my new normal. I created my own value set and reframed all of this in my mind.

Over time, I slowed down my automatic behaviours and started to make conscious decisions about what I needed to eat to be a healthy, happy woman. Learning the skill of acceptance helped me find my peace. I had empathy for my former self, and the wee girl who went through that horrible stuff. I reached out to her in meditation. I told her all the comforting, compassionate words she needed to hear at that time long ago, and I let her know she would be okay, that I was holding her hand, and I wouldn't let go. I learned how to trust myself and maintain my boundaries. My self-talk is now loving and kind, and it embraces my ethos that every day is a school day. I have chosen to be celibate for a while; my intimate relationship is with myself, and that is the most rewarding and beautiful experience I have had to date. And like I have said before, every night, I give myself a hug, wrapping my arms around my shoulders to grab the backs of each arm, and I squeeze and think, "You did well today; well done." My body is not perfect now, but it's feminine and it's all mine.

Thankfully, I still love creating food for pleasure and enjoyment only. Food is my friend. I enjoy healthy cooking and creating wonderful, nutritious food to ensure my body thrives and bounces out of bed each day feeling grateful that I am where I am.

> My body is not perfect now,
> but it's feminine and it's all mine.

25. Reflection Time

Reflection Time: Exploring Your Food Story

Okay, my friend. Let's take a gentle journey together, exploring your parents' eating habits and how they shaped your own relationship with food. This is a safe space to consider the lasting impact of your upbringing – how it has subtly (and not so subtly) influenced your dietary knowledge, behaviours, and beliefs.

> **"Perhaps the greatest kindness we can offer ourselves is to hold our story, with all its mess and beauty, in a space of gentle acceptance."**
> – Glennon Doyle

These reflection questions will guide you as we delve into the heart of your relationship with food. We're going deep, touching upon the beautiful, messy, and real origins of how you relate to food – the behavioural, physical, cognitive, and emotional dimensions. It's a powerful, layered process, and together we'll peel back those layers to truly appreciate how you've come to be who you are today.

We'll also consider your social context around eating, often influenced by your family's habits. This exploration can bring clarity and insight, helping us understand those subtle ways your upbringing still whispers in your ear when it comes to food in social settings.

Take your time with this, dear one. Allow yourself to see the connections between your parents' styles and your own food and drink behaviours right now, today. This isn't about pointing fingers or placing blame – it's about gaining more clarity. It's a tender space to express gratitude for all that has brought you here. There is no judgement here, only a compassionate holding of your unique and beautiful story. If this reflection brings up any discomfort or anxiety, please pause. Honour what you can manage in this moment, and know it's always okay to stop, breathe, and come back to this when you feel more settled.

> Remember: Read your reflections aloud, let your voice carry the words, so you hear and feel them deep in your heart, so you truly believe and embody what you say.

Let's Begin

1. How do your current food and drink choices reflect the eating habits and styles you learned from your family?

   Journal Prompt: Describe a recent meal or snack that forms part of a pattern you can connect to your childhood experiences.

2. How might your parents' eating habits and styles have shaped your relationship with food and body image?

   Journal Prompt: Write what first comes to your mind, giving as much detail as you can. How can you gently challenge and shift any negative eating habits or body image whispers you might have picked up from your parents? How can you cultivate a truly positive and healthy relationship with food and your body, a relationship filled with self-love and acceptance?

3. How did your parents' approach to healthy eating and nutrition influence your understanding of a balanced diet?

   Journal Prompt: What did "good" look like in your home? It's vital to acknowledge when the messages we received in childhood might not have been accurate or healthy, even if they came from a place of love.

4. Emotional Eating: How did your parents' attitudes and beliefs about food influence your emotional connection to eating? (Part 1)

   Journal Prompt: What patterns did you witness your parents go through? When they were triggered or stressed, what did they do with food and drink?

5. Emotional Eating, Differentiating Hunger: How can you differentiate between emotional hunger and physical hunger, and how can this help you challenge emotional eating? (Part 2)

Journal Prompt: This could be tough, but try to connect to what happened when you were hungry versus when you felt vulnerable and wanted to eat to suppress your feelings.

6. How did your parents' approach to mealtimes and social gatherings impact your sense of self-worth and body image?

   Journal Prompt: Consider if you felt worthy of certain foods, or if your worth was tied to how you looked or ate at family and social events. Did you feel judged or valued based on your food choices or body size in these settings? Can you recall specific instances where you felt your self-worth or body image was affected by how your parents treated food or talked about your body during meals or gatherings?

7. Conflicting Messages: Did your parents have conflicting messages about food at home versus food in social gatherings?

   Journal Prompt: Did any contrast between strict home rules and more relaxed social eating create confusion? Describe how that felt. How did your parents' approach to mealtimes at home differ from their approach at social gatherings (e.g., strict rules at home, but more lenient at parties; different foods allowed at each)? What conflicting messages did this create for you about food (e.g., "Certain foods are only for special occasions," "Eating rules don't apply when others are around," "Food is a reward for social behaviour")?

8. Social Interactions and Food: How did your parents' approach to mealtimes and family/social gatherings influence your relationship with food and your social interactions?

   Journal Prompt: Take a trip down Memory Lane. Think about specific scenarios at family gatherings or social events involving food that stand out. What comes up for you? What did your parents do or say? Who else was there? What was the atmosphere? Describe a typical holiday meal at your childhood home. Who was there? What was the food like? How did your parents interact with food and with others?

Think of a time when your parents made a comment about someone else's eating at a social gathering. How did that make you feel?

Recall a time when your parents' behaviour around food at a party embarrassed or confused you. What happened? How did you react?

9. How can you create a supportive, nurturing environment for yourself that encourages healthy eating habits and a positive body image in social settings?

For You to Think About

Can you think of some small, manageable steps you can take this week to make some tiny, powerful shifts in your attitudes? Use this reflection time as a creative space to brainstorm, to jot down notes, to discover one small way you can make a difference for yourself, for just this week. It doesn't have to be a grand gesture, just one gentle step toward your own beautiful transformation.

•••

After the Reflection Questions

Please, take a pause and reflect. Take a moment to reread your answers. What stands out to you? What emotions are coming up?

As you deepen your self-awareness and gain more clarity, it's vital to hold yourself with compassion and allow yourself to be comfortable with all aspects of your upbringing. I know this isn't always easy, my friend. You've journeyed through many cycles of change in your life, experienced both losses and gains within your family – these are the unique and precious seasons of your life so far.

Through this work, you might feel a tug of resistance, a desire to push away certain truths. I encourage you, with gentle kindness, to sit with this for a while. When we deny our true feelings, that denial can lead to automatic behaviours and a sense of disharmony within our mind and body. It can cause us to suppress and stall ourselves, our needs, and our deepest desires. Let's be brave, together, and honour the truth within.

I hope this reflection has been helpful.

26.
Your Food and Drink Reality

A Real Look at Your Daily Choices
Bringing Clarity to Your Everyday Patterns

Okay, I think you are ready for this deep dive and personal review into your current relationship with food and drink. You have already made connections to how your childhood experiences and family of origin have influenced your behaviours, so I feel you are ready now to take another brave step forward and investigate what's happening right now with you. The purpose of this exercise aims to deepen your inner connection and bring awareness to what you are doing automatically (perhaps unconsciously) with food and drink and how it makes you feel.

Be honest in answering these questions, allow your authentic voice to come out, and be open to the answers you receive, even if they feel a little challenging. In your most compassionate way, give yourself permission to be vulnerable. You are in a safe place.

It is okay to have responses that aren't all in the positive camp. It is okay to be where you are right now. Everything you are facing right now is an opportunity to learn something, to grow, and to evolve.

Right, so why are we doing all this? It's simple really. By tuning into how you're actually behaving, you'll start to see those patterns pop up.

Once you're onto those patterns, you can spot them a mile off before they cause a drama. In other words, this whole thing will help you hit the brakes on those automatic reactions and make some thoughtful changes, so you can catch yourself before you trip up. This is where you find the real gems that light the way to the changes you're after. So, rest assured, understanding your patterns better lets you take little steps towards making changes in the future, and not get stuck in those endless loops of behaviours you'd rather ditch when it comes to food and drink.

Remember: Read your answers aloud so you hear yourself speak the words – so you believe what you say. There are no right or wrong answers here.

> So, here's why we're doing this together: We're building the skills that give you the freedom to make choices that feel good. This is your chance to build trust in yourself and a clear sense of what's truly important for your health and happiness.

Let's Begin

1. How would you describe your number one challenge with food and/or alcohol?

   Journal Prompt: What struggles/stressors are relevant to this challenge?

   What are the costs of this challenge in your life? How do you feel when you read this question out loud?

2. How can you cultivate a sense of curiosity to see if you can take action to make small steps of change in this situation?

   Journal Prompt: What is one small thing you can do this week to make a shift in your behaviour? How would you rate your ability to make this a successful change?

   Give yourself a score from 1 to 10.

3. What do you feel you are ignoring about your relationship with food and/or alcohol?

   Journal Prompt: Why don't you want to see the situation and its impact on your life? How does it feel when you read this out loud to yourself?

4. Be honest about what you are ignoring. How can you cultivate a sense of curiosity to see if you can take action to make small steps of change with this situation?

   Journal Prompt: What is one small thing you can do this week to make a shift in your behaviour? What would you like to do to change this situation?

   What lesson is this challenge trying to teach you? What do you feel you need help with in this scenario?

5. How would you rate your ability to make this a successful change?

Journal Prompt: Give yourself a score from 1 to 10. How does it feel when you give yourself a score?

6. When you feel vulnerable, have you experienced a feeling of being out of control with food and/or alcohol?

   Journal Prompt: Can you describe the situation leading up to it? Can you connect with how it made you feel afterward? When you consider this scenario, can you see the consequences of this situation? (What are the costs to you from these behaviours?)

7. How does your relationship with food and/or alcohol impact your physical health?

   Journal Prompt: What specific physical symptoms do you experience related to your food and/or alcohol choices? How does your energy level feel? What other areas of your physical health do you notice are being affected?

8. How would you say your relationship with food and/or alcohol impacts your mental health?

   Journal Prompt: How does your mood fluctuate based on your food and/or alcohol consumption? Do you experience anxiety, depression, or other emotional challenges related to your choices? How are your self-esteem and self-worth affected?

9. Think about times when you have felt confident and in control. What would you like to do to repeat the behaviour that made you feel that way?

   Journal Prompt: What would that situation look like, do you think? What small shifts in your mindset could you make to help you in this scenario? (Think about the times you have made a successful decision and done something well; how did you go about that?)

   How would you rate your ability to make this a successful change?

Give yourself a score from 1 to 10. How does it feel when you give yourself a score?

10. What have you experienced when you have had a preoccupation with your weight and body image?

    Journal Prompt: How do you feel this drives your behaviour with food and drink? For instance, when you get stuck in negative self-talk, what are your behaviours with food and drink?

    What do you think is happening to your confidence? What are the costs to you from these behaviours?

11. What specific behaviours or habits do you engage in when you are struggling with your relationship with food and/or alcohol?

    Journal Prompt: Do you isolate yourself? Do you eat in secret? Do you find yourself constantly thinking about your next meal or drink?

    How do these habits make you feel in the moment? How do they make you feel afterward?

12. How can you embrace shifting your perspective about your weight and body image and be open to more loving and compassionate self-support?

    Journal Prompt: How could you make room for your mind to shift from the tainted perception of your body image to loving your innate qualities?

    What can you say about how liberating it is to be comfortable with imperfection? How can you cultivate a sense of freedom by letting go of what you think you should be and accepting who you are today?

    How could you make space in your daily routine to spend a few minutes appreciating and loving your physical body for what it is right now?

13. If you were to practise these skills and make small changes, how would you rate your ability to make this a successful change?

    Journal Prompt: Give yourself a score from 1 to 10. When you read that score out loud, how does that make you feel?

14. When you feel out of balance in your physical self (e.g., having poor digestion, headaches, brain fog, joint-back-hip-neck pain, feeling sick, lethargic, bloated, gassy, acidic, swollen), have you used rigid rituals and routines on yourself, especially surrounding food and drink?

    Journal Prompt: Can you describe what it feels like? Now go deeper and think about your domains of life. How does this impact your: Relationships? Working life? Mental health? Exercise practices?

15. What happens when you experience chaos in your work life?

    Journal Prompt: What are your behaviours with food and drink?

    How can you find a calm and peaceful centre and practise living by your values to help you avoid using these pain-numbing tactics in the future?

    How is your sleep?

    Now answer the same questions for what happens when you experience chaos in your relationships.

16. As you become more confident in your ability to shift and implement new changes in your life, how would you rate your ability to make this a successful change?

    Journal Prompt: Give yourself a score from 1 to 10. When you read that score out loud, how does that make you feel?

•••

After the Questions

So, I'm really curious, how are you feeling about those insights you uncovered through those thought-provoking questions? What really stood out to you? Anything feel surprisingly familiar? What feels important to you now? How does this newfound awareness make you feel about wanting to make a change, even if it's just one small step forward?

"Between stimulus and response there is a space. In that space is our power to choose our response. In our response lies our growth and our freedom."

– Viktor Frankl

The great thing here is, when you're consciously thinking about all this great information you've uncovered, you gain clarity on the reasons why you want to change. Trust that any step you take from here is in the belief that you know what's right for you. With a deeper understanding of why you struggled in the past, you can hold yourself with more compassion and love.

Sit with that for a while.

Your Springboard for Real-Life Change

There are three things I want you to contemplate this week:

1. If you could pick one little thing from all this that you could do a bit differently, starting today, what would that be? Remember, you reshape your reality as you do this work.

2. You are awakening a part of your consciousness and your authentic self; expect a stronger inner dialogue to start to become more present in your quieter moments, which will bring you even greater clarity.

3. Change is never a straight line. With each little shift, you may experience struggle. Tell yourself that it is okay. Notice what comes up for you and make room for that. This is all a normal part of your Change Experience, and you'll learn and grow with each step.

Remember: Embrace any lessons that come your way and use them to fuel your journey forward with your newfound grace.

27.
The Social Maze of Change

Food Is Social – Change, However, Is Not
Navigating the Social Landscape to Move Forward

Let's explore what happens when you decide to make changes, especially when others in your life are used to you staying the same. You might find, my dear friend, that changing in a social setting can be tricky. Food is often a social experience, yet personal change is a different matter.

It's important to be prepared for how your social circle – friends, family, partners, and community – may react to your need for transformation. People expect you to show up as you always have. You play a role in their life, and that routine behaviour is established; it's something they rely on. Why? Because people generally prefer consistency and are invested in maintaining the status quo. When you start to change, it can make others uncomfortable because it shifts their world, not just yours, and they may not be ready for it. The crux of this matter is most people are naturally focused on their own needs first. So, don't be surprised if they don't immediately understand or support your journey. You may need to clearly communicate what's important to you. Be prepared; this can be a moment when you discover who your true friends are.

People aren't always supportive of change because it can be inconvenient for them. When you decide to change your eating habits or your relationship with alcohol or other substances, you'll need strategies and awareness of those you can continue to spend time with and those you can confide in. Changing ingrained patterns within social settings is challenging. It's not always easy because others can unintentionally make it harder or be insensitive to deflect how your choices are making them feel about theirs. The deflection may present itself as someone making a joke or a judgemental comment. This can be destabilising. Hence, why you may need to hand-pick your inner circle for a while.

The sheer need for acceptance from our tribe can make any change feel daunting, even terrifying. The weight of the deep psychological need for human connection can make trying these changes on for size in social settings feel like a ghastly weight around our necks or a target on our backs. I understand; I've been there. We all want to belong. You might feel vulnerable, like you're standing on the edge of a diving board, unsure whether to dive in. You have an internal desire for change, but the external world can feel overwhelming. If you're not ready to take that leap, it's okay to limit exposure to challenging social situations until you feel more secure in your resolve.

When you try to step outside your usual behaviour in a social setting, feeling judged or criticised can hinder your progress. It might make you second-guess yourself and falter. This is exactly what you're trying to move away from. Is the need to fit in greater than your need for authenticity and living a life that is true and balanced, living within your values, taking care of your needs? That is up to you to decide.

> The key is to be aware of this possibility of discomfort.

When you anticipate these reactions, you can prepare yourself. You can think, "When someone makes a joke or criticises me, I will ground myself, acknowledge the feeling without letting it overwhelm me, take a breath, and step away for a few minutes." You will say to yourself, "This negativity is with them; it is their discomfort being projected onto me. I believe that what I am doing is right for me." You might even give the anticipated criticism a name to take away its power.

Throughout this book series, you will learn more strategies to manage these situations, and as you practise them, each scenario will become easier. But until your skills are really developed, a simple and quick way to catch yourself, when emotions arise, is to tell yourself, "I'm going to ground myself so I can slow down, regain clarity, and choose my next steps." That person who is criticising you, perhaps because they feel insecure, won't derail you or send you back to old patterns. You are in control now, and that's empowering!

> **"Change will not come if we wait for some other person and some other time."**
> – Barack Obama

In the next section, I'm going to ask you to think about the people, places, and situations that might challenge you. Identify those who might make comments and the environments that feel precarious. When you're prepared, you can handle these moments and protect yourself. You can also choose to limit your contact with those people or places until you feel more confident. Wait until you feel empowered by your new changes before engaging with those who tend to judge. This is about taking control and mastering your path forward.

People, Places, and Situations: Identifying Your Triggers

Relationships with those close to us, whether family, friends, or partners, can act as mirrors. They can reflect what's happening within you if you're open to seeing it. These reflections can guide your learning and growth.

Those you spend time with are essential for your Future Self. The people around you can influence and normalise behaviours that may or may not serve you. Understanding your behaviour in these situations and identifying your triggers allows you to develop strategies to avoid them in the future. This process opens the door to making small, sustainable steps towards your desired life, living by your values and breaking free from unwanted patterns related to food and drink.

I'm going to ask you some questions to help you reflect and build that internal connection. More building blocks, more skill-building, more rewiring of neural pathways, more clarity, and stronger coping mechanisms for when you're triggered.

Navigating Emotional Triggers: A Go-To Guide

It's completely normal to sometimes use food as a way to cope with emotions. But when this becomes a regular pattern, it can steer us away from the balanced life we truly desire. Let's explore some healthier ways to respond to those emotional triggers.

 1. Anxiety – Using food to calm yourself

Instead of: Reaching for sugary or processed foods, or an alcoholic drink for a quick fix. Try:

- Your grounding techniques: Dropping Anchor, by pushing your feet into the floor, connecting to the room around you, noticing five things in the room, saying them out loud, and connecting to your body. Practise deep breathing with your 4-7-8 Breathing technique. Remember to do this slowly and gently. Repeat a few times.
- A calming walk or gentle stretching.
- Herbal tea, like chamomile or peppermint.
- Journalling. Write down your anxieties; sometimes, getting them out of your head can really help.

 2. Boredom – Eating to pass the time

Instead of: Automatically snacking or drinking out of boredom. Try:

- Engaging in hobbies. What are yours? Painting, drawing, reading, Pilates, listening to some tunes, home DIY, getting into your garden?
- Calling a friend or family member for a chat.
- Going for a walk or doing some light exercise. Try listening to a podcast while you walk or work out.
- Learning something new online. Get creative with AI.

- Organising a drawer or completing a small task around the house you've been putting off.

🔍 3. Feeling hollow – Eating to fill a gap in your life

Instead of: Eating to fill an emotional void. Try:

- Identifying what's missing. What do you truly need? Connection? Purpose? Creativity? Get your journal out and give form to what you think is missing. This will help you see what actions you can take to "fill the gap".

- Engaging in activities that bring you meaning. Volunteer, pursue a passion, or spend time in nature (take your shoes off and stand on the grass and feel the energy of the earth! More on this in Book Three).

- Connecting with loved ones. Schedule quality time with friends or family.

- Self-reflection. Explore your feelings and needs, honestly and without judgement.

- Mindfulness exercises. Focus on being present in the moment and ask yourself, "What am I avoiding?" Listen for the answer; it will always come.

🔍 4. Rewards – Eating and drinking to celebrate a win; food and wine play hand in hand

Instead of: Overindulging to celebrate. Try:

- Non-food rewards. Treat yourself to a massage, a new book, or an experience you enjoy. Go back to your rewards list that we created earlier in the book.

- Sharing your success with others. Celebrate by spending quality time with loved ones, with activities that are non-food and non-alcohol related.

- Creating a playlist of celebratory music and playing it loudly.
- Setting new, exciting goals to work towards. What's something new you've wanted to try?

5. Feeling alone – Using food to give you comfort and companionship

Instead of: Eating to cope with loneliness. Try:

- Reaching out to someone. Call a friend, send a text, or join an online group.
- Engaging in social activities. Join a club, attend a class, or go to a community event. Get connected to new people.
- Getting a fur baby for companionship. Animals can provide a wonderful source of love and joy.
- Practising self-compassion. Remind yourself that you are worthy of love and belonging, and that this feeling will pass.

6. Feeling low – Using food to give you a temporary high

Instead of: Eating to numb sadness or depression. Try:

- Talking to a trusted friend or family member. Share how you're feeling in that moment. Talking about it can often release the blockage you're feeling.
- Engaging in activities that lift your mood. Listen to music, spend time in nature, or do something creative. Do something using your hands!
- Exercising. Physical activity releases endorphins, which can improve your mood.
- Seeking professional help. If the above isn't working for you, finding a therapist or counsellor can provide support and guidance.

🔍 7. Avoiding – Using food as a way to procrastinate and shift focus

Instead of: Eating to avoid a task or difficult situation. Try:

- Breaking down tasks. Divide large tasks into smaller, more manageable steps. Or just choose five small tasks a day, tick them off as you complete them, and feel satisfaction as they are finished.
- Setting a timer. Work on the task for a set amount of time, then take a break.
- Identifying the root of avoidance. What are you really afraid of? What would happen if you leaned into this thing you are avoiding? Answer that question with factual responses, not fear stories.
- Seeking support or guidance from a mentor, family member, or colleague.

🔍 8. Stress – Food offers a distraction and numbness from the pain

Instead of: Using food to cope with stress. Try:

- Stress-reduction techniques. Sit for five minutes in silence at the beginning of your day. Write pages of reflections for fifteen minutes when you wake up. Try some gentle movement to music for fifteen minutes. (Wiggle your bum as you get ready in the morning!)
- Time management. Prioritise tasks and avoid overcommitting. Keep time for yourself.
- Setting boundaries. Learn to say "no" to things that add to your stress.
- Spending time in nature. Take a walk or a hike in a garden, park, or forest.

9. Anger – Food and drink numb that intensity

Instead of: Using food or drink to suppress anger. Try:

- Healthy outlets for anger. Exercise, hit a pillow, or yell in a safe space. Break an old mug outside; it will feel satisfying.
- Communicating assertively. Express your feelings in a healthy way. Anger is a healthy feminine energy.
- Journalling. Write down your anger to process it. Give it a name.
- Taking a time-out. Step away from the situation to cool down.

10. Happiness – Food is a contributor to the sense of happiness lasting longer

Instead of: Overeating to prolong happiness. Try:

- Savouring the moment. Fully enjoy the experience without overindulging.
- Sharing the joy with others. Celebrate with friends and family without having to use food to express your happiness.
- Creating happy memories. Take photos, write in a journal, or make a scrapbook.
- Manifesting your Future Self. Make a vision board of what you want in your life.

11. Feeling rebellious – Food vindicates you, so there are no boundaries

Instead of: Using food to rebel against restrictions. Try:

- Understanding the root of the rebellion. What are you really pushing against? Be honest with yourself. Write it down, and give it a name.
- Setting healthy boundaries for yourself. You are in control of your choices. And trust that you will maintain them.

- Finding alternative ways to express your independence. Revert back to your values and stay true to them.

12. Feeling under threat – Food can comfort and give you validation and a temporary sense of calm

Instead of: Using food for comfort when feeling threatened. Try:

- Assessing the situation. Is the threat real or perceived? Ask yourself to be honest in that moment. Is this a reminder of an old fear story, or truly something that can harm you in the present moment?
- Seeking support. Talk to a trusted friend or family member.
- Practising grounding techniques. Bring yourself back to the present moment.
- Self-care. Engage in activities that make you feel safe and secure.

> Remember, my friend, these are just suggestions. The key is to find what works best for you.

Questions for Reflection

Let's explore how you can navigate social situations while making meaningful changes in your life. These reflection questions are designed to help you connect with yourself and develop strategies for those challenging moments. Find your cozy spot, private corner, or moment alone, and grab your journal and pen. Let's get into this.

Identifying the Triggers

1. Think of three specific occasions where you may find it hard to stick to your new behaviours surrounding food and drink choices. Consider:

    Dining at a favourite restaurant or eating out in general.

    Attending family functions, cultural events, or a friend's house for a gathering.

    Being on holiday or in public situations at work.

    Take a moment to really picture these situations. And write them down.

2. Next, for each of those occasions, write down the people who might challenge you with making a change. It's helpful to also consider why you think they might create objections. Understanding their potential motivations can strengthen your own resolve and help you prepare.

    For example, you might encounter:

    Someone who uses jokes to implement peer pressure.

    Someone who uses humour and charm to coerce you to do what they want.

    Someone who wants you to normalise what they are doing.

    Someone who uses guilt or shame to try to keep you from changing.

3. Next, using the same three occasions, what committed action or strategy could you use to stay true to your values and stand by your choices?

   For example, consider:
   > How could you set a healthy boundary?
   >
   > How could you communicate what your choice is?
   >
   > Are you feeling strong enough to confront this change, or perhaps it is best to find a convenient exit?
   >
   > How can you prevent yourself from getting thrown off course in these situations and falling back into old patterns?

4. Next, using each of the same three scenarios, write the name(s) of the person/people (friends, family, colleagues) you know you can rely on to support you throughout your changes with food and drink.

After the Questions

Throughout your life, you'll have many different relationships. Some may be brief, and some may last a long time. Whatever their role, appreciate the reflections they offer. Nothing or no one must be permanent in our lives.

With each exercise you complete, your skills develop, and you build a stronger foundation for yourself. You are growing in this beautiful connection to your true self. Please acknowledge that your dedication to this journey is a precious gift you're giving to yourself.

You are doing challenging and confronting work here; be proud. This is all truly terrific stuff! Take a moment and give yourself a little credit. Being patient with yourself and acknowledging every small step you take is a testament to the incredible inner strength you have.

> So please, say it out loud: "Well done, me!"

Stress, Sleep, and Your Food and Drink

28. When Stress Takes Over

How Stress Drives Your Choices
Transforming Your Stress Responses for Healthier Habits

If you've come this far and have decided you're ready to make changes in your life, then we need to talk about gaining some more clarity on what can throw you off course. Stress, my friend, is a big one. Stress is that messy stuff that often leads us into behaviours that pull us away from our values and the life we truly want.

When we get stressed, we often slip into automatic behaviours. These are the habits we use to numb, distract, and take away the pain we're experiencing. So, to help you steer away from these unhelpful automatic patterns, we need to become aware of what triggers us and how the chronic stress in our lives impacts our choices.

This world is fast-paced. We're constantly bombarded with information and demands. Things are always changing – trends, expectations, the constant rush of where we have to be and when we have to be there. It's a lot. One of the most important things you can do right now is to understand where stress shows up in your life.

Let's look at how stress impacts the main areas of your life. When you're stressed at work, your relationship with food and drink often changes. You might come home and grab something quick and not so nourishing, or reach for that drink (or bottle) to unwind.

If you're stressed in your relationship, you might reach for the tub of ice cream or something else that feels comforting in the moment but doesn't align with your healthier choices. Think about when your physical world feels compromised, or when your emotional and spiritual worlds are struggling. What do you do? Throw in the towel, perhaps, and say, "Stuff it. I am going to dial a pizza!"

What do you do in those times? For me, when I'm upset about something in my relationship, I don't reach for a healthy juice or a vibrant salad. I crave those "naughty pleasure foods" to momentarily take away the pain – and a truckload of them, to be honest. For me, it was about bangs of flavour, and an abundance of it.

Trigger/Event Eating

Stress can be a chronic challenge, especially for those who have experienced trauma. Why? Because our ability to control stress responses and emotionally regulate can be affected by what we've been through. That small space between a trigger and a response can be hard to navigate, and without conscious awareness, we can fall into patterns that don't serve us.

As I have pointed out before, trauma, combined with the negative stories we tell ourselves, can make us feel isolated and stuck with shame, guilt, and self-punishment – and when stress takes centre stage, it can trigger old patterns, sending our nervous system into fight, flight, fawn, or freeze mode. This is why regulating stress can feel so difficult.

Chronic stress permeates all areas of our lives – relationships, exercise, work, sleep, and spirituality. When these areas are out of balance, our relationship with food and alcohol often suffers too.

If you're living with the effects of complex trauma, you likely have a set of triggers that can set you off. These triggers can lead to behaviours that have consequences, impacting what and how you eat and drink, which affects your nutritional intake and, ultimately, your health.

> **"Beware the barrenness of a busy life."**
> – Socrates

Emotional Eating

It's common for those who have faced challenges and experienced complex trauma to become emotional eaters. I was one too. I know those walks to the fridge, the speed dial for home delivery, and the familiar drive-through windows all too well.

So, let's ask a few simple questions to get you thinking:

- Have you noticed that when you feel stressed, your appetite changes?

- Have you noticed that your behaviours toward food and alcohol have changed? Have you experienced times of emotional eating?

- Have certain events triggered you, creating internal anxiety and stress, leading you to indulge in food or drink you don't usually choose?

Sometimes, anxiety can also cause a loss of appetite, leading to a different kind of unhealthy pattern – depriving yourself of the nutrition you need.

My friend, it can be a messy cycle. These extreme eating habits often create more stress, self-loathing, self-pity, and disgust, significantly impacting emotions and raising stress levels further.

> **NOTE:** Some foods, especially those high in sugar or caffeine, can increase stress, while others, rich in omega-3s or magnesium, can help decrease it. So, stress levels can influence your daily diet choices.

I Was an Emotional Eater for Years

I used to find it very hard to regulate my emotions. I was highly sensitive and hypervigilant. When I was upset at work, I would overeat. I indulged in large servings of takeout or fast food.

If I was having a tough time with my boss, which was often, I drank too much wine and smoked a pack of cigarettes in an evening. This led to poor sleep, feeling terrible the next day, and hating myself. I denied this behaviour for many years, doing it all behind closed doors, and turning up the next day, shiny, happy, super high-energy, and wearing a mask of a big smile.

Urgh, it was all so fake, as I look back at it now, and I have a lot of compassion for my former self. But this is not my secret anymore, and I do feel privileged that I can stand before you and tell you all of this pretty confronting stuff about myself.

Helpful Tips

My friend, if you're ready to dive deeper and explore more ways to support your body while managing the effects of chronic stress, I have you covered.

I've created downloadable resources on my website, filled with more in-depth nutritional guidance, mindful eating techniques, and other tips to help you on your Change Experience journey.

You can find all of this and more on the Resources page of my website at **www.fleurelizabeth.com**.

You are not alone; I'm here with you.

29. Reflection Time

Stress and Food Choices

In this next exercise, I want you to take a moment to truly reflect on what you do when you're stressed in different areas of your life. Think about those times when you're at work and feeling the strain, when you're unhappy in your relationship, or when you're facing challenges in your physical and emotional world. Picture those moments clearly. Then, list the specific things you do with food and drink in those situations.

Once you've written them down, read your list aloud. Really listen to yourself as if you were hearing a dear friend share this with you. What advice or words of comfort would you offer them? This exercise is about bringing awareness to your relationship with food, so be brave, be compassionate, and be honest with yourself. Remember, this is a safe space for your thoughts and feelings.

This Reflection is designed to help you explore the triggers, behaviours, and consequences in four key domains of your life. By understanding these patterns, you can begin to slow down those automatic responses and make conscious changes. When you recognise the patterns, you can start building strategies to avoid these

> **"The food you eat can be either the safest and most powerful form of medicine or the slowest form of poison."**
>
> – Ann Wigmore

triggers in the future. This process opens the door to taking small, sustainable steps towards the life you truly desire, a life aligned with your values, where you're no longer trapped by unwanted behaviours related to food and drink.

The next time you set your intentions for a more effortless life (remember?), you'll be ready to put these strategies into action. When you see these habits written down, and you gain more clarity and truly understand them, you can identify those areas that need your attention – those moments when you tend to stray from your values.

> Remember: You are not alone in this. What you're experiencing is very normal, and you're taking a courageous step towards change.

Let's Begin

1. **When you're stressed in your relationship:**

   Think of three specific examples of what you do with food or drink. Which one feels like the biggest challenge for you?

   What are the real consequences of these behaviours? (What is the cost to you, your relationships, and your wellbeing?)

   How would you truly love to change these behaviours and experiences? What would feel more aligned with who you want to be?

2. **When you're stressed at work:**

   Think of a few examples of what you do with food or drink. Which one feels most problematic for you?

   What are the actual consequences of these behaviours? (How does this affect your work, your health, and your happiness?)

   How would you ideally want to shift these behaviours and experiences? What would bring you more peace and balance?

3. **When you're feeling stress related to low self-esteem, a loss of identity, or negative self-worth:**

   Think of a few examples of what you do with food or drink. Which one feels most difficult to manage?

   What are the deeper consequences of these behaviours? (What is the emotional and psychological toll?)

   How would you truly desire to transform these behaviours and experiences? What would it mean for your sense of self?

4. When you're experiencing physical challenges (i.e., illness, injury, chronic pain):

   Think of three examples of what you do with food or drink. Which one is the hardest to deal with?

   What are the true consequences of these behaviours? (How does this impact your healing and your overall health?)

   How would you like to modify these behaviours and experiences? What would support your body's needs better?

   ・・・

After the Reflection Questions

Stress is definitely unpleasant, and yet, it's a normal part of life. But it's also communicating something important to you. How can you listen to what your stressors are trying to tell you? How can you deepen your clarity and understanding of what you can work on to change or shift the presence of stress in your life?

Where have you been neglecting your own needs? In your heart space, what steps can you take, after answering these questions, to pay closer attention to the aspects of your life that you may have neglected? The answers you seek to reduce your stress lie within these insights.

If you can view stress as a form of communication, it becomes easier to soften and surrender to what your needs are for change.

> Please take a moment to remind yourself that you're doing wonderfully well. Acknowledge your efforts and your courage!

30.
The Sleep-Food Dance

How Your Sleep Influences What You Eat
Unpacking the Night's Influence on Your Day

Do you get eight hours of sleep at night? I do now (I never used to, though, for years), and honestly, those eight hours set me up for a brilliant day, every day! It's amazing how sleep impacts our choices, isn't it? Have you ever stopped to consider the connection between how you sleep and what you choose to eat and drink? It's something many people overlook, but I'm here to tell you, there's a strong link between the two. Having clarity within this connection can empower you to make more conscious food and drink choices.

> **"Sleep is the single most effective thing we can do to reset our brain and body health each day."**
>
> — Matthew Walker, Professor of Neuroscience and Psychology at the University of California, Berkeley, and Director of the Center for Human Sleep Science

Maintaining optimal sleep habits is what we now call "good sleep hygiene". It's about improving the quality and quantity of your sleep and reducing behaviours that disrupt it. Good sleep undeniably improves brain performance, lifts your mood, and keeps your health balanced.

When we're sleep-deprived, our hunger hormones get thrown off balance. This can lead to overeating and craving foods high in sugar, fat, and salt. Regularly choosing these foods can lead to type 2 diabetes, heart disease, and other health challenges. Good sleep boosts your immune system, supports a healthy heart and blood flow, and can even prevent diseases from developing. Lack of sleep increases susceptibility to inflammation, obesity, heart attack, stroke, diabetes, hypertension, and more.

Your sleep habits influence the amount and types of food you eat and whether you gain or lose body fat. Experts have found that even adding just one more hour of sleep a night can improve eating habits and support healthy weight management.

> For example, if you get only five hours of sleep a night, your body produces the stress hormone cortisol, which creates inflammation, increases water retention, and the net result is, you can literally put on 2 kilograms overnight.

When you're sleep-deprived, the reward centre in your brain responds strongly to "junk foods", high-sugar treats, and calorie-dense foods. Your brain releases hormones that trigger food cravings, making you reach for something that will give you a quick boost. This can create a cycle where you're choosing against what you truly want and what you know is good for you.

Sleep directly affects your endocrine system. Two key hormones involved are ghrelin, which makes you feel hungry, and leptin, which suppresses your appetite and signals to your brain that you're full. When you don't get enough sleep, your circadian rhythms are disrupted, suppressing leptin and increasing ghrelin. This results in more cravings, especially for sweet and fatty foods. Sleep loss also decreases activity in the parts of your brain that regulate food intake, making it harder to exercise self-control. This makes us more likely to eat fewer vegetables and opt for high-fat, high-sugar foods. The higher the

> **"Sleep is the golden chain that binds our health and body together."**
> – Thomas Dekker

calorie density, the more appealing the food is to a sleep-deprived brain, which explains the link between poor sleep and weight challenges.

Losing sleep triggers the brain, and hormonal changes stimulate food cravings, driving us to consume more calories, especially junk foods. It's a tough cycle, but we can break free from it. There is no doubt, healthy eating habits encourage healthier sleeping patterns – full stop. Increasing the fibre in your diet with plenty of fresh fruits, vegetables, whole grains, and lean proteins, while reducing foods with added sugars, is ideal.

> I'm here to help you every step of the way, my friend!

Food and Drink to Support Restful Sleep

Sometimes it's hard to know what foods are right for your sleep. Research shows that eating the following foods daily can improve your chances of a good night's sleep:

- Follow a Mediterranean eating plan that includes whole grains, vegetables, fruits, legumes, nuts, fish, and olive oil and minimises red meat and processed foods.

- Include protein foods that contain tryptophan, such as chicken, eggs, cheese, fish, peanuts, pumpkin and sesame seeds, milk, turkey, tofu, and other soy products.

- Choose high-quality carbohydrate foods, such as whole-grain bread and cereals, brown rice, and oats.

- Eat plenty of fresh, seasonal vegetables and fruit.

- Include foods high in B vitamins, such as fish, lean poultry and meat, legumes, eggs, and dairy, to help regulate melatonin.

- Maintain a balanced diet that supports healthy weight management, which leads to better sleep and reduces daytime fatigue, insomnia, and obstructive sleep apnea (OSA).

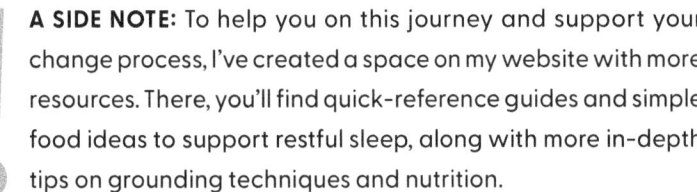

A SIDE NOTE: To help you on this journey and support your change process, I've created a space on my website with more resources. There, you'll find quick-reference guides and simple food ideas to support restful sleep, along with more in-depth tips on grounding techniques and nutrition.

You can find all of this on the Resources page of my website at www.fleurelizabeth.com.

So, What to Do Now?

There are many things you can do to improve your sleep. Becoming aware of your pre-bedtime routine can make a big difference. Things like blue light from screens, overstimulation, certain beverages, sugar, and spicy foods can all interfere with your sleep. When you have this knowledge, you can decide what's truly important for you at that time of day. As you carry on reading, you will see I offer some simple "get more sleep" hacks. And some gentle, "what to do when you wake up and can't get back to sleep" hacks. I like to call them strategies, though, because nothing about this is hacking your life; it is being smart about making sustainable improvements!

A lack of sleep could be one of the underlying reasons for those automatic behaviours with food and drink. And it's okay to concede that it is something you may have taken for granted or overlooked. But now that you know this information, it is your duty to your Future Self to get your seven to eight hours of sleep per night, and protect it and make sure it happens, just as you would for a three-month-old infant.

> **"The role of sleep health in the development and management of chronic diseases has grown. Notably, insufficient sleep has been linked to the development and management of a number of chronic diseases and conditions, including type 2 diabetes, cardiovascular disease, obesity, and depression."**
>
> – CDC (Center for Disease Control and Prevention)

Think of it as your ticket to a healthy, balanced life. It's one of the core foundations of keeping the equilibrium in my life, to be honest. It's another essential building block in mastering your relationship with food and drink.

Maybe some of this is familiar, but you've chosen to ignore it. Or perhaps some of it is entirely new to you. Either way, approach this with an open mind and a willingness to learn. You'll start to see the direct connection between your nutritional choices and your sleep, and you can take charge of this for your own wellbeing.

> Take some time to reflect and gain more clarity on how these ideas relate to your own routine.

31. Your Sleep Toolkit

Finding Your Way to Restful Nights
Practical Steps for Deeper, Healthier Sleep

Okay, let's be real – there's no one-size-fits-all solution when it comes to sleep. What works wonders for me might be a complete flop for you, and that's perfectly okay! The key here is to explore, experiment, and adapt these strategies to fit *your* unique needs.

Remember, what doesn't work tonight might be exactly what you need next month, when you're in a different headspace or dealing with a different stress level. It's all about flexibility and finding what resonates with *you*.

Your Homework

Over the next couple of weeks, pay close attention to how these strategies impact your sleep. Keep a journal, jot down your observations, and really *notice* what difference they make to your sleep quality over time. This is how you gain more clarity.

Let's dive into these new skills to help you improve your sleep.

1. Avoid Eating Too Close to Bedtime

Try to keep that last 1.5 to 2 hours before bed free from food and drink stimulants.

Fatty or High-Protein Foods: Digestion naturally slows down when you sleep. So, going to bed too soon after a hearty steak dinner or other high-protein meal can leave you feeling uncomfortably full and disrupt your sleep. Foods high in saturated fat can also throw off your sleep patterns.

Spicy Foods: Oh, how I love spice! But spices can cause painful heartburn, making it hard to lie down comfortably and fall asleep. Heartburn can also worsen the effects of obstructive sleep apnoea (OSA) because that backed-up acid can further irritate your airway. Plus, some spicy foods can raise your body temperature, and your body then has to work harder to cool down enough to fall asleep, which can definitely disrupt your sleep.

Large Meals: Eating a big meal right before bed is a major sleep disruptor. Your body needs time to digest and process everything. Sugars and high-intensity sweeteners might taste amazing going down, but they can often wake you up in the middle of the night as your liver and kidneys work on processing those sugars.

2. Stop All Stimulants Before Bed

Alcohol, coffee, and cigarettes are really not helpful before bed as they can act as stimulants.

Alcohol: Winding down with a glass of wine or beer at dinner can be nice, but not right before trying to sleep. It might make you feel sleepy at first, but alcohol will often wake you up in the night as your liver starts processing those toxins. It's not fun, and it really messes with a good night's sleep.

Caffeine: We all know that caffeine late in the day is a sleep saboteur for many because it contains properties that keep you alert. Avoid products containing caffeine (tea, coffee, and chocolate) for at least four hours before bedtime. (Caffeine-free tea and coffee are okay, but watch out for sugary plant-based milks!)

Smoking: Oh gosh, having a smoke before bed? Please, please, try to avoid nicotine (cigarettes, vaping, joints, etc.) for at least one hour before bedtime and if you wake up during the night.

3. Maintain Regular Sleeping Hours

Having a consistent bedtime and wake-up time each day is so important. Sticking to regular hours helps keep your body clock, your circadian rhythm, on track. The more consistent you are, the better your sleep quality will be. The more irregular your sleep, the higher the risk of broken, poor-quality sleep.

For instance, sleeping in too late or staying in bed longer than you normally do really can mess with your healthy sleep pattern. No joke.

4. Your "Wind-Down Ritual" Before Bed

The last 1.5 to 2 hours before bed should be your peaceful time. This is such an excellent and effective habit to develop.

Apple phones now have a cool feature that turns off all notifications one hour before bedtime.

Try to finish all texting, notifications, and interactions 1.5 hours before bed.

I recommend avoiding phone conversations for 1.5 hours before bed.

Instead of watching action shows on TV and absorbing blue light from the screen, try listening to some chilled-out, relaxing music.

Start a habit of reading in bed or listening to an audiobook.

Take a warm bath or shower in dim light.

Practise the 4-7-8 Breathing technique five times before bed to calm your nervous system.

Figure out what works to soothe your nervous system and avoid those stressful, chaotic, high-intensity TV shows in your space within one to two hours before bed.

5. Blue Light Before Bed

Our phones can be so addictive, and that constant exposure to blue light from phones, computers, and TVs right before bed really messes with our ability to fall asleep.

Can you try to put your phone away one hour before bed? It makes such a big difference.

If you have to work, and use your phone, fine, but allow yourself at least forty-five minutes away from the screen before bed, as your brain will likely keep going over things while you're trying to get to sleep.

6. Exercise During the Day

Go for a walk and do your movement practices each day. Regular physical exercise during the day, even mild exercise, helps improve sleep quality. Getting your daily dose of vitamin D from the sun also helps you sleep well at night.

Avoid crazy cardio (to the point of sweating) for at least one hour before bed. A gentle walk after dinner is a great way to release any extra energy and helps regulate your blood sugar after eating.

7. The Bedroom Is the Passion Paddock Only

Your bedroom is for passion and sleep – those are its primary functions. Relaxing by reading a book or listening to peaceful music is also acceptable.

Watching TV, using your phone, working, or studying – not on the primary needs list. Avoid these as much as possible in bed.

You want your brain to associate your bed with sleep and *only* sleep.

So, try to avoid other activities in the bedroom, such as watching TV, working, eating, doing yoga, or lifting weights.

8. Make Your Bedroom Sleep-Ready

Keep your room clean, tidy, and free from clutter. You want to create a calm and sleep-conducive space.

Regularly changing your sheets, using comfortable pillows, and having free flowing bedding all help.

Keep your room dark at night (use blackout curtains) and minimise noise. Make sure your phone is on silent.

If your partner snores, try earplugs. If they get up earlier than you do, use an eye mask so you don't wake up when they turn on the lights.

Keep your room temperature moderate, around 18 degrees Celsius (64 degrees Fahrenheit). Make sure it's cool in the summer before you sleep. Avoid extreme temperatures. Anything above 19.5 degrees Celsius (67 degrees Fahrenheit) can disrupt your sleep.

9. Cat Naps: Half an Hour or Less

The Spanish love their afternoon siestas, but they keep them short – no more than half an hour. A short twenty-to-thirty-minute nap in the late afternoon can be invigorating and restorative, but longer naps usually mess with your nighttime sleep quality.

Experts say just twenty minutes of sleep can revive and refresh the brain. Why not try that next time you need a little pick-me-up during the day?

10. Don't Try to Force Sleep

If you're in bed and can't sleep, don't lie there frustrated. Don't let yourself ruminate over those swirling thoughts.

Your brain will start associating your bed with those spiralling thoughts and as a place to send warning messages.

Get out of bed, sit in your living room, put your feet on the floor, and connect to the feeling of sitting in the chair. Simply removing yourself from the bed and bedroom environment can rewire your neural pathways.

Or try the grounding exercises I outline below.

Even if you're not sleeping, you're building valuable skills that will help you manage an overactive mind and those recurring thoughts.

Exception: If You Need a Snack Before Bed

If you really need a snack before bed, here are a few ideas:

- Warm plant-based milk with a spoonful of natural protein powder (no high-intensity sweeteners or preservatives).
- Complex carbohydrates, like oatmeal or whole-wheat toast, which digest quickly.

Sweet, beautiful dreams, my friend!

Grounding Techniques for Sleep Difficulties

Visualisation: Creating a peaceful mental image

How: Imagine a place that feels safe and calming to you. It could be a beach, a forest, or your favourite cozy room. Engage all your senses in this visualisation: what do you see, hear, smell, feel?

Why: This provides a mental escape from anxious thoughts and helps create a relaxed state.

Progressive Muscle Relaxation: Tensing and releasing muscles

How: Start with your toes. Tense the muscles in your toes for a few seconds, then release. Move up to your feet, calves, thighs, and so on, until you've worked your way up to your head.

Why: This releases physical tension, which can also have a calming effect on the mind.

Body Scan: A mindfulness practice

How: Start at your toes and slowly move your attention up through your body, noticing any sensations without judgement. If you find tension, acknowledge it and gently try to release it.

Why: This increases body awareness and helps to identify and release physical tension that might be contributing to restlessness.

And ... as we have previously discussed, here are some techniques you already know but can also be helpful with sleep.

Name and Tame: A helpful way to quieten the mind

How: Acknowledge the thoughts that are keeping you awake. Mentally label them ("worry about work", "to-do list", "that conversation"). Then, tell yourself that you've noticed the thought, and you can return to it tomorrow. You can visualise putting the thoughts in a box to open the next day.

Why: This helps to break the cycle of rumination. By acknowledging the thoughts without engaging with them, you reduce their power.

4-7-8 Breathing: A breathing technique to calm the nervous system

How: Inhale deeply through your nose for 4 seconds. Hold your breath for 7 seconds. Exhale slowly through your mouth for 8 seconds. Repeat this cycle several times.

Why: This technique activates the parasympathetic nervous system (your "rest and digest" response), which counteracts the stress response that can keep you awake.

∙ ∙ ∙

Rest well, my friend.

32.
Your Plate, Your Rules

Fit Out. Don't Fit In
Think About Your Food Choices as Small Steps to Big Food Shifts

The focus here is to make a choice to "fit out" with your food habits and help the change process become a lot easier.

When you're making changes to your food choices or how you're drinking, or anything like that, tell yourself it's okay to fit out – to not be the same as everybody else. Tell yourself it's good to fit out and be your unique, beautiful self! It can be hard to be the odd one out at any gathering, but give yourself permission to be different and fit out! You may not always be popular, but you will be happier.

When you give yourself permission to be different, it makes the whole process of change so much easier. You can say, "I don't need the acceptance of everybody else because I accept myself for who I am today and what I'm choosing to do. I'm good with that. Thanks very much."

When you are making changes, my message to you is: Don't try to fit in all the time.

> **"Champion the right to be yourself; dare to be different and to set your own pattern, live your own life, and follow your own star."**
> – Wilferd Peterson

> So, fit out. Do it for you.
> Don't do it for everybody else.

Crowding Out: Your Strategy to Change

This is all about learning how to replace the "not-so-good stuff" with a healthier option. The best way to change a habit of eating is to stay within the routine of that habit but substitute that chocolate bar, for example, for a bowl of blueberries. Change the junk for the healthy stuff that can feed the need you have at the time of the craving. Keep your eating schedule the same, just change what's in it.

When you're changing the unhealthy to the healthy, it can feel boring and can lead to ambivalence. You feel like you want to change, but your perception is that "bland tofu" instead of a "juicy, lip-smacking burger" doesn't appeal to you. Look, I'm not a believer in total denial. I don't think it works. It's not sustainable because your mind and body are saying, "Yum, yum, yum, I want that burger." Tofu isn't going to cut it. Denial creates desire, so what do you do here?

What has worked well for me and many others is the process of small, incremental changes to get you to a place where your body starts telling you the healthier choice actually feels better. This process is called "crowding out". If you're eating a hamburger for lunch or dinner, and your cholesterol is getting a bit high, and your heart rate is going up, or maybe you just have a bit of a "muffin top", instead of a hamburger with cheese and mayo, swap it for something different. Swap it for something that is still going to give you that yummy, juicy, pleasurable, "wrap your mouth around something" feeling, but it's not going to have the same calories, fat, and triglycerides that are going to impact your health.

For example, swap the burger for a lean chicken, tofu, or fish (low-carb, high-protein) wrap, with salad and hummus. Still pretty damn tasty!

To make this sustainable, you do this gently, gently. You don't do it all at once. Choose one meal or one snack at a time. Start by introducing the healthier, yet yummy, lip-smacking stuff.

> **NOTE:** There are many chefs and websites all over the internet showing how to make healthy, delicious foods that satisfy like the unhealthy ones do. You can start there and just try! (I follow loads of chefs on Instagram; it's an awesome source of inspiration when I want something different from my usual repertoire.)

With more nutrient-dense and healthier food, your body will change. Your internal computer tells you what is going on – how it is responding to the better-for-you consumption. "Ding, ding, ding, ding, ding, I'm feeling good. Those pleasure hormones start to come, and then, ding, ding, ding, I'm starting to sleep better. I'm starting to wake up feeling good. Ding, ding, ding, the muffin top isn't so noticeable anymore. Oh, I'm starting to feel good. Ding, ding, ding, a little bit of cholesterol has gone. Fantastic."

When you measure your progress, it motivates you. It's like pulling that thread, as I've said. Just keep pulling it. Little by little, you'll see improvements.

Crowding out is a fantastic strategy to change your relationship with food, with alcohol, with coffee, and all these substances we think we need. But maybe they aren't the best thing for us all the time. Give it a go. See how it feels.

Planning For Better-For-You Food

This work we are doing here is all about giving you the right information so you can make the right choices for your bio-individual type. And if you're like most people, you actually don't know exactly what to change, right? What do you need to be doing to eat the right type of food? So, here's how it works:

> VITAL: Remember, none of this will happen overnight.

- First, you are getting to know the right ingredients to introduce.
- Next, you will take it slow and work on a couple of meals each week that you will replace with healthier options (i.e., replacing the cheesy

burger with an equally delicious, better-for-you option – changing a quarter-pounder with cheese for a kid's burger, no cheese).

- And then build on your repertoire of options.
- The key here is not to overwhelm yourself and your body with too many changes or denial – because you will swing back to the unhealthy stuff, without a doubt.
- Create small goals to help you succeed in this crowding-out transition!
- Listen to your body; it will tell you what it likes, and it will respond in kind.
- Notice the differences in your physical and mental self as you go through this process.
- Keep a journal. How is your sleep? Your skin, your brain fog, your energy? Make a list of things to monitor, and check in and see what happens in one month's time.

So, while it is easy to say, "Replace your burger with an organic chicken wrap with fresh lettuce and homemade hummus," you first have to understand the basic principles of the ingredients that you should be thinking about.

> **MY MESSAGE TO YOU HERE:** Choose what you prefer to eat, within the parameters of "the good stuff" rather than the "inflammatory, problem stuff".

> Please check the resources section on my website: Here, I share with you details around proteins, carbohydrates, fats, and oils to help you deepen your nutritional understanding. It may be that you have a lot of nutritional knowledge already, but sometimes, it is helpful to be reminded.

Okay, this is a lot to take in – don't stress. This is the stuff you sit with and just slowly work through. Practise trusting your body's signals to direct your food choices. Your body will tell you what it likes. Hunger means you must eat, appetite tells you what foods taste good, and satiety tells you when you've had enough. Your body is the most highly tuned machine – if you listen to it enough, it will guide you through this process.

> I am still here – holding your hand.

Strategy for Changing Beyond Crowding Out

So, you may be asking, "How can I make the transition to healthier eating more enjoyable?" Let's work on that. Let me assure you, though, that the tried and tested concept of crowding out is a genius step in your change experience, no doubt. But let's take it to the next level. So, for all of you who want to carry on from here, I'd like to help you make the transition to healthier eating enjoyable and approachable. This really is the key to sustainable and long-term success with your eating choices.

> Okay, my friend, here are some simple ways to make that shift a more pleasurable experience:

 Focus on Flavour

Experiment with herbs and spices: These can transform simple dishes into culinary delights. Have a "Sri Lankan week" and look up different dishes to try.

Roast or grill your vegetables: This brings out their natural sweetness and adds a delightful caramelisation to the vegetables. Add goat cheese, herbs, or some Japanese mirin to create another layer of flavour.

Always use fresh ingredients: The vibrant flavours of fresh, seasonal produce are often much tastier, packed with more flavour, and so much better for you than processed foods.

🔗 Make It a Fun Process

Try new recipes: Don't get stuck in a rut! Explore cookbooks, websites, and food blogs for exciting and healthy recipes. Follow some home cooks on Instagram that you like, cook what they do, and congratulate yourself for trying something new.

Cook with others: Invite friends or family to cook healthy meals together. It's a great way to bond and learn new skills.

Visit farmers' markets: The lively atmosphere and beautiful produce can inspire you to try new things. I literally go each week for my fresh vegetables!

🔗 Embrace Variety

Eat the rainbow: Aim for a variety of colourful fruits and vegetables. Each colour group provides different nutrients.

Explore different styles of cooking: Trying foods from various cultures often means cooking in different ways – a wok, a hibachi grill, the barbecue, a smoking oven – and can introduce you to new, healthy, and delicious options from a different cooking platform or cooking utensil (eating with chopsticks, for example).

Mix and match textures: Combine crunchy, creamy, and chewy elements in your meals for a more interesting experience.

🔗 Mindful Indulgence

Allow yourself treats: Remember, denial creates desire. Deprivation can backfire. Enjoy small portions of your favourite treats occasionally, but be mindful of how often and how much. And tell yourself, that's okay!

Upgrade your treats: Instead of a regular chocolate bar, try dark-chocolate-covered fruit or a healthy homemade dessert. Make your own chocolate mousse with melted dark chocolate folded into natural yogurt with fresh raspberries. Yum.

Savour every bite: When you do have a treat, eat it slowly and mindfully, focusing on the flavours and textures. Take your time; don't rush!

 Small, Sustainable Changes

Like I said, start small: Don't try to overhaul your entire diet overnight. Begin with one or two changes each week.

Celebrate successes: Acknowledge and reward yourself for reaching small goals.

Be patient: It takes time for your taste buds to adjust to healthier foods.

 Practical Tips

Keep healthy snacks on hand: When you have healthy options readily available, you're less likely to reach for junk food.

Meal prep: Spend some time on the weekend preparing healthy meals or components of meals for the week.

Make it visually appealing: A beautifully presented meal can be more enjoyable.

 Remember

Listen to your body: It is the most communicative computer on the planet – pay attention to what makes you feel good.

Don't be afraid to experiment: Find what works for you. Practise new things.

Focus on the positive: Shift your mindset from "I can't eat this" to "I choose to eat this because it makes me feel good." And rest easy after that.

I don't expect you to remember all these things, but you can keep this book with you in the kitchen and use it as a reference guide if you like. By incorporating these tips, you can start to transform the journey – from the darker times of getting lost in automatic behaviours to healthier eating – into an enjoyable and fulfilling one.

> It's okay to feel whatever you're feeling right now. What you need to do is just believe in yourself.

Portion Control: A Strategy for Change

I have to admit, I'm a little passionate about the topic of portion control. You see, I need to have full disclosure here and tell you that I am what I would describe as a "voluptuous eater". When I see and taste something I love, it's all, "Yummy, I want more, I want, I want, I want, I want!" What can I say? I love my food.

As you already know, my Mum was a chef, caterer, and cooking schoolteacher, my younger self was always attached to a kitchen in some way – and I was raised on what some might call "gourmet food". My whole life has been about food, experiencing everything through flavours. Cooking relaxes me. A lot of the time, I will cook and create in silence; it is like a meditation. Creating new dishes is purely for pleasure – my own personal, dinner-for-one pleasure! I dive right in, and I adore it. And without sounding conceited, I think my food is pretty darn delicious! So, I've always struggled with portion control. I've never been a small eater.

So, motivated by my own challenges, I came up with some steps that helped me take back control of my eating habits. I found these to be super helpful and successful in terms of making a new habit. I want to share some ways to manage portion control because I know many of us eat to soothe. I want to offer strategies that can act as your "stop button".

In the past, my rationale was, "I eat because it makes me feel better." And it did, temporarily. But I realised I was eating like that to feed the sorrow of my inner child. I was feeding the one who suffered – the pain, the trauma, the hurt. I ate to soothe all of that. The gift of acceptance helped me understand this and come to terms and make peace with it (in Book Two: *A New Perspective*, I will share with you my inner child practices that aided this process). That's when portion control became a big part of my healing journey. Because when we eat too much, too fast, we don't give our brains the time to register with our bodies that we're full. So, in other words, I found a way to slow down that process and allow my brain to catch up and communicate with me.

This technique is all about practising breathwork while you are eating. It gives your brain that valuable time to connect with your body and receive the signals that tell you when you've truly had enough. You're cultivating a deeper awareness of the beautiful connection between your body and mind.

> **HOW PORTION CONTROL WORKS BETTER WHEN EATING IS THE ENTIRE ACTIVITY:** My friend, before you begin this exercise, I want to invite you to remember one simple but powerful thing: eating is the entire activity.

In our busy lives, it's so easy to eat while we're reading, scrolling, or watching TV. But when we're distracted, we lose the ability to truly listen to our body's signals of fullness.

For this exercise to be most effective, I want you to be fully present at the table. Put the devices away, turn off the television, and simply focus on the food in front of you. When you pay attention to the textures, the flavours, and how your body feels, you'll be amazed at how much easier it is to manage your portions. This is about reconnecting with yourself, one meal at a time.

I have detailed my process here to help you get to where I did – a place where I have control over my portions and still love my food. Seriously, this was another link in the chain towards my freedom, so that's why I am feeling privileged to share this with you.

> See how it works for you.
> See how it feels.
> Slow the whole process down,
> like I did, and give it a go.

Portion Control Exercise

Use this technique at home, at work, or adapt it for when you're dining out. The four basic principles can help you manage portion control in most situations.

1. Eat with consideration.

2. Inhale/exhale before each mouthful.

3. Chew your food thoroughly before swallowing.

4. Use the 4-7-8 Breathing technique to help your mind and body connect and assess your satiety before eating more.

Step 1: Prepare your food as you usually would.

Easy. Got it.

Step 2: Prepare a plate of your normal portion.

When you make your dinner, make it like you usually would, with your normal (generous) portion size, and put it on a serving dish, like one you would use for a shared meal with a loved one. Put it in the middle of the table, or in front of your place mat (where you would sit). On your place mat, you should have an empty dinner plate for you to serve up your (smaller) portion of the meal. Almost like being at a restaurant where they serve the food to you from a dish in the centre of the table. This little extra step works wonders for me!

Step 3: On a separate plate, start small.

Start by serving yourself a helping of your yummy food in a smaller portion. (Take a smaller amount of each item you have prepared on the main plate and add it to the empty plate in front of you.) This is how you rewire your brain and connect to knowing when you are really satisfied.

Step 4: Your first serving

Eat that amount of food you served up, but this time, slow down the pace at which you would normally eat. (This is called a mindful approach. This doesn't need to look like a cow slowly chewing her food; just don't scoff it, okay?) As you take each bite, notice the colours, the textures, and the aroma. Feel the food in your mouth. Savour the flavours as they unfold. Then happily swallow that mouthful. Then smile.

Take a breath in and exhale before the next mouthful. And repeat.

The idea is to chew each bite thoroughly.

Step 5: Do you want another?

When you've finished the food on your plate (the first portion you gave yourself from the larger serving), do the 4-7-8 Breathing exercise once.

Breathe in quietly through the nose for 4 seconds. Hold the breath for a count of 7 seconds. Exhale through the mouth for 8 seconds. As you exhale, imagine releasing any tension or stress you're holding onto.

Then ask yourself, "Am I full? Am I satisfied? Or do I want more food?"

Step 6: Listen to your body and respond

Wait and listen to what your body tells you. (Give this ten to fifteen seconds.) Tune into the subtle sensations. Is your stomach still growling? Do you feel a pleasant fullness, or an uncomfortable tightness?

If your body says it's still hungry, serve yourself more food. Repeat Steps 3 and 4.

Step 7: Listen to your body and respond

After your second helping, repeat Step 5. This time, do the 4-7-8 Breathing exercise twice. Then ask yourself again, "Am I full? Am I satisfied? Or do I want more food?"

Step 8: Listen to your body and respond

Wait and listen to your body. (Feel, observe, and listen!) If your body still feels hungry, serve yourself more food. Repeat Steps 3 and 4.

Step 9: Connect to what you are feeling

Be honest with yourself. Allow time for your body and mind to connect. Give yourself thirty seconds to a minute now.

If your body says it's still hungry, repeat the process again. And then truly listen to what your body is saying. If it tells you that you're satisfied, stop eating.

Even if there's food left in the bowls on the table, stop eating.

Step 10: Feel good about your control

Put any remaining food in Tupperware containers and store it for later.

Things to Be Aware of:

You might find that your mind wanders, and that's okay. Gently bring your attention back to your breath and your food.

I know it can feel awkward to breathe so deliberately while eating, especially in public (or if you live with other people). But trust me, with practice, it becomes second nature.

If you find that you are still hungry after waiting, and then asking your body, that is all good; I do not want you to see it as a failure. This is your body communicating what you need. Give yourself permission to finish all your food.

This isn't just about controlling portions; it's about reconnecting with your body's wisdom. It's about learning to trust the signals it's sending you.

As you practise this, you'll start to notice how your emotions and stress levels impact your hunger cues. This awareness is invaluable.

I had to practise this a lot! I found it easier to start in my own space at home. I felt silly trying this in public or even telling anyone I was doing it. But practising at home gave me the confidence to do it automatically and silently.

For Me …

When I did this exercise myself, I want to share with you this: My inner child wasn't screaming, "I want, I want, I want, I want, I want," anymore. The adult had stepped in and said, "Okay. I'm in control of this. I'm making the decisions here." My body told me what it needed. We were good. Everything was working, and all the endorphins in my brain made the right decision a pleasure for me, too.

For me, the pause between each breathing practice was essential. At first, I had to ask myself aloud if I wanted more. (Now, I can do this silently.) Listening to the response also took practice. At first, it felt like a flirtatious dance with my food. I still desired it, but did I need it? By the second check-in, I was unsure if I wanted more, but it wasn't an absolute craving. Then, after the third breathing routine, I'd wait for the answer. I can absolutely guarantee you, without a doubt, that every time I did this, by the third breathing practice, the message was clear: "I am done, finito. That's all good now. Enough." Then, I would feel grateful and thank myself. And that was it. I'd put what was left on my plate in a container and put it in the fridge. That felt really good. I was in control.

> "Health is a relationship between you and your body."
> – Terri Guillemets

There was this one time I was at a friend's gathering, and everyone was going for seconds and thirds. In the past, I would have jumped right in and followed suit, but I remembered this technique, caught myself, and smiled from within. I knew what to do. Now, if I get tempted by a trigger, or that internal dialogue from the past rears its head when I am in public, I can sit in a café or restaurant and go through this process without anyone noticing. Of course, there are times when I slip up. Triggers can happen that shake us all. I have learned it's okay to fall over. And the next day, I get right back on track.

Over to You

Imagine how empowered you'll feel when you're in control of your eating, rather than the other way around. Picture yourself feeling lighter, more energised, and at peace with food.

> This is a journey, not a race. Be patient with yourself, celebrate your progress, and don't give up if you have a setback. You've got this!

33.
Your Food Story

What Your Plate Reveals
A Daily Practice for Clarity Through Connection

Now I would like to share with you another tool I have personally used, and many others I have worked with have gotten great benefit from. Here is your next tool, the Food Diary.

Using this diary is a brilliant way to become aware of how your eating patterns are impacting your mind and body. It's a simple tool that can help you understand so much about yourself – and track, frankly, a lot of the stuff that gets missed or overlooked because of how busy life is, packed with so many digital distractions. That, and we have become a society where we normalise negative bodily reactions to foods and don't really pay attention to what it means to us.

For example, I have a friend who always said, "Oh well, just another case of the runs; I always get that after coffee in the morning!" Then she would go on to complain further, "Urgh, I am so sick of feeling tired every day." You see, my lovely friend never stopped to think about the ingredients in her morning coffee and why she was having this reaction. Milk, coffee, sugar. I recommended she remove the milk for two weeks to see what happened. Hey presto, no more "water bottom", and she started feeling more vibrant and awake in the morning. No more sluggish starts to her working day. Interesting, isn't it?

When I coach people about relationships, I always ask the question to help them gain clarity, "What is this relationship adding to your life, or is it taking something away?" I always delve deeper, asking the same question in different ways: "Does it contribute to your life in a good feeling way? Or is this relationship making you feel drained and worn out?" I then ask the same questions when we talk about their relationship with food and drink. "Is this food contributing to your life in a good way? Is it creating energy? Does it make you feel good? Or is it making you feel sluggish, tired, grumpy, moody? Does it hinder your sleep?" These questions are critical when you delve into the nitty-gritty of self-awareness about what you are feeding yourself. They are relevant to all that we keep close to ourselves as our life support systems.

So, these are the questions you can ask yourself, when feel like coming back to look closer at what's happening to you when you eat and drink.

So, What Is the Food Diary?

The main reason for keeping a food diary, my friend, is really to become more aware of your eating habits and how they truly impact your overall wellbeing. It's about understanding yourself better, from the inside out.

I've created a really simple format for you to use to start this process in the course of the next week. (There is a sample at the end of this section.)

This is about you tracking what you're eating and drinking, from when you wake up until you go to bed. You'll be tracking the sensory feeling and experience you're having after you've eaten or drunk something. The more you capture, the more you'll learn. The more you do it, the better off you are. Do this for just two weeks and be amazed by what you learn about yourself.

When you start this journey, it can be super helpful to keep your diary – whether it's a notebook or an app – right there in your kitchen. Having it handy makes it so much easier to use! You could give it a whirl for a couple of days and see what you discover. Or maybe you're ready to dive in for two weeks and really feel the benefits. What do you think would work best for you?

And you know what? You can always come back to it later, maybe in a few months, if something throws you off track. It's like saying to yourself, "Okay, it's time to check in with myself again." Use this as your way to understand what's going on. Because when you can see it, you give it form – you take away that scary, out-of-control feeling and step back into the driver's seat. You get to be in control, instead of it controlling you.

All this effort you're making? It's really helping you make more informed choices, break free from old habits, and move towards a healthier, more balanced lifestyle. It's about creating that real, meaningful connection to what you put in your body and how it makes you feel – whether it's serving you well or maybe not so much.

How to Use the Diary

To truly get the most out of your food diary, I've put together some helpful suggestions to keep you on track. These are practical tips to make your food journalling really work for you:

 1. Be Consistent

Daily Tracking: The key here is consistency. Try to record everything you eat and drink each day, without skipping a beat.

Set a Routine: Choose a time of day to update your diary, like after each meal or at the end of the day. Making it part of your routine makes it so much easier to stick with.

 2. Be Honest and Detailed

Record Everything: Yes, everything! No matter how small. That includes snacks, drinks, sauces, condiments, and even "just a little taste". (You're only cheating yourself if you leave something out!)

Portion Sizes: Be as accurate as you can be. Use measuring cups, spoons, or a food scale if that helps. If you're eating out, just do your best to estimate.

Ingredients: List all the ingredients, especially if you're tracking specific nutrients or have food sensitivities.

Cooking Methods: This isn't always needed, but it can give you some great insights. Frying versus baking, for example, can make a difference. So, jot down how the food was prepared – baked, fried, grilled – as that can affect things.

 ### 3. Note Your Moods and Feelings

Emotional Eating: Write down how you felt before, during, and after eating. This can really help you see those emotional triggers.

Physical Sensations: Note any physical feelings or reactions after eating, like bloating, fatigue, or changes in energy.

Sleep: How are you sleeping? Are you waking up during the night?

Mental State: Jot down your mental state – stressed, bored, lonely, tired, happy, sad, moody, full of beans?

 ### 4. Be Specific About Timing

Time of Day: Record when you eat each meal and snack. This can help you find patterns in your eating and energy levels.

Consistency: Try to eat around the same time each day if you can.

 ### 5. Choose a Method That Works for You

Paper Diary: Use your journal, keep a notebook, or create a special homemade food diary.

Keep It Handy: Have your diary within reach, so you can jot things down right after you eat.

6. Don't Judge Yourself

Observation, Not Judgement: This is about understanding, not criticising. Focus on seeing patterns, not judging your choices.

No Perfection: It's okay to have an "off" day. Just keep tracking and learn from it.

7. Review Regularly

Weekly Review: Take some time each week to look back at your diary. Spot those patterns, triggers, and areas where you could make changes.

Reflect on Progress: Celebrate your wins! Acknowledge the positive changes you're making.

Adjust as Needed: Use what you learn to adjust your eating habits and make healthier choices.

8. Use It as a Tool, Not a Punishment

Positive Approach: See this as a helpful guide, not a way to punish yourself.

Focus on Learning: Focus on what you're learning about yourself, rather than feeling guilty or ashamed.

9. Be Patient

Long-Term Perspective: Building new habits takes time. Be kind to yourself and trust the journey.

Small Steps: Focus on small, sustainable changes, not trying to do everything at once.

By using these tips, your food diary can become a powerful tool for improving your relationship with food and your overall wellbeing.

Please, Do This for Two Weeks

When you have finished the two weeks, you'll have a more global view of what's happening. You can see your patterns and look at how your feelings and moods were related to particular foods or drinking episodes. You can map out how your body responded to the food you gave it.

It's also for you to track how your mind is feeling and functioning. Are you getting brain fog? Is your memory poor? Are you feeling confused? Are you feeling moody? Are you feeling like things are going a little bit off course emotionally?

My friend, you will start to see more about your relationship with food and drink than you ever anticipated. This ultimately will enable you to ask more essential questions like "What do I want to hold on to?" and "What is creating a new desire for change?"

I have a friend who always complained about having a runny tummy. She's an A blood type. After the third complaint, I worked out that there was a pattern to when she said this. I asked her what she ate the night before, and it was a creamy pasta carbonara. It was her favourite dish after a bad day at work. She was blind to the reason for what came next. She had never connected the two things before. She had carried on taking pills, suffering poor sleep, and putting up with her discomfort because of her need to soothe the bad day. Now, after we had an enlightened discussion about what was happening, she has made some changes. She now makes pasta with zucchini, peas, and Parmigiano Reggiano. That gives her a yummy fix but with no more uncomfortable and harmful aftermath.

As you do this exercise, pay attention to how you feel when you wake up. Take a look at the questions at the start of your diary: Did you wake at two o'clock in the morning after you'd eaten something sugary? Or perhaps you were up at three o'clock after you'd had red wine?

Even these small insights can help you make simple changes that improve how you feel.

> All of these things are there for you to track how your body responds. Write it all down and then look at which foods are associated with what responses, to help you gain more clarity.

To Make This Easier for Yourself

I would recommend keeping your food diary in your kitchen, committing to this for the week, and really, really using this as a time to appreciate, learn, and observe the food and drink that you're choosing.

When you're really honest with yourself about this type of stuff, when you write it down, it's just this beautiful way for you to clearly see what it is that you're doing in your relationship with food and drink and how it's showing up for you. When it's good, notice what you were doing at the time, what you were consuming, and how much. When it wasn't so good, also notice what you were doing at the time, what you were consuming, and how much.

Also, note your style of eating. Are you eating fast, shoving food in your mouth like there's no tomorrow? Are you taking time to chew thoroughly? Are you pushing food around on your plate and fighting against eating? What are you choosing to eat first – the veggies, the meats, the salad?

When you write this stuff down, and you see it over a couple of weeks, you may find that you want to keep doing it for longer. Your body is the most communicative being

> **"People will do anything, no matter how absurd, in order to avoid facing their own souls. One does not become enlightened by imagining figures of light, but by making the darkness conscious."**
> – Carl Jung

on this planet. We have just become so damn good at ignoring it. And let's face it, who likes to be ignored, right?

Really, it's up to you. When you get it out, and you put it on paper, and you speak the words out loud, you soon find out what your truth is. This is you being 100% honest. It's your relationship that's happening in the here and now. When you see it, and you know it, and you look at it like this, it becomes undeniable. It's like the bad boyfriend who is cheating on you. You were ignoring the signs before, but now that you know, you can't sign up for this rubbish behaviour anymore.

> Give yourself the gift of self-awareness. Commit to it for a while. Bring it into your life. See how it feels. This is a strategy for you, and it helps you decide what's in and what's out.
>
> See how you do. It's a fascinating exercise.

Sample Food Diary

Day 1
Morning

Date: _____
Time: _____

How did I wake up feeling today? (e.g., rested, groggy, energised, stiff)
_____
_____
_____
_____

Sleep quality last night: (e.g., deep, light, interrupted, time taken to fall asleep)
_____
_____
_____
_____

Food and drink: (Be specific about what and how much)
_____
_____
_____
_____

How did my body feel *immediately* after? (e.g., comfortable, energised, heavy, bloated, thirsty, heart racing)
_____
_____
_____
_____

My energy level (1–5) *about 30 minutes after eating/drinking*:
☐ 1 ☐ 2 ☐ 3 ☐ 4 ☐ 5

My mood *about 30 minutes after eating/drinking*: (e.g., content, focused, irritable, sluggish)

_____
_____
_____
_____

Mid-morning snack (if applicable)   Time: _____

Food and drink:

_____
_____
_____
_____

How did my body feel *immediately* after?

_____
_____
_____
_____

My energy level (1–5): ☐ 1 ☐ 2 ☐ 3 ☐ 4 ☐ 5

My mood:

_____
_____
_____
_____

Lunch   Time: _____

Food and drink:

_____
_____
_____
_____

How did my body feel *immediately* after?

_____
_____
_____

My energy level (1–5): ☐ 1 ☐ 2 ☐ 3 ☐ 4 ☐ 5

My mood:

_____
_____
_____

Afternoon Snack (if applicable)   Time: _____

Food and drink:

_____
_____
_____

How did my body feel *immediately* after?

_____
_____
_____

My energy level (1–5): ☐ 1 ☐ 2 ☐ 3 ☐ 4 ☐ 5

My mood:

_____
_____
_____

Dinner

Time: _____

Food and drink:

_____
_____
_____
_____

How did my body feel *immediately* after?

_____
_____
_____
_____

My energy level (1–5): ☐ 1 ☐ 2 ☐ 3 ☐ 4 ☐ 5

My mood:

_____
_____
_____
_____

Throughout the day

Drinks – include timing if relevant:

_____
_____
_____
_____

Did I notice any specific times I felt particularly thirsty or had cravings?

_____
_____
_____
_____

Any other notes or observations for today: (e.g., digestive issues, headaches, skin changes, emotional eating, social context of eating):

___

NOTE: You can either use the diary available on my website or simply use your own journal or notebook to copy the prompts I've shared here. Whatever works best for you is okay!

I recommend you continue for a second week to really see what patterns are happening. There is also a helpful reflection exercise for you to do after your seven days of observation. This is designed to help you create a deep connection to how your food and drink choices impact your overall health and vitality.

Where to Find the Diary: You can download the food diary from the Resources page on my website at **www.fleurelizabeth.com**.

• • •

After Your Seven Days of Observation

Now, when you have completed your seven days of journalling, I'd like you to connect with what you've learned about yourself. This is how you really understand what's working for you and what's not. This is really powerful information, and incredibly insightful. So, when you're all done with seven days of observation, it's time for thoughtful reflection:

Body Signals: What physical sensations did you notice after eating certain foods? Did any patterns emerge? What were your body's clear messages to you?

Energy Fluctuations: Did specific meals or snacks consistently give you energy or make you feel drained? Were there noticeable energy highs and lows?

Mood Connections: Did you see any links between what you ate and your mood? Were there comfort foods that didn't actually make you feel better in the long run?

Sleep Impact: How was your sleep quality this week? Did your evening food and drink choices seem to affect your sleep or how you felt when you woke up?

Cravings and Triggers: Did you have any recurring cravings? What do you think might have triggered them? (Stress, boredom, time of day, etc.)

Overall Wellbeing: Considering your body's responses, energy levels, mood, and sleep, what insights did you gain about how your current eating habits are affecting **your overall wellbeing?**

Small Steps Forward: Based on what you've noticed, what two to three small, specific changes could you make this week to better support your overall health? What feels truly doable for you?

"The Why": Why Bother Doing This?

Okay, okay, I get it. Keeping a food diary might seem tedious at first, but it really does offer so many benefits, my friend! It can truly transform your relationship with food and your wellbeing because it's giving you complete clarity on what's happening to you after you eat each day. And, really, what is two weeks in your whole life? Not very much, when there is a lifetime ahead of benefits for you, hey? Doesn't seem like much of a sacrifice, when you look at it that way.

To make it even more certain for you, here are some key advantages:

> **"To eat is a necessity, but to eat intelligently is an art."**
> — La Rochefoucauld

1. **Increased Self-Awareness**

   Identifying Patterns: You'll start to see patterns in your eating. Maybe you overeat when stressed, or certain foods affect your mood.

   Understanding Triggers: You can pinpoint those triggers – emotional, environmental, social – that make you eat even when you're not hungry.

   Connecting Food and Feelings: You'll see the connection between what you eat and how you feel, both physically and emotionally.

2. **Improved Portion Control**

   Visualising Intake: Writing things down makes you aware of portion sizes, which helps with control.

   Accountability: Knowing you have to record it can stop you from mindlessly grabbing extra.

3. **Enhanced Nutritional Awareness**

   Tracking Nutrients: You can track things like protein, fibre, and fats. Google is your friend if you're not sure about nutrient content.

Evaluating Diet Quality: You can see what might be missing and where you can improve, like adding more fruits and veggies.

4. Better Weight Management

Monitoring Progress: It helps you track progress towards your goals. While it's not just about weight loss, this is often a happy side effect of becoming more aware.

Identifying Obstacles: You'll spot the things that get in your way, like stress, late-night snacking, or sugary drinks.

Losing Weight When You're Not on a Diet: Honestly, one of the coolest things about keeping a food diary is that it gently nudges you towards making changes – no strict dieting required! When you start noticing and removing those foods that make you feel sluggish, puffy, or bloated, your body naturally responds. You might see that puffiness go down, the bloating disappear, and even that water retention fade away. Plus, you'll be helping your body lower its cortisol levels – that's the stress hormone – and that, in turn, can help you shed some kilos without having to do any of that awful, restrictive dieting. It's like your body starts to find its own natural balance again, and the weight loss? Well, that just becomes a lovely side effect.

5. Have Better Emotional Regulation

Track Your Moods: Record how you feel before, during, and after eating to identify your emotional connections to food.

Spot the Patterns: Regularly reviewing your diary reveals patterns between emotions and food choices.

Gain Mindful Control: Awareness of these triggers allows you to develop healthier coping strategies.

Connecting the Dots: Once you identify those patterns, you can start to connect the dots between your emotions and your eating habits. This awareness is the first step in making positive changes. By understanding your emotional triggers, you can begin to develop healthier coping mechanisms for dealing with those emotions, rather than turning to food.

NOTE: This is what Book Two: *A New Perspective* is centred around – helping you take more control over your triggers, behaviours, and consequences. So, by doing this work now, you are giving yourself a head start for the next phase of your evolution!

34.
Drink: The Silent Destroyer

Drinking Seems Fun, But …
It's Your Social Highway to Nowhere Good

Shall we agree that alcohol is a widely used "numbing agent" when people get stressed, angry, sad, happy, pushed around, or are struggling with anxiety or depression? It's that liquid gold that takes the pain away – until the next day, that is. It's one thing to say this is the go-to antidote for triggers and emotional storms, but it's another to recognise that this damn thing is ingrained in us from birth. Our parents did it, our grandparents did it; it's a social norm, the lubricant for most relationships coming together and sharing each other's company – which rarely happens without the chink of a glass, now, does it? For me personally, it took over my life, and then one day, when I decided to end my dependent relationship with the bottle, I lost the keys to the club. I wasn't invited anywhere, and all of a sudden, my world became very different. More on that later.

We Aussies love to get stuck into our booze on any occasion, really, as do the Brits and, in my experience, so too the Americans. The French sip, savour, and classically match wine to enhance a gourmand experience. The Italians do aperitivo, a drink after work or at the end of the day, to pair with flavourful creations. While the Italians are known for their beautiful wines, they certainly don't guzzle them like we Aussies do. I remember my wine professor during my master's study in Florence. He held up a bottle of Sangiovese Grosso and said to the class, "This bottle is too good to open because my wife and I wouldn't finish it." I remember thinking, "Wow, I could easily finish that myself!"

In my generation, many of us started drinking alcohol quite young, often influenced by peer pressure or wanting to fit in. (Even talking to my fourteen-year-old godson, I see how drinking has become normalised among young people today.) My parents enjoyed their drinks, and I was allowed to have some alcohol from the age of fourteen. I'd join my mother for a game of gin rummy, and she'd share her manipulative stories about my father and caution me about trusting men.

Drinking is so intertwined with how we socialise. It's there at celebrations, or sometimes it's just seen as a way to relax. Yes, it can feel like a reward after a hard day or a temporary escape. That initial "high" can make you forget your troubles for a bit. But that high is often followed by a sense of numbness, brain fog, confusion, and disorientation. It doesn't solve anything; it often just creates new problems.

Regular drinking can also put you on a path towards serious health issues. We all know alcohol is a toxin, yet so many of us keep drinking. Social influences play a big role. The connection between alcohol, friends, and family has made drinking, even heavy drinking, seem normal. It can be hard to say "no" because we don't want to feel left out or rejected by our social group.

> **"When you quit drinking, you stop waiting."**
> – Caroline Knapp,
> *Drinking: A Love Story*

We see drinking on TV and in movies all the time. Characters clink glasses of wine or beer to celebrate. It's portrayed as a sign of success, happiness, enjoyment, even being cool and attractive. This creates a positive impression of alcohol in our minds and further normalises it. Many people find it hard to admit that drinking isn't working for them. They ignore the potential harm, wanting to appear "normal" and be accepted. I even have friends who've survived cancer and still drink, despite it being a known contributing factor. (Clinicians now often refer to cancer as a "lifestyle disease".)

Alcohol can lower your inhibitions and lead to poor decisions, especially about your lifestyle and diet. It can cloud your judgement, making you reach for sugary foods that trigger inflammation. These choices often lack the nutrients your body needs to stay healthy.

Drinking is a social norm, but there are many myths about it that keep us from making healthier choices. Years ago, we heard that small amounts of wine could be good for the heart. Suddenly, everyone was saying, "But wine is good for you; let's drink all the wine!" The cardio-protective properties of wine come from polyphenols, antioxidants that help neutralise free radicals in your body. These free radicals can cause damage, and polyphenols can help reduce that. It sounds impressive, right? All those big words make it seem like drinking wine is a healthy choice.

> But here's the catch: It's not that simple. It's easy to be misled into thinking, "The more I drink, the better!" But that's not true. We need to consider the sugar. One large glass of red wine is roughly equal to three Tim Tam biscuits, for my Aussie friends. (A Tim Tam biscuit is the rough equivalent of an Oreo cookie in the USA. In the UK, it is the same as a Penguin biscuit.)
>
> **So, three glasses a night? That's like eating nine Tim Tams! That's a LOT of sugar.**
>
> One Tim Tam has roughly 8-9 grams of sugar = +/- 2 teaspoons of sugar. Three Tim Tams have 25-27 grams of sugar = +/- 7 teaspoons of sugar. Nine Tim Tams have 81 grams of sugar = +/- 20 teaspoons of sugar.
>
> **Imagine eating 20 teaspoons of sugar with dinner!**
>
> That level of sugar can really outweigh any benefits from the polyphenols. Drinking more than one glass of wine in a sitting can be risky for your health.
>
> In my days of chronic hip pain (before my hip replacement), I could easily drink a whole bottle of red wine in an evening. That's like eating seven Tim Tams a night. If I drank like that five nights a week, that's thirty-five Tim Tams. In a year, that's 1820 Tim Tams. Over 2.5 years, that's 4550 Tim Tams contributing to my poor health! (No wonder I was struggling and carrying extra weight.)

Speaking of weight gain, too much alcohol can make your liver less efficient at processing fats. This can lead to fat buildup, especially around the abdomen. It's why regular drinkers often develop that "muffin top" look after forty. This can also lead to other health problems.

Alcohol Is a Drug

Alcohol is linked to chronic health issues. It can cause poisoning and contribute to inflammation or even death.

- It can affect your immune system.
- It can slow down healing.
- It can speed up heart, liver, and digestive problems.
- It can cause brain damage and affect memory and emotions.
- It can worsen arthritis.
- It can contribute to type 2 diabetes and increase the risk of stroke and heart attack.

It's so important not to be fooled into thinking drinking alcohol is always healthy. We need to understand the fine print and remember that any potential benefits are only associated with small amounts.

Trust me, poor health can be a lonely and dark place. Alcohol can trap you inside your head, playing on your fears and anxieties. It can feel like chains holding you back. This can lead to other unhealthy habits, like eating junk food, to distract from the pain. But those habits lead to more weight gain, making things worse.

How does all of this sound to you so far?

Giving Up Versus Progressive Change
True Progress Is Found in Gentle Steps

Okay, so you might be thinking about giving up alcohol, or maybe you've recently tried and then had another drink? Or perhaps you've made those big declarations like, "I will never drink again." The thing is, declaring total abstinence can sometimes create an unrealistic expectation of perfection.

Telling everyone you're giving up completely can actually put more pressure on you and leave no room for the inevitable challenges. The stricter the "I must be perfect" rule, the more likely you are to feel like you can't have a bad day, struggle, or "fall off the wagon" – which, let's face it, is part of the journey for many people. We often end up creating the very thing we're trying to avoid. Ironically, the more you restrict yourself with a rule of absolute abstinence, the harder it becomes to be honest if you do slip up. In your mind, you've failed. That need to be in control and the pressure to be perfect creates so much internal conflict, and then comes the shame.

We often pretend everything is perfect because we don't want to admit to slipping up or going back on our word. "No one needs to know. I don't need to face this." Relapse can bring on guilt and shame, but that's really just your perception. A relapse is simply a mistake, and it doesn't have to be something you carry around like a heavy weight. These are two very different things – making a mistake and carrying around shame. We often make those big commitments of abstinence because we're already carrying shame about drinking. But is that realistic? And then, of course, we feel guilt and shame over a relapse, which we often see as a total failure. But, again, that's just not true.

> The word "relapse" carries so much guilt with it. In your mind, it wipes out all the progress you've made because you think not relapsing means perfection, and relapsing means complete disaster.

When you say you want to give something up completely, when you say you're going to stop drinking and never touch it again, that's a lot of pressure. We often make those grand promises about giving up everything because we feel shame and embarrassment.

Your drinking might feel out of control, and maybe you've made some choices you regret. You might be carrying shame as a result of something that happened when you were drinking. Then, when you do have a drink, you'll probably feel like that relapse is a million miles away from the commitment you made to yourself.

> Here's the thing: We humans really need to get better at celebrating our progress, no matter how small. If you didn't drink for a couple of days, and you used to drink every day, that's progress! If you went a week without drinking, and you used to drink a lot, that's huge progress! So, if you do have a drink, or maybe a "cheeky" one at home, that's understandable. Let's normalise that. It's okay to make a mistake. If you've decided that reducing your drinking is what you want, need, and desire, then make that your next small step forward.

The most important commitment is the one you make to yourself and your own journey of change. If you need help with this, reach out and ask for it. There are many excellent resources available to you. It's important to connect with the people around you – that's where you can find acceptance, feel loved, and experience a different reality. You're not alone. People can and will support you through this.

Remember, taking small steps towards living by your values is key. That's how you make lasting progress. Normalise those times when you get triggered and have a drink. And be sure to celebrate every single step of progress you make along the way.

> **"A man who wants to lead the orchestra must turn his back on the crowd."**
> – Max Lucado

The Number of Drinks a Week

Okay, why would you change this habit? If you enjoy a drink, maybe even a few more than you'd like to admit sometimes, have you ever really stopped to ask yourself: "What are the long-term costs if I keep going like this?"

When you start thinking about changing your drinking habits, really understanding what alcohol is actually doing inside your body is such a powerful first step. When you truly grasp the cost to your health, you might just find a deeper, more genuine desire to make some real changes.

Remember when we talked about needing that burning desire to change? Having a strong reason why you want to change, and truly believing that you can change? Those are the key ingredients, right?

So, when you're looking at shifting your drinking habits, it's so important to cement that desire. Because this isn't about making empty promises or trying to please other people. This is about the cost to you – your health, your wellbeing – if you don't make a change. Getting really clear on what drinking is doing to your body and your health is what creates that real, personal motivation and desire for change that's specific to you. Clarity is your friend, remember?

Three Drinks a Week

Hmm, I know this sounds really unfun, but can you hear me when I tell you that alcohol is not your friend? It's a messy, silent destroyer of your peace, happiness, and Future Self.

Okay, let's talk about what just three little drinks a week (not a day!) can do to your mind and body. Three glasses of wine might not seem like much. But you've probably normalised that icky feeling of a hangover, right? So, you've kind of brushed over what feeling unwell actually means to your body. There's so much that happens inside us, the damage that alcohol does to our internal organs, that we just don't see. We just don't really appreciate what this fun-loving, temporary-high-inducing, toxic substance is doing to us. And then, sometimes, we find out – when it's too late.

It's really important to understand that even moderate alcohol consumption carries risks, and those risks increase with heavier drinking. Here's a breakdown of how drinking more than three drinks a week can affect your health:

General Impacts: Increased Risk of Chronic Diseases

Alcohol is a known carcinogen, which means it can cause cancer. It raises the risk of various cancers, including mouth, throat, liver, breast, and colon.

It disrupts blood sugar regulation, which increases the risk of type 2 diabetes.

It contributes to heart disease by damaging the heart muscle and increasing blood pressure.

Inflammation: Alcohol promotes inflammation throughout the whole body. Chronic inflammation is linked to a whole range of health problems, including heart disease, arthritis, and some cancers.

Specific Bodily Impacts

Stomach: Alcohol irritates the stomach lining, leading to gastritis (inflammation of the stomach lining), ulcers, and heartburn.

It can interfere with the health of your microbiome, which impacts nutrient absorption.

Liver: The liver is responsible for processing alcohol. Regular alcohol consumption can overwhelm the liver, leading to fatty liver disease, alcoholic hepatitis (inflammation of the liver), and cirrhosis (scarring of the liver).

Kidneys: Alcohol can impair kidney function by affecting their ability to filter waste.

It can also lead to dehydration, which puts extra strain on the kidneys.

Hormones: Alcohol disrupts hormone balance. In women, it can affect estrogen levels, increasing the risk of breast cancer.

In men, it can lower testosterone levels, leading to sexual dysfunction.

Brain: Alcohol impairs brain function, affecting memory, concentration, and coordination.

Long-term regular drinking can lead to brain damage and increase the risk of dementia.

It can also exacerbate short-term memory loss and mental health conditions, like depression and anxiety.

🔍 **Heart:** Alcohol raises blood pressure and can damage the heart muscle, increasing the risk of heart disease, stroke, and arrhythmias (irregular heartbeats).

🔍 **Blood Pressure:** Alcohol consumption is directly related to increases in blood pressure. Regularly drinking too much can lead to chronic hypertension.

Key Considerations

To have optimal health, the data now suggests that no drinking is what experts recommend – however, "no more than three drinks a week" is a more widespread guideline. Individual risk varies based on factors like age, sex, genetics, and overall health.

- Binge drinking (consuming a large amount of alcohol in a short period of time) is particularly harmful.
- The cumulative effect of regular alcohol consumption over time significantly increases health risks.
- While moderate alcohol consumption is sometimes portrayed as harmless, or even beneficial, the medical consensus is that alcohol consumption has many negative health effects. Drinking more than three drinks a week greatly increases the risk of many chronic diseases and organ damage. It's always best to consult with your doctor about your alcohol consumption and any health concerns.

Do you see what I am getting at here?

The Killer of Your Emotional Regulation

But wait, there's more. If you are drinking more than three drinks a week, it's not just your physical health that gets impacted; your ability to emotionally regulate yourself also becomes impaired. Make no mistake, alcohol significantly impacts emotional regulation, and consuming more than three drinks a week can exacerbate these effects. Here's a breakdown.

How Alcohol Disrupts Emotional Regulation

Impaired Brain Function: Alcohol affects the brain regions responsible for emotional control, particularly the prefrontal cortex. This area is crucial for decision-making, judgement, and regulating emotional responses.

As a result, individuals may experience increased impulsivity, making it harder to manage emotions like anger, sadness, or anxiety.

Disrupted Neurotransmitter Balance: Alcohol alters the balance of neurotransmitters like serotonin and dopamine, which play a vital role in mood regulation.

While alcohol may initially provide a temporary sense of euphoria, it can lead to long-term imbalances that contribute to mood swings, irritability, and increased susceptibility to negative emotions.

Heightened Emotional Reactivity: Alcohol can amplify existing emotional states. If someone is already feeling stressed or anxious, alcohol can intensify those feelings.

It can also lower inhibitions, making individuals more likely to react impulsively to emotional triggers.

Increased Anxiety and Depression: While some people may use alcohol to cope with anxiety or depression, it often worsens these conditions over time.

Alcohol can disrupt sleep patterns, which further contributes to mood disturbances.

Alcohol can create a cycle of dependency, where someone drinks to try to regulate negative emotions, but the drinking itself makes the negative emotions worse.

🔍 **Reduced Ability to Cope:** Regular alcohol consumption can diminish a person's ability to develop and utilise healthy coping mechanisms. This means that when faced with emotional challenges, they are more likely to turn to alcohol, creating a negative cycle.

So, when you get triggered by an event, and your response is to throw your arms up and say, "Stuff it; I'm having a drink, or three," the consequences of those choices, stemming from poor emotional regulation, are:

- Increased conflict in relationships.
- Difficulty managing stress.
- Increased risk of anxiety and depression.
- Impulsive and potentially harmful behaviours.

> **"Since we cannot change reality, let us change the eyes that see reality."**
> – Nikos Kazantzakis

It seems like a lot to take in, doesn't it? Just three little drinks can do all that. But this isn't made up, or a story I'm spinning. These are all medical, science-based facts. So, while those three little drinks might seem like a temporary solution for managing emotions (by numbing them and pushing them away), it ultimately undermines the ability to regulate emotions effectively.

The next time you fancy a drink, grab a warm non-alcoholic drink or a cool soda water with some frozen raspberries. Then, have a read of the next section, which provides you with some fascinating information and helps you get prepared for taking some small steps of change within your relationship with drink.

> No matter how crap you feel, remember, every little step is progress, my friend. You can do this!

35. Staying On Course

Why Motivation Can Be Tricky
Reminding Yourself Always ... That's Okay!

It's totally normal to need a little help with motivation when you're thinking about changing your drinking habits. Seriously, it's not just you! There are some real reasons why this can be tough.

🔍 **Dopamine and that Pleasure Feeling:** You know that good feeling you get when you have a drink? That's dopamine, a chemical in your brain that makes you feel happy and rewarded. Alcohol triggers it, and that's why it can feel so appealing. But, over time, your brain can start to rely on that feeling, which makes it harder to get motivated by other things.

🔍 **Brain Chemistry Changes:** When you drink regularly, it can actually change how your brain works. This can affect your mood, your decisions, and even your impulses. All of that can make it harder to stay motivated and say no to those cravings.

🔍 **Withdrawal Symptoms (Ugh, Right?):** If you try to cut back or stop drinking, you might get those yucky withdrawal symptoms – anxiety, irritability, trouble sleeping ... the list goes on. It's no wonder it's hard to stay motivated when you're feeling that way, and it's so easy to just want to drink to make it stop.

Alcohol as a Coping Tool: A lot of us use alcohol to deal with stress, anxiety, or other tough emotions. It can feel like you need it to feel okay. Breaking that emotional connection takes a lot of motivation and support.

Fear of Change (the Big One): Let's be real, change can be scary! Even good change. You might worry about social situations without alcohol, or maybe you're afraid of facing some things you've been avoiding. That fear can really mess with your motivation.

Staying Motivated – Your Fuel for Change (Let's Keep that Fire Going!): It's totally okay if your motivation dips sometimes. Life happens, right? Some days, sticking to your goals is just going to be harder. But don't worry; here are some ways to keep that fire lit:

Remember Your "Why"

You may already be familiar with some of these strategies – and that's a great thing! Consider this a refresher and a way to check in with yourself as you commence changing your drinking habits. These simple ideas will help affirm your choices and set you up for success.

Reconnect: Go back to those reasons you wanted to make a change in the first place. Write them down, stick them where you can see them, or make a vision board. Reminding yourself of the bigger picture helps you stay focused.

Focus on the Good Stuff: Think about how much better you feel physically and mentally. Celebrate the little wins – better relationships, more energy, more productive at work, and feeling good overall.

- **Connect with Your Values:** Link your goals to what's important to you. If family is your priority, remind yourself that changing your drinking habits will make you a better parent, partner, or family member.

Track Your Progress

- **Celebrate Milestones:** Every week, every month, every milestone – mark it! Seeing how far you've come is a huge motivator. Even the small victories count!

- **Journalling:** Jot down your journey. Write about your challenges, your successes, and how you're feeling. Looking back can really boost your spirits.

- **Reward Yourself:** Celebrate with little non-alcoholic treats or activities you love. It reinforces the good stuff and keeps you going.

Find an Accountability Partner

- **Team Up:** Connect with a friend, a family member, or a support group. Having someone to share this with makes a big difference.

- **Check In:** Schedule regular check-ins to talk about your progress, any challenges, and celebrate those wins together.

Re-evaluate and Adjust

- **Be Flexible:** If something's not working, change it up! Don't be afraid to try new things.

- **Set New Goals:** As you reach your initial goals, set new ones. Keep challenging yourself and keep that momentum going.

Remember the Long-Term Benefits

🔗 **Health is Wealth:** Think about the long-term health benefits. You're lowering your risk of diseases, improving your mental health, and adding to your life.

🔗 **Better Life Quality:** Imagine the positive impact on your relationships, your career, and your overall happiness. A healthier you leads to a happier, more fulfilling life.

Staying motivated is all about remembering why you started, celebrating your progress (big and small!), building a support system, and being kind to yourself.

> Think of self-compassion as a precious gift, and self-acceptance as the invaluable treasure. Self-empathy is the gold that gets you through your stumbles, and your self-awareness is the greatest prize of all. Regardless of where this journey takes you, I'm right here with you.

36. My Trauma Experience

Fun Times, Shameful Secrets
How I Found Peace Behind the Bottle

Wow, looking back, I'm truly grateful for the turning point I reached with my drinking. Changing that relationship has brought so much peace into my life. Now, I'm not going to pretend it was a walk in the park. It meant shaking things up, especially my social life, and saying goodbye to some old friends. But honestly? What came after was extraordinary. It was like shedding a skin, and I finally got to connect with me – the woman, the heart, the soul that had been hiding behind the bottle all along. Today, my life is less chaotic, more peaceful, and so much more balanced, and I absolutely love the woman I've become.

It all really started to shift when I had my hip replacement in August 2020. As part of my recovery and knowing what I know as a health coach about how inflammatory alcohol is, I decided to stop drinking. Though, I have to be honest, for the two years I was in chronic pain, on crutches for nine months, barely able to walk due to the intense pinching in my hip, I wasn't really caring about the inflammation factor! I was hurting so much, and alcohol was my way of numbing that pain.

And, truthfully, I'd been using alcohol to numb my pain for all of my adult life. It was how I fuelled this "Fleur Jazz Hands" persona I'd created – this untouchable, awesome character. I used alcohol to power her relentless energy and zest for ... well, maybe chaos. I had a whole world of friends who loved to drink and party, and I became this kind of pied piper, creating fun (and maybe trouble) so everyone could keep the drinks flowing.

I used to beat myself up for that. Then, when I stopped drinking, I realised something big. Those same friends who blamed me for their hangovers? They were still drinking just as much! They didn't need me to be the ringleader. That was a huge "aha" moment. My whole social circle revolved around alcohol, and everyone was making their own choices. Finally, with the perspective of being sober, I realised it wasn't my responsibility to carry that burden.

In that world, binge drinking was just normal. I could hide in plain sight. It was fine to joke about "drinking all the wine" the night before. Everyone would just laugh, and that was that. No one asked if I was okay, or if something deeper was going on that made me want to drown myself in alcohol. The truth was, I was often emotionally distraught about something that had triggered me, but no one knew.

It's kind of scary to think back now, but I could hide the fact that I'd be out until 3 or 4 a.m., then come home and open another bottle, chain-smoke cigarettes, and get lost in these fantasies in my head. I lived in this little glass bubble where everything seemed fabulous, happy, and full of "warm and fuzzy love". There was "success", and all these elaborate scenarios I'd dream up while listening to movie instrumental songs on repeat, fuelled by more wine and cigarettes. I was a master at distracting myself from the deep trauma and turmoil I was holding inside.

Needless to say, with all that "magic", I could do anything with liquor running through my veins. I engaged in incredibly risky behaviour. I got myself into some tough spots, both sexually and physically. I carried a lot of shame about some of those times for a long while after I got sober. Then, I realised: Every single mistake I'd ever made involved alcohol. Every. Single. One. Every major issue, every life blow-up – alcohol was right there in the middle. And, boy, have I had a few of those.

Every time I hit a rough patch, alcohol was involved. But at the time, I didn't think I had a problem. I thought it was all just ... fabulous. I'd justify blacking out. I'd explain away my ridiculous behaviour, the things I'd said, the arrogance, the anger, the risks. I'd justify it by just ... forgetting about it.

It just didn't happen. I'd keep moving on, keep being "Fleur Jazz Hands". I didn't have to take responsibility or be accountable because "Hey, it never happened." I'd shove all those experiences into a box and carry on as if I had alcohol amnesia. It's terrifying now to think about how I used to live.

Having that hip replacement at forty-seven? It was a complete life shift, and honestly, from the bottom of my heart, I'm grateful. That period of physical healing cracked open a space for profound emotional healing too. It pushed me, gently but firmly, to face all those feelings I'd been denying, hiding, and burying deep within. I had to let myself feel them, truly feel them, not just numb them away. It was scary, incredibly scary, at first, facing my emotions completely sober, and I won't lie, also utterly exhausting in those initial days. But something shifted. Those things that were triggering me? I started to see they were trying to tell me something. What I'd been resisting, avoiding at all costs, was exactly what I needed to embrace, to see for what it truly was – the core of who I am. And you know what? When I finally stopped running and just sat with those feelings, they weren't the monsters I'd made them out to be. They were just … parts of me, yearning to be seen, to be heard. My former self was reminding me she felt pain, and she needed support, needed me. And I gave that to her. So now, when those emotions bubble up, I lean in, I quiet the noise, and I listen to the messages from within. I've learned that when you give something form, a voice, it somehow dissolves the fear. That old resistance, that refusal to acknowledge, it just … faded away. When an emotion surfaces, I hold it, I tend to it with kindness, and the anxiousness softens, passes. I no longer get lost in those old distraction patterns I'd once mastered. Life isn't this chaotic storm anymore. Life just … flows, smoothly, gently. And I can honestly say, with my whole being, that giving up alcohol was the most transformative, the most loving thing I've ever, ever done for myself.

Sure, I lost friends. I lost my old social circle, my "scene". I lost the keys to the club. I wasn't invited out anymore. That was the cost of change for me, and it was a cost I had to pay. But as one part of life ended, it made space for something new to begin. I've made some wonderful new friends who don't need alcohol to connect or have a good time. And they actually care enough to ask if I'm okay, and if I need to talk. About anything!

These days, I call myself an "event drinker". I might have a dirty martini for a special milestone or a worthy celebration. That's fun. But I no longer feel the need to drink wine every time I see someone or use it as a crutch in any relationship. I hate hangovers. I hate what alcohol does to my brain the next day, how it messes with my productivity. I feel short tempered, impatient, and exhausted. It's just not worth it for me.

I broke up with alcohol. I said, "Bye-bye. You and I, we're not together anymore." I didn't want to hang out or share my secrets with it anymore. That relationship ended, in a good way. Now, we're like distant friends. We say hi every once in a while. We still appreciate each other, but we don't depend on each other. That deliciously fun and dangerously unhealthy relationship is gone, and I can say with confidence that this is a beautiful and much more comfortable place to be.

> It's lovely to have one martini or a lovely glass of red wine and a little giggle, but that's it. Tick. But, honestly, I can have a wonderful night out without it.

37. Drinkies Discovery

The Change Process with Drinking Questions

These questions are a warm invitation to explore the role of drinking in your life and uncover the hidden costs tied to your current habits. I encourage you to approach this with bravery and openness, fully embracing this meaningful journey of self-discovery. As you thoughtfully consider the full spectrum of costs connected to your drinking habits, see each insight as a chance for growth and an opportunity to create the life you desire for yourself now, and for your Future Self.

This is your moment to reflect and connect with those deeper aspects of yourself that might be trying to reach you. Pull out your journal and let your pen flow. And remember, **read each question and your response aloud** – letting the words resonate can bring incredible connection and motivation.

Give your thoughts and feelings the space to form. You might just uncover the clarity you need to guide you on your Change Experience journey. Remind yourself, though, that in this safe space, there's no judgement. You're simply exploring aspects of your life to gain more clarity, decide what truly serves you, and see what changes you'd like to make.

> "Follow your bliss and the universe will open doors where there were only walls."
> – Joseph Campbell

Remember, you have the power to shift your perspective at any moment. If you need guidance, recall the qualities of your Future Self for support and wise counsel.

Exploring the Ripple Effect: Uncovering the Impacts of Drinking in Your Life

It's time to gently delve into the impacts, the echoes, and the unseen costs that drinking might have woven into the most significant threads of your life. This isn't about judgement, but about illuminating your path forward.

Relationships: The Heart of Connection

1. How has drinking subtly, or not so subtly, created a sense of unease or distance in your most important relationships – especially those intimate connections that mean the world to you?

2. Can you bring to mind a specific moment when drinking shifted the dynamic in a relationship, perhaps causing a misunderstanding or a moment of regret? How did that specific instance make you feel afterward? What deeper truths about yourself and your relationship patterns are asking to be seen and accepted right now, so you can truly feel more grounded and secure?

3. Imagine your relationships as fertile ground for growth. How can you consciously nurture them, not just for connection, but as a mirror for self-discovery – revealing more about who you are and who you're becoming?

4. As you move forward, how can you intentionally draw closer to those who genuinely uplift your spirit, celebrate your strengths, and champion your evolving self? What kind of relationships truly nourish your soul?

Family: Unpacking Our Roots

1. When you reflect on your family experiences, what patterns or unspoken dynamics might have quietly encouraged or reinforced automatic drinking behaviours for you? How have these "family scripts" played out in your life?

2. Recall a specific time when drinking led you to act in a way that felt out of alignment with your deepest values or who you truly aspire to be. What did that scenario teach you about where your boundaries might need strengthening?

3. Creating healthy boundaries with family isn't about building walls, but about cultivating respect and fostering authentic connection. How can you thoughtfully establish and communicate these boundaries in a way that truly nourishes everyone involved?

4. Our families, imperfect as they may be, often reflect parts of ourselves back to us. How can you look at what your family members present – both the challenging and the supportive – as profound lessons for your personal growth and evolution? What insights are waiting for you there?

Work and Vocation: Finding Your Flow

1. Do you often feel the weight of your work life, perhaps finding yourself overwhelmed by demands or navigating tricky workplace dynamics? How do these pressures trigger stress, and where does drinking fit into that cycle?

2. When difficult thoughts or intense feelings arise at work, has drinking become a go-to coping mechanism? What inner resources or new practices can you begin to cultivate to find genuine calm and balance, even amidst chaos, without turning to alcohol?

3. How can you actively ground yourself and reconnect with that deep well of inner peace, even when your professional life feels demanding? In those stressful moments, what clear, kind, and effective boundaries can you begin to set and communicate to protect your energy and wellbeing?

You: Nurturing Your Physical and Mental Balance

1. Let's get really honest here: When you wake up after drinking, how does it genuinely impact the way you feel about yourself – mentally, emotionally, physically? What messages does your body send?

2. You hold incredible inner wisdom. How can you tap into this wisdom to gently shift your perspective towards profound self-love and radical compassion for yourself, especially when you're feeling vulnerable or triggered? What would truly loving yourself look like in this moment?

3. Taking small, consistent steps can create profound change. What tiny, manageable shifts could you introduce into your drinking habits right now that would immediately enhance your overall wellbeing – both physically and mentally?

4. If you were to embrace these changes, what tangible actions would you take to ensure they not only stick but become a sustainable part of your journey? How will you lovingly support yourself through this process, celebrating every step forward?

Your Health: A Solid Foundation

1. Let's gently explore the physical side of things. What specific health signals or challenges have you experienced that might be directly linked to your drinking habits? (Take a moment to truly consider examples like brain fog, heart rate shifts, restless sleep, digestive discomfort, changes in skin or hair, energy dips, etc.)

2. Recognising these signals is the first step. How can you actively seek the right kind of support – whether it's medical guidance, a trusted friend, or a new wellness practice – to lovingly realign and restore your physical health? What does "support" truly look like for you?

3. As you choose to make changes, what clear and personal signs will tell you that your health is genuinely improving? How will you truly feel the progress? How will you enthusiastically celebrate every small step forward, and equally important, how will you compassionately accept any setbacks as simply part of this courageous journey?

And now, dismount!

After the Reflection

Take a load off. You're doing so incredibly well! Please, acknowledge the effort you're putting into this journey with me.

It's not easy, and you're new at building skills to develop your inner strength it can make you feel a little tired at times. That's okay. I want you to take a pause now, and really just let all this sink in for a while.

If I were there with you, I'd give you a big hug, wrapped up in a warm smile, and encourage you to tell yourself, "You're awesome!"

> Perhaps you could try that yourself; why not stand in front of the mirror and do just that?

YOU ARE NOT ALONE

You do not have to suffer in silence.

While I sincerely hope these pages offer you support and guidance, I also understand that sometimes we need more – more personalised, hands-on help. If you're feeling overwhelmed or that you're navigating this journey alone, please reach out.

Help is available: Speak with someone today.

There is support available, and you don't have to carry this burden by yourself. If you're in Australia, know that help is just a phone call away:

1800RESPECT – Call 1800 737 732 or text 0458 737 732.

Alcohol and Drug Information Services: In Sydney, you can call (02) 9361 8000, and in country areas, you can call the toll-free number 1800 422 599.

If you live outside of Australia: I encourage you you to explore the support services within your local community or country. You are not alone, and there are people who care and want to help you through this process. Please, reach out and allow them to.

38. Reflection Time

Food and Drink Questions
For Your Thoughts and Observations

You've almost reached the end of Book One: *Project Clarity* – well done! Now, it's time to pause and reflect. This is an opportunity to pause and process everything that came up for you. What did you learn? What did you feel? What challenged you, and what did you feel resistant to? What surprised you?

This reflection is all about connecting with your experience as you explore these new ideas, learn new skills, and build your toolbox for making empowered choices in your relationship with food and drink. Remember, there are no right or wrong answers. This is your time to honour your feelings. Whatever you're feeling today, write it down. It might shift tomorrow, or next week, as you continue to process. You might find yourself holding onto a new insight, feeling grounded and confident. Or it might take time for things to truly sink in.

> "The purpose of life, after all, is to live it, to taste experience to the utmost, to reach out eagerly and without fear for newer and richer experience."
>
> **– Eleanor Roosevelt**

In whatever ways you process this information, it's all with you; take your time, as needed. Once again, please follow the process of reading the questions out loud. Then, once you have written your answers, speak your words aloud. This helps your brain and body connect, and you hear your own wisdom. It's a powerful way to solidify your connection to yourself.

> **"The only journey is the one within."**
> – Rainer Maria Rilke

I've created some questions to guide your reflection, both now and in the coming weeks, as you continue to integrate what you've learned. You may not want to answer everything right now, and that's perfectly okay. I encourage you to sit with the questions, let them percolate, and return to them later.

Find a cozy spot to do this exercise, and a place where you feel safe to read it aloud to yourself. Allow all those wonderful (and, yes, maybe a little "crunchy") imperfections – the ones we all have – to settle in and marinate.

Your Reflection Process

Using your journal, I would like you to contemplate what has stirred within you as you've read these pages. Can you let it all out, give it form, allow the words to flow onto the page and speak to you?

Our relationships, work, family, and mental and physical health all play a role in how we approach food and drink. These domains of our lives are where we get thrown off course and feel challenged, which in turn creates the messy relationship with food and drink.

A healthy relationship with food and drink involves making space for the challenging stuff and accepting parts of ourselves we may have ignored or denied. It also includes aspects of an intuitive eating mindset, listening to your hunger and fullness cues, and letting your body guide you on how much and when to eat.

On the flip side, then, your work, relationships, physical/mental health, and your exercise practice can become your primary sources of nourishment, feeding your mind and body while you allow yourself to enjoy food and drink (your secondary sources of nourishment) for sustained energy, health, and wellbeing. Do you see the difference?

I hope by now you're beginning to see how your automatic responses around food or alcohol might be gently nudging you away from living in alignment with your deepest values – and the behaviours that genuinely support them. There's undoubtedly quite a lot to ponder here, so please, take all the time you need to gently sit with it all.

> This is your life's work, and it's a journey we all embark on as we learn to pay loving and compassionate attention to our needs. I wonder, are you starting to appreciate more what your needs are now?

Let's Begin

Starting From Today

1. What does a healthy relationship with food and/or drink really feel like to you?

2. Imagine looking in the mirror and truly, deeply accepting yourself, just as you are. What would that be like?

3. What if you stopped trying to please everyone else and started tuning in to your own needs first? How would that feel? And what would change for you?

4. What if you could confidently say "no" when you needed to, without guilt or hesitation? What possibilities would that open up?

5. Picture waking up every morning full of energy, practically bouncing out of bed! What would that feel like?

6. What would it be like to fully embrace your new values and really live them out in your daily life?

7. If you could step into the shoes of your Future Self right now, how would your life be different? What would you be doing, feeling, and thinking?

8. How might your life transform if you no longer drank, or if you became a confident, mindful social drinker only?

9. If you could give one piece of advice to your past self about developing a healthy relationship with food and/or drink, what would it be?

...

After the Reflection

If You Struggled with the Above, Here's Some Help

A healthy relationship with food and drink means:

🔗 **Making Space for the Challenging Stuff:** Acknowledging and accepting that emotions and life circumstances can affect eating habits.

🔗 **Accepting Parts of Ourselves:** Embracing aspects of ourselves that we may have ignored or denied, including our emotions and needs.

🔗 **Intuitive Eating:** Listening to hunger and fullness cues and allowing your body to guide you on how much and when to eat.

🔗 **Mindfulness:** Being present and aware of the experience of eating and drinking, rather than acting on automatic behaviours.

🔗 **Nourishment:** Recognising that food and drink serve as secondary sources of nourishment, while primary sources include relationships, work, physical/mental health, and exercise.

🔗 **Alignment with Your New Values:** Making food and drink choices that support your overall wellbeing and align with your values.

🔗 **Self-Compassion:** Approaching your relationship with food and drink with kindness and understanding, rather than judgement or restriction.

Be patient and kind with yourself. This isn't about perfection or restriction; it's about learning to listen to your body, honouring your needs, and finding a balance that feels good for you in the long run. It's a journey of self-discovery, not a race to the finish line.

With acceptance, start to appreciate your body size and image just as you do your shoe size. It's your genetic blueprint. With love, compassion, and self-respect for your body, you can begin to see yourself with clarity and feel even better about who you are.

Think about this for a while: Your mind is in a relationship with your body, and your brain is the matchmaker. By the end of this, I would hope that you will be feeling like saying this:

> My relationship with food and alcohol has become more mindful and intentional. I'm paying attention to my hunger and fullness cues, and I'm making choices that nourish my body and support my overall wellbeing.

39. From Here to Clarity

Now, Going At Your Own Pace
This is Your Final Check In

My friend, I fully appreciate that the journey you have just taken is a lot to process. It might feel like you've taken on more than you ever imagined. So, as you approach this final part, please take your time with these questions. There is no rush here.

This really is a profound journey, and sometimes, as I said at the very beginning, it can feel like you need a crowbar to prise these truths out of yourself. Give yourself full permission to take as long as you need, while also remembering that these questions are designed to help you create a deeper, more profound connection within. They are here to reinforce your learning and acknowledge the building blocks of change you have already made, coming this far.

I often say to my clients, once you start this process and see glimmers of change, you can't go back. There is a force inside that will work its way up and spur you along your Change Experience – I see this in every person I work with.

Your Project Clarity Evolutionary Sense Check

Drawing on all the insights you've gained. Imagine yourself as the evolved woman you're becoming, not just today, but one month, three months, six months, even a year from now. You see things differently now, don't you? There's a deeper awareness, a richer understanding of yourself and clarity on the journey that has shaped you. This is an opportunity to offer yourself encouragement, to visualise how you'll step into these next months, embracing your new strengths.

Let's be real, this growth takes practice, and there will be stumbles along the way. You might find yourself slipping back into old patterns, and that's okay. It's all part of the process. You'll notice, you'll learn, and you'll come to appreciate that healing is never a straight path. So, approach these questions with an open heart and a wise spirit.

A LITTLE SIDE NOTE: It's perfectly fine to tackle these questions now, or you can revisit them later when you feel you've processed things a bit more. No pressure; just go at your own pace!

In one month:

1. When stress creeps in and sleep feels far away, what gentle steps can you take to care for yourself and navigate those emotional triggers?
2. Life can get wonderfully messy sometimes. How might you carve out space for a solid eight hours of sleep each night, knowing it's a real gift to yourself?
3. As you align with your values and choose to pause before reacting, how do you see food and drink fitting into this new space? (And it's okay to admit, will there be a little part of you that misses those old, automatic responses?)
4. If something at work feels unsettling, how can you gently bring yourself back to centre? Would you consider setting a kind boundary to support yourself and avoid slipping into old patterns?

In three months:

1. In your heart space, take a moment to recall a time when you felt triggered in a significant relationship and it led to some destructive automatic behaviours in how you approached eating and drinking.
2. With the clarity and new skills you've gained, what gentle steps might you take to make conscious choices and pause those automatic reactions?
3. As you move forward with more discerning choices, how do you envision food and drink fitting into this new picture?

In six months:

1. Picture a moment when you're feeling challenged by your reflection. What kind of inner dialogue comes up? Perhaps recall those less kind words you might have said to yourself about your appearance.

2. Now, keeping your values in mind, when you look in the mirror, how might you offer yourself validation? What does acceptance of your image look like for you in this new light?

3. With these new skills you've been exploring, how might you respond to that mirror moment now? What feels like a supportive and gentle approach for yourself?

4. If you have recognised a tendency to react negatively in the past, how will you compassionately catch yourself in the present? How will you shift towards seeing food and drink as nourishment, rather than a punishment or a denial of your pain?

In one year:

1. Think ahead to a year from now. A challenging work situation arises, the kind that used to really bother you. What internal changes do you feel might be there now? And how do you see yourself navigating it, especially regarding how you've used food and drink in the past?

2. Imagine a time when a physical setback happens. What will you do to adjust, and how will you find new ways to care for your wellbeing? How will you be mindful of the patterns you might have had with food and drink in these situations?

3. When those familiar family dynamics stir up those old "I'm not enough" feelings, what strategies will you naturally turn to now?

How will you work towards change in those moments, keeping in mind how your relationship with food and drink has shifted?

4. What does self-compassion look like for you when things get tough? If you imagine a scenario a year from now, what does that look like? How will you find a way to comfort yourself during any struggles, without turning those previously used numbing or distracting coping mechanisms?

5. How will you approach conversations when you feel a boundary has been crossed? How can you speak your truth, being respectful to your needs and communicating them to others?

6. Thinking about how you're taking care of your health, how will you feel about your role in what you choose to put into your body? How will your understanding of nourishment, in terms of both food and drink, influence the choices you make?

7. If you have a setback and feel embarrassed, what story will you tell yourself about it? How will you find a way to acknowledge your worth and value?

8. What personal rituals or intentions might you create to acknowledge and appreciate the journey of change you're on?

9. Now that you have a clearer sense of how your actions affect your health, think about how much your body does for you. What's one genuine way you can appreciate and honour that relationship with your body?

After everything we've explored together, I find myself wondering what's changed for you? What does it feel like to look at these questions now, through the lens of your deeper connection and greater self-awareness? What's shifted for you?

...

After the Questions

You are who you are – a powerful woman with many layers of beautiful colours. Embrace them, lean in, and love them. Close your eyes for a moment and feel that.

> **"We are what we repeatedly do. Excellence, then, is not an act, but a habit."**
> – Will Durant
> (paraphrasing Aristotle)

If anything else has come up for you this week, please write down your thoughts, opinions, and ideas. This is your time to reflect, digest, process, and acknowledge your feelings and decide how you can create positive changes in your life. Use your journal to freely express yourself.

In Book Two: *A New Perspective*, we will delve deeply into managing emotional triggers, and in Book Three, we will explore how to set and define your boundaries. Therefore, these questions will serve as a valuable gauge to measure your progress or assess how your approach to them might change as you develop further skills in these areas throughout the coming books.

40. Until We Meet Again, Friend

It is Just "Bye For Now"
With Some Words For Your To Ponder

My dear friend,

I want to acknowledge your hard work, your effort, and your bravery in looking deep within, and the commitment you have made to yourself. This journey of developing a new form of clarity in your life has been immense, and that should never be underestimated. So, before you continue to the next part of this series in Book Two, I encourage you to pause. Let all of this information settle within you for a while. I suggest taking a good month before diving into new topics. This will give you time to practise these new skills, build your strength, and try out strategies to make small, meaningful changes that will bring more balance, peace, and joy into your life.

The Change Experience Within You

If this part of the journey has awoken your curiosity, I have a feeling you'll be ready for what's coming next.

When you are ready get online and order your copy of Book Two: *A New Perspective*. In it, we'll delve deeper into how your unmet childhood needs and past experiences can shape your adult life, influencing your behaviours and emotional patterns. I'll be sharing easy-to-understand insights and real-life stories you can truly relate to.

After a short break, I imagine you'll be prepared to dive deeper – to understand your triggers, examine the emotional hooks that have kept you stuck, and recognise the real consequences of your behaviours. My aim is to equip you with simple, practical techniques that will help you manage those difficult moments and become more grounded in yourself.

Until then, I want to leave you with these thoughts:

Finding Your Happiness

Remember how we talked about many destructive behaviours being driven by a desire to escape pain and constantly chase that "happier" feeling? It's a common misconception, but here's the truth: Happiness isn't just a feeling; it's a profound experience. Happiness, my friend, in my opinion, isn't simply a feeling you arrive at; it's something far more expansive. While feelings like joy, contentment, or peace are beautiful *evidence* of happiness, they aren't the final destination. Instead, true happiness blossoms from finding deep meaning and genuine connection in your life, discovering joy in the everyday, and cultivating satisfaction in who you are and what you're doing. It's a holistic tapestry, not a quick fix or fleeting sensation.

True happiness involves a sense of deep contentment with your life, regardless of momentary ups and downs. It's an inner peace that remains even when you are faced with challenges.

A core component of lasting happiness is having a sense of purpose. This means living a life that aligns with your values and contributes to something larger than yourself. And it means living a fulfilling life for what is important to you, no one else.

Strong, healthy relationships are vital for your mental wellbeing. True happiness often involves deep connections with others, feeling loved and supported, and contributing to the wellbeing of those around you.

So, what does this mean for us here? Well, this investment you're making by doing this work, reading through these pages, and engaging in the exercises means you're becoming much more skilled at enjoying your life. By practising these techniques I'm sharing, you're practising getting more satisfaction from what you're doing – this is my opinion, is the doorway to experiencing true happiness. And by making choices aligned with your values and being committed to your Future Self, you're giving meaning to your purpose and existence.

How does that sit with you?

Healing Your Pain

To be able to walk down this path towards happiness, there is something we have to deal with first, though, right?

You can't outrun your past. Those automatic behaviours, the self-medicating, the numbing, the distractions, the self-sabotage – they're all whispers from wounds you haven't truly acknowledged. Until you trace those whispers to their source, you'll remain trapped in a cycle.

A lot of the time, we can't face these past experiences because of our fears. Well, this is another fear, of feeling. Any feeling you have is a gift because it's an experience of yourself for you to connect with, learn from, and grow beyond. Be curious about your feelings. Even if you're curled up in a ball and feeling all torn up, there's a message in that feeling for you. Connect to it, listen to it, and experience the gift that your body is giving you.

Now, I'm not asking you to relive every agonising detail of your past. You can't rewind time, change the actors, or rewrite the script. Can you?

Nor is it about forcing forgiveness or denying what happened. It did happen, and it was difficult, perhaps profoundly so. But it's part of your journey, not its entirety. Appreciating that you can't alter the past is where you find acceptance.

It's about tenderly reshaping the story you tell yourself about those moments, right here, right now.

> Until you can meet your pain with a spirit of kindness, it will continue to shape your present.

Instead, let's give that pain a gentle presence. Give it a name, a shape, a feeling. When it arises, acknowledge it with compassion. "Ah, there's that 'foggie feeling' again," you might say. (I named mine that because it always seemed to pop up unexpectedly!) Make it personal. By acknowledging it, you soften its power to overwhelm you. You give yourself a moment to pause and ask: Is this a current threat, or is it a past echo?

That "foggie feeling" is a messenger, a sensation in your body, trying to communicate. In the beginning, allow it to speak. Let the tears flow; even let the anger roll and surface. Healing is a dialogue between your mind and body. Only by listening to your body can you rewrite the fear-based narratives that hold your mind captive and replace them with stories of peace, safety, and empowerment – stories where you are in control.

HERE'S THE TRUTH: Until you make peace with your pain, until you're willing to face its roots, every healing technique, every empowerment strategy, will fall flat. Yes, sister, the only way forward is through.

Once you name your pain, once you see it for what it is – a narrative, not something that can hurt you now – you'll begin to understand why you've been running. You'll see how avoidance has created its own chaos.

This inner work, this courageous act of facing yourself, will unlock the doors you thought were sealed. You'll finally have clarity on the "why" behind your patterns, the reasons behind your self-destructive habits.

And here's my promise: In the next book, we'll delve deeper into these processes. We'll explore the tools for letting go, the practices of acceptance, the ways to soothe that wounded inner child. If this feels overwhelming, know that you're not alone. I've been there. And when you're ready, these techniques will transform your life. I'll be there to guide you, to hold your hand, as you embark on this journey of healing and self-discovery with clarity and a new perspective. These are the skills that will define your Change Experience.

> **One final question for you ...**
> Let me ask you, with all honesty: Have you ever shown up for yourself at this level before? Have you ever truly chosen you?

Until next time, take good care of yourself, and trust the process.

With warm and loving healing energy.

Fleur Elizabeth

I. Appendix: Methodology

My Coaching Practice

My Approach

I use an integrative coaching method that blends nutritional health with psychological principles. Rather than focusing on restrictive diets, we'll explore your emotional relationship with food and drink to create personalised, sustainable changes. The goal is to equip you with the tools and motivation to live a healthier life you truly desire. My work draws specifically on evidence-based practices such as trauma, addiction, and anxiety-focused Acceptance and Commitment Therapy and Motivational Interviewing.

Our Focus: The coaching process is designed to help you understand your behaviours and the triggers behind them. We will work together to identify and connect four key areas of your life – relationships, vocation, mental/physical health, and exercise – to your choices around food and drink. This will empower you to set boundaries, protect your energy, and make choices that align with your core values.

Change Talk: A core component of my coaching is a technique I call "Change Talk," which is scientifically based on the principles of Motivational Interviewing. You'll be encouraged to read your responses to self-assessment questions aloud. This simple yet powerful practice significantly increases the likelihood of lasting change by allowing you to hear and internalise your own arguments for it. My role is to provide the knowledge and support, while your role is to engage with the process openly and with self-compassion.

My Credentials

I've earned the following credentials, which provide a knowledge base that I draw from in my coaching practice:

- Master's in food, wine, and tourism branding and management
- Nutritional health coaching diploma
- Certificate in Acceptance and Commitment Therapy (ACT) and an advanced certificate specialising in depression and anxiety
- Certificate in trauma-focused ACT (TFACT)
- Certificate in Motivational Interviewing (MI) and an advanced certificate specialising in alcoholism and addiction
- Certificate in Emotional Focus Therapy (EFT): Attachment Science in Practice
- Certificate in Dialectical Behaviour Therapy (DBT), specialising in mindfulness, acceptance, and change skills
- Certificate in Executive and Transformation Coaching
- Certificate in Food as Medicine
- Certificate in Food and Mood: Improving Mental Health Through Diet and Nutrition

II. References and Research

General Research

Fletcher, T. (n.d.). *Trauma Series*. YouTube.

Sapolsky, R. (2003, November). Stress and plasticity in the limbic system. *Neurochemical Research, 28*(11), 1735-1742.

Scaccia, A. (2017, May 18). Serotonin: What you need to know. *Healthline*. Retrieved September 15, 2017.

Headlight. (2020, November 29). Your Brain Thrives on Positivity. [Blog post].

Koosis, L. A. (2024, June 25). The Science Of Affirmations: The Brain's Response To Positive Thinking.

De Franco, D. (2022, July 18). The Four Functions of Behaviour: Understanding Your Child's Actions.

McClelland, D. (2019, August 27). *Trauma And The Brain*. [Blog post].

National Library of Medicine. (2021, October 22). *How Does the Family Influence Adolescent Eating Habits in Terms of Knowledge, Attitudes and*

Practices? A Global Systematic Review of Qualitative Studies. [Study publication article].

Fraser Stillpoint, L. (2018, July 26). *Empathetic Witnessing.* [Blog post].

Gibson-Judkins, C. (2019, October 9). *The Link Between Childhood Trauma and Eating Disorders.* Eggleston Youth Centre. [Article].

University of Melbourne, MAEVe. Melbourne Research Alliance to End Violence against women and their children (MAEVe). [Google Research site].

The Anxiety Recovery Centre Victoria (ARCVic). *Anxiety Disorders.* [Google Research site].

Cleveland Clinic, Ohio, USA. (2022, November 1). *What is the Vagus Nerve?* [Article]. [Google Research site].

Types of violence against women – Intimate-partner violence. (2024, June 27). [Blog post]. [Google Research site].

Palumbo, L. (2018, February 26). *The Connection Between Eating Disorders and Sexual Violence.* [Blog post].

Chapple, R. (2023, February 2). *What Is Generational Trauma? Signs, Causes, & How to Heal.* [Blog post].

Rigby, A. *Family values: 24 Examples to strengthen your family bonds.* [Blog post]. [Date not defined].

[Acceptance and Commitment Therapy, Motivational Interviewing, DBT, Emotional Focus Therapy, Dialectical Behavioural Therapy]. [Online resources].

Food and Drink

D'Adamo, P., & Whitney, C. (2016). *Eat Right 4 Your Type (Revised and Updated): The Individualised Blood Type Diet® Solution.* New American Library.

Glazier, E. M. (2024, November 15). Junk food cravings tied to hormones, circadian cycle. *UCLA Health.* [Blog post].

National Sleep Foundation. (2020, November 12). The Link Between Nutrition and Sleep. [Blog post].

O'Connor, A. (2022, September 13). Just one hour of extra sleep each night can lead to better eating habits. *Washington Post online blog.*

Healthy Sleep. (2024, May 15). How Sugar Before Bed Ruins Your Sleep. [Blog post].

Healthify. (n.d.). Sleep – how food and drink affect it. [*Online resource blog*].

Body Ecology. (n.d.). The links between your blood type, personality, and diet, explained. [*Online resource.*]

Lee, K. (2023, September 13). Why Alcohol Disrupts Your Sleep. *Everyday Health.* [Blog post].

Medical News Today. (n.d.). What to know about diaphragmatic breathing. [Blog post].

www.ingramcontent.com/pod-product-compliance
Lightning Source LLC
Chambersburg PA
CBHW071950070526
44583CB00015B/1136